CW01649683

THE JANUS ASPECT

Also by John Tusa

Conversations with the World

A World in your Ear

Art Matters: Reflecting on Culture

On Creativity: Interviews Exploring the Process

JOHN TUSA
THE JANUS ASPECT

Artists in the twenty-first century

Methuen

First published in 2005 by Methuen

10 9 8 7 6 5 4 3 2 1

Copyright © 2005 by John Tusa

The right of John Tusa to be identified as the Author
of this work has been asserted by him in accordance
with the Copyright Designs and Patents Act 1988

Extracts from *The Sunday Feature: The John Tusa Interview* © BBC 2003
and 2004 by arrangement with the BBC

Published in Great Britain in 2005 by Methuen Publishing Ltd
215 Vauxhall Bridge Road, London SW1V 1EJ

Methuen Publishing Limited Reg. No. 3543167

This book is sold subject to the condition that it shall not,
by way of trade or otherwise, be lent, resold, hired out,
or otherwise circulated in any form of binding or cover
other than that in which it is published and without a
similar condition, including this condition, being imposed
on the subsequent purchaser

A CIP catalogue record for this book is available
from the British Library

ISBN 0 413 77472 4

Designed by Bryony Newhouse

Typeset by SX Composing DTP, Rayleigh, Essex

Printed and bound in Great Britain by
Mackays of Chatham plc, Chatham, Kent

CONTENTS

INTRODUCTION: THE JANUS ASPECT

For the last five years, I have been talking to leading figures in the arts for the BBC Radio Three series, *The John Tusa Interview*. In that time, I have had the privilege of meeting almost fifty major figures in disciplines as varied as painting, sculpture, cinema, poetry, architecture, photography, literature. They have included people such as Howard Hodgkin, I. M. Pei, Louis Andriessen, Frank Gehry, Tom Stoppard, Frank Auerbach and György Ligeti, to name only a handful of them. The present volume contains the texts of the interviews with Bill Viola, Atom Egoyan, Simon McBurney, Gilbert and George, Merce Cunningham, William Forsythe, Anish Kapoor, Heiner Goebbels, Bernardo Bertolucci, Michal Rovner, Michael Craig-Martin, Renzo Piano and Rachel Whiteread.

The purpose of the interviews has been to put on record conversations that assess at serious length as much as possible of the total career to date of the particular person – for while some are established and senior, others are in an even more interesting mid-career phase. I have, for the most part, deliberately avoided the format of the interview directly related to a show, a play, or a publication. These have not been opportunistic publicity exercises. I believe they have benefited from such an approach, from being conducted in such an atmosphere.

In 2003, Methuen published a collection of thirteen of the

interviews which, once selected, revealed themselves to have a common, though not dominating, theme: the nature of artistic creativity.

The successor volume takes a different – perhaps a more proactive – approach. As my BBC producer, Philip Sellars, and I went through the stimulating process of identifying artists to interview, and the sometimes still more stimulating process of persuading them to be interviewed, we became aware of an emerging pattern in the subjects we approached.

A significant number of them were artists working in fields that fell outside the customary artistic categories. There were, for instance, visual artists who worked in and with video, yet whose work was clearly 'on the gallery wall'. There were theatre creators – more than mere interpretative directors of existing texts, important as they are – who created work using a plethora of artistic disciplines from the spoken word to music, lighting, film and video projection. There were choreographers who used computer techniques and skills to enlarge the range of the possibilities available to them.

In grouping them together for this volume, I have identified two broad themes that might be said to constitute a common ground for most of the artists included here. These themes do not make up a dogmatic, theoretical basis for their work: the book certainly does not claim or intend to push them into some conceptual or philosophical grouping. But they do emerge sufficiently often as constants to deserve identifying and attempting to articulate in a more considered way.

The first connection between many of the artists, then, is a readiness to use new techniques to achieve the traditional ends of deepened, heightened artistic expression. Those techniques – computers, industrial materials, video, digital simulation – would, not so long ago, have been considered to lie, purely or largely, in the experimental field. What is significant is that none of the artists represented in this volume should have the tentative, qualified label of 'experimental' applied to him or her. That would be far too provisional a judgement.

Each has taken on, worked with, and finally achieved a body of work where the new techniques or materials have opened up for the artist – and for us, the audience – new ways of expression and understanding. The refreshment of expression that flows from these new modes of creation has been huge and revivifying.

In searching for a word, an idea, capable of embracing this aspect of an otherwise diverse grouping of artists, I have settled on the term 'crossovers'. Here, in short, are artists who resist placement in any of the traditional categories of art – painter, writer, sculptor, artist. They do not accept the formal boundaries of expression that these historic categories imply. They leap over the old boundaries, or simply decline to recognise them.

Of course, the word 'crossover', as it is customarily used, often has a disparaging quality to it. It's commonly applied either to a classical artist who courts popularity by trying to embrace the sounds or values of rock or pop music; or, just as scornfully, to a rock artist who tries to acquire respectability by dabbling in the classical. I think nevertheless that the idea of 'crossing over' in the way I have outlined above is too appropriate, too illuminating, to be limited by its use elsewhere.

The second insistent theme to emerge here is that of the relationship between innovation and a consciousness of historical roots. There is an increasingly compelling sense of the near-necessary connection between true innovation and an active awareness of the past. Ultimately, that is why the book is called *The Janus Aspect*: to acknowledge the many ways in which past and present interlink in the most innovatory of artistic processes. Being linked to the past does not represent some sort of defeat, some reflection of a lack of creative power. Rather, a respect for and understanding of what has gone before emerges almost as a condition of the truly new. That is the predominant theme of this collection, a theme found, too, in some key conversations in the previous collection, *On Creativity*.

Yet the companion idea of 'crossovers' is also worth examination. In what ways do some of the artists interviewed in this volume defy conventional boundaries? Many reach out to techniques that would either not have been available a decade ago, or would not have been regarded as suitable for the discipline in which they work. Rachel Whiteread's choice of 'unfashionable' materials for sculpture is one instance, using plaster, resin, rubber and cement to explore not so much physical spaces as the unconsidered volumes in between. In adopting such materials, Whiteread has rejected – or certainly moved beyond – the classical, 'fine' materials of her predecessors. In doing so, she redefined the very notion of what sculpture 'ought' to be.

A similar process can be seen in Atom Egoyan's evolution from the ethos of the hand-held, home video to the fully crafted world of the arthouse movie; the final, formal version is heavily influenced by the original, informal inputs of the home video. The resulting, considered artistic form derives originally from the most casual kind of personal capture of images. Egoyan, too, is using 'unfashionable' materials as a raw base from which to craft a refined product. He refuses to draw a line between a medium that an amateur can handle and one where only a professional can survive.

Equally, both Heiner Goebbels and Simon McBurney have carved out a new kind of theatrical form, where all the art forms that appear on the stage are shaped by the creator–director – my term – to produce a fascinating theatrical hybrid that now contributes some of the most stimulating creations to the musical–theatrical stage. Do they write the texts? Sometimes. (In Goebbels' case, even the music). Do they direct the performers? Always. Do they mastermind the ultimate collection of artistic inputs into a form for which they are finally responsible? Undoubtedly. Above all, they are not mere interpreters – however important that role is – of the ideas and words of others. This is what sets them apart and makes them distinct.

When Michal Rovner starts her creative process with film or video, her end point may be video, but it may also be graphic prints, or digital screens the size of a small glass bowl in which wonders of human observation reveal themselves. Yet her work – like that of the video artist Bill Viola – is clearly in the graphic tradition of the visual arts.

For 'crossing over' also involves breaking out of existing conventions, established rules and agreed norms. Everyone interviewed here has had to experiment – but each artist has reached a point of mastery of the forms in which he or she once did so. The first tentative thrusts of experiment have been transformed into actual innovation, a more finished result. This is not to say that the individuals have stopped either experimenting or innovating, but to suggest that the transitional period of discovery has matured in some degree into actual expressive achievement.

This breaking out through techniques, materials and forms creates new freedoms for expression. It permits the deconstruction of forms into fresh shapes and categories. For all the artists, it reveals a curiosity, a refusal to be bound, a readiness to take risks that is usefully included in the idea of 'crossing over'. For audiences, such breaking of conventional lines, such crossing of disciplines has immeasurably enriched the range and type of artistic expression that we can enjoy.

Yet engaging in such innovation, toying with the rejection of past traditions, raises urgent questions about the place that tradition usefully and necessarily plays – if any – in the creation of the new, in the ability to innovate. Do the innovators, the 'crossovers', only succeed when they have consciously and deliberately rejected the past, when they have abandoned tradition, when they have started from scratch?

To the contrary, I believe that the work of the 'crossovers' – and not only those interviewed here – reveals, among many other things, how intimate are the umbilical ties between knowledge of the past and reaching out to the new.

Take the evidence of the video artist Bill Viola. For some, perhaps, the very phrase 'video art' is a contradiction in terms, a forewarning of mediocrity, art-college modishness, shortcuts to expression. And true, the number of quality practitioners in this field is dauntingly small. Bill Viola is certainly one of them. His trade-mark work is of super slo-mo, wall-mounted videos of human figures doing some very familiar, yet also eternal things.

Crying, running, walking, relating, greeting or facing one of the apocalyptic cataclysms such as fire or flood. Viola could not do what he does, could not express what he wants, without harnessing the latest technology: the highest-definition plasma screens, digital editing, cameras that slow down action to the point at which the movements as they unfold in the finished work are almost indistinguishable from the movements that went before; they appear to have become a series of held, animated tableaux, at once apparently still and consequently monumental, yet retaining their powerful aspect of motion.

At college, Bill Viola had reacted against conventional teaching of the art-school curriculum. He was the classic rebel until he discovered for himself the fifteenth-century Siennese masters – such as the Master of the Osservanza – an unlikely discovery, you might think. From that time, he decided that his subject matter as an artist would be the reinterpretation of Christian iconography. This was about as uncool as you could get among his Californian colleagues and classmates.

Yet once he had set that course, the integration of the modernity of his techniques with the openly historical nature of his sources could not have been more overt and complete. The fifteenth-century painting by Pontormo, *The Visitation* about the Annunciation, inspired Viola's work called *The Greeting*. A sequence of studies of a woman alone in a convent-like room at different seasons, with the light changing as the seasons outside change, is a meditation on spiritual devotion itself, based on echoes of Vermeer.

On other occasions, Viola explores the scene surrounding the tomb of Christ, when the sleeping soldiers completely miss the epic event of the Resurrection; or the quiet drama of the journey through life, including saying farewell to a dead parent, humanity's common links in facing apocalypse, or the experience of birth – or rebirth – through water.

These are not pious pastiches, however; not holy archaisms, devotional pictures, or mere modern tweaks on ancient beliefs. Viola is not, I think, proselytising. But his sustained, almost timeless re-examination of these great scenes of Christian mythology does throw a different, contemporary and wholly serious light on them. There isn't a great deal of convincing – or even attempted – new religious art around; few painters today undertake it or are inclined to do so. Viola employs the most modern techniques to express his meanings; but he uses these techniques as an instrument to explore the great themes of two millennia ago, giving the resulting work a strength, a contemporary resonance and an originality which mere technical tricks would not achieve.

In this respect, Viola is a leading witness in support of the argument that connection with the past is a source of strength to the modern artist, part of the lifeblood of creation. For it is not a slavish act of homage and mere dutiful reverence to what has gone before, but an indication of the depth that the crossover artist can achieve by both reaching out to the future and reconnecting with the past. Viola would not be the artist he is without his historic sources of inspiration. His expression of them would not be what it is without his mastery of contemporary technology. Matter and materials create a new, enriched synthesis.

At first glance, the case of the choreographer, Merce Cunningham, appears very different. He was a young man who loved to dance, a charismatic figure on the stage: tall, strikingly good-looking, with a feral yet lyrical athleticism. Cunningham was trained in the Georges Balanchine–Martha Graham tradition. At a very early stage he decided that he wanted to part company from what he felt was a too heavily narrative-based model of choreography. His instincts drove him towards a more abstract style of dance, one where the exploration of movement itself was the principal driver.

It was in 1944 that he met John Cage, with whom he had a relationship for almost fifty years. Together they explored the idea that the ingredients of dance performance – music, movement – did not need to be tied together as they had been in the past. Each had its own autonomy; each had its own integrity; each would gain from the context of the other. But music did not follow the movement or vice versa. They were equal and separate. In Cage's view, for the dance to follow the music represented a kind of slavery.

This was a startling concept. As John Cage wryly explained it: 'Merce does his thing and I do mine, and for your convenience we put them together.' We should not be fooled by the flippant tone of Cage's remark, characteristic as it is. It conceals the reality that in creating each work together there were – as Cunningham recalls – time milestones, which laid down a necessary structure. Cage was strong on structures, leaving maximum room for freedom to operate in between them.

When the autonomous, parallel creation of set and costumes was added to the mix, with the arrival of artists such as Robert Rauschenberg, the radical nature of the Cunningham work was there for all to see. On the famous European tour of 1964, it was greeted with boos, hisses and catcalls in Paris. In London, when I first saw it, there was a breakthrough of recognition. I won't pretend it was easy. For Cunningham represented an apparently total break with the past, with the way ballet, dance, had been created. That was the challenge he presented. He was overturning a tradition.

But there was a further stage of innovation to go. It came when Cage introduced Cunningham to the medieval Chinese Book of Changes, the I Ching, the tradition of turning to random choice to determine future actions, future directions. On the face of it, nothing could be further removed from the Western idea of the artist having a sense of purpose, an idea of direction, exercising detailed control over the order, structure and development of his/her work. The very idea of letting chance determine anything creative, let alone be the deciding factor, could hardly be more alien to the Western creative approach.

In his most recent work, *Split Sides*, there are two sets of choreography, two designs, two lighting plots and two sets of music. Before each performance the casting of the die determines which goes with which on the night. There are thirty-two possible permutations of all the artistic elements.

It should be a formula for chaos or incoherence. Yet far from being either chaotic or incoherent, the piece regularly draws the response that all the elements, though separately created and randomly assembled, emerge with an extraordinary sense of discipline, controlled form and inner order.

On this evidence, is Merce Cunningham an instance of the artist who has broken from his roots, ignored tradition, and thereby succeeded in creating something truly original, unfettered by the traditions of a discipline – that of dance – quite extraordinarily bound up with ancient practices of a particularly restrictive kind?

It is not, I think, quite as simple as that. To begin with, Cunningham never rejected Balanchine and Martha Graham. He set out to go beyond them, to find out more on the journey of discovery that they had started. That is quite different from pure rejection. While rejection has its place as a gesture in the armoury of innovation, it seldom works as a creative driving force by itself. Continued evolution is a very different matter. No one can watch Cunningham's work without recognising in it an utterly familiar classical discipline but with a dramatically enhanced language of movements and connections.

Then, too, Cunningham's use of chance deserves further thought. The automatic reaction to the very idea of the random is that it destroys order, especially when aleatory techniques are applied to ordered forms. Usually the random is used to disrupt order. Cunningham uses it in an entirely different way – to increase choice and to indicate new directions of discovery. In this, too, he seems to me to be a very radical but also very traditional kind of artist. Like Bill Viola, he uses the contemporary tools to help him explore, renew and extend traditional forms. Within the spirit of the I Ching, says Cunningham, there is a very strong sense of 'going forward'. I do not think it is fanciful to say that, for him, the forward path also stretches back to deep roots.

The comparison with his partner and mentor, John Cage, is worth considering in order to make the case for the 'crossovers' and their awareness of continuity. Cage's open assault on the past was explicit. It was all Beethoven's fault, specifically his sense of structure, logic, purpose and intense rhythmic drive that Cage couldn't abide. In one of his most controversial statements he declared: 'Was Beethoven right or were Webern and Satie right? I answer immediately and unequivocally, Beethoven was in error and his influence, which has been as extensive as it is lamentable, has been deadening to the art of music.'

In January 2004 the BBC mounted an entire weekend of music by John Cage and his contemporaries at the Barbican. By the end of the weekend – which was undoubtedly full of diversions and fun – the universal conclusion was that while Cage was highly significant as an influence – 'There's a bit of Cage in all of us,' said one composer – he was not important as a composer. Cage was fundamentally limited by his inability to understand the past. Cocking a snook at Beethoven gave him no ground from which to move and develop. Cage was left marooned and rudderless.

At this stage, let me introduce into the argument two composers whom I interviewed in *On Creativity* – Harrison Birtwistle and György Ligeti – and contrast their connection with the past with that of the apparently wholly innovatory school of the so-called American Minimalists: Philip Glass, Steve Reich and John Adams. I believe the very different experiences of these sets of composers throw a strong light on the role that a sense of the past plays in the challenging process of innovation.

Let us begin with the American composer, John Adams. He, after all, deliberately left music school at Cambridge, Massachusetts, because he found the atmosphere too intellectually prescriptive and restrictive. Obeying the time-honoured injunction to 'Go west, young man', Adams did just that, finding on the West Coast of the United States the freedom to innovate that he found difficult, if not impossible, in the East Coast conservatoire. Did Adams reject the main stream of the classical musical canon? Perhaps it was more a case of just leaving it behind, parking it for future reference once he had found himself and his voice in a more untrammelled atmosphere.

Is there a distinction to be made between the more elaborate development of Adams's music and that of the minimalist musicians with whom he was once bracketed, Steve Reich and Philip Glass? Both these have achieved significant creations. Reich's renovation and would-be reinvigoration of opera form in *Three Tales*, for instance, is ambitious and highly serious. Similarly, Glass's composition of a film opera, writing music to the pre-existing words of the text of Cocteau's *Beauty and the Beast* is a considerable achievement. By contrast, listening to an evening of Glass's symphonies can be a thoroughly dispiriting experience. Lacking any deep connection with or belief in symphonic form, the works emerge as pallid, formal studies expressed without commitment or conviction.

So what is the problem with minimalism, with what Steve Reich himself admits is 'repetitive music'? Is it that it lacks precisely those deep roots in the past that feed and nourish the most adventurous new growth? For surely – to continue the botanical image – the newest growth needs the deepest tap roots. Cutting the roots stunts real growth.

For some, such as Harrison Birtwistle, listening to minimalist writing is like 'waiting for the bus to arrive; you see it coming from a long distance' – in other words, there's absolutely no surprise left by the time it reaches you. (For Birtwistle's interview, see *On Creativity*, chapter 3.) For others, such as Elliott Carter (*On Creativity*, chapter 5), minimalism's rejection of formal, traditional disciplines, and their replacement by surrender to what he sees as 'fake orientalism', carries disturbingly totalitarian overtones. Carter rejects the element of repetition in minimalism as akin to trying to persuade audiences with the techniques of advertising or political propaganda. 'This is a way,' he told me, 'of destroying intelligence.'

Perhaps the reliance on a single formula, of insistent repetition, and harmonic repetition at that, is just too limited expressively to take you very far creatively. Of course, repetition is an important gesture in music, from Rossini to Ravel at least. But to take a single gesture and to attempt to build it into an all-inclusive system seems to me to sideline the other available lessons of the past. Rather like a simple act of rejection, repetition is finally not rich or complex enough by itself as a code for composition.

Yet even rejection, as a way of setting a new artistic course, has its part to play in the search for originality – but it must be informed rejection, not blind, unconsidered indifference. Take the cases of the Hungarian, György Ligeti (*On Creativity*, chapter 10), and the Briton, Harrison Birtwistle.

In 1956 the young Ligeti emerged from the ruins of Budapest and the would-be Hungarian Revolution suppressed by the tanks of the Red Army. Such was the control exercised by the Communist Party that Ligeti's access to contemporary music was almost entirely through the broadcasts of the Western radio stations. Despite that, and despite being Hungarian, Ligeti came to West Germany – as it then was – never having been able to hear the third and fourth of Bartók's string quartets.

His fledgling reputation led him to Darmstadt, where he found himself the centre of attention. Very flattering, no doubt; Pierre Boulez wanted him in his school; Karl Heinz Stockhausen wanted him in his.

After an entire lifetime living under Fascism during the war and Communism after it, Ligeti was not ready for more control of how he thought, how he wrote. Besides, serialism was not what he heard in his own head. It might have been the prevailing theory, but it was not for him. Moreover he hated its totalitarian overtones. He quotes with contempt Schoenberg's claims for the influence of the twelve-tone row: 'I made sure of the domination of German music for the next hundred years.' In Ligeti's view, those who place no value on the past are to be dismissed as egocentric and self-important in their concern only for the future.

In rejecting serialism, however, Ligeti had somewhere else to turn. There was his own Hungarian past, with the folklore tradition captured, codified and enhanced by Bartók and Kodály. But his roots went much further, back to Renaissance polyphony, to Gesualdo, Monteverdi and – as he disarmingly but inclusively puts it – 'to any good music'. Ligeti's rejection of serialism, of everything that was presented as the most contemporary and advanced way of writing music, could only work because he had foundations in the past that informed his unique personal sensibility, his sense of how he needed to compose. Turning to the past involved an understanding of the past as anchor. It had nothing to do with cheap pastiche, mere nostalgia, pallid revivalism.

'I am deeply linked to tradition,' Ligeti told me. 'I don't think we discover new styles from a zero point. We are always continuing, whether we want to or not.'

A comparable experience affected the British composer, Harrison Birtwistle. As a music student at the Royal Northern College of Music in Manchester, Birtwistle's contemporaries were people such as Alexander Goehr and Peter Maxwell Davies. In the pecking order of the day, Sandy Goehr and Max Davies were the clever ones, the composers, the young Turks, the confounders of the English pastoralist or cow-pat school of music. For Sandy and Max were serialists. Harry Birtwistle was just a clarinet player.

In fact, Birtwistle *was* composing but serialism meant nothing to him. He recognised it as one of the most important movements of the twentieth century. But it simply did not square with what he heard in his head. He couldn't make it work. So he put composition to one side.

It was only when, as a musician, he played in Messiaen's *Quartet for the End of Time*, that he had his revelation. If Messiaen could write with such personal freedom and originality, so could he. It gave Birtwistle the courage to write as he heard. Interestingly, in talking to Messiaen, Birtwistle got the strong sense that his music, however wholly personal it sounded, was in the main tradition of music from the beginning of time.

In acting as they did, Birtwistle and Ligeti were taking a stand on the great issues of twentieth-century music: whether to sign up to the Second Viennese School or not. Certainly, in passing up the opportunity, each of them had major resources of intellectual understanding to turn to: in Birtwistle's case, the rich veins of classical mythology – everything from *The Masque of Orpheus* to his latest work, *The Io Passion* – and the earthier traditions of English music hall and folklore.

The powerful importance of this historical dimension can be

observed in close, physical detail in the new Disney Concert Hall in Los Angeles, designed by Frank Gehry. (I interviewed him in Los Angeles in November 2004 for a BBC Radio Three broadcast in January 2005.) To the casual viewer, no buildings constructed today could have more of the contemporary feel to them, seem less anchored in the past, than those by this architect. From his Guggenheim Museum in Bilbao onwards, Gehry has created dazzling sculpturally shaped buildings that seem to exist in the now, and to be utterly dependent on the most modern materials, the latest design techniques and concepts. As he told me, without access to the computer design systems used by Dassault aircraft in France, his buildings could not be modelled, planned, costed or the construction managed. Can any connection with the past be traced in these extraordinarily sinuous shapes? Not obviously.

Yet Gehry has always acknowledged, and insisted on, two huge influences that he came across as a young student on his first visit to Europe. They were the Romanesque churches of France, and the Baroque extravaganzas of southern Germany. In the first he discovered great internal volumes enclosed in stone; in the second he revelled in the pierced vaults and the dazzling illumination of the internal spaces. Gehry told me that when he first saw Notre Dame in Paris, he felt a sense of rage that his teachers had not shared this building with him except in a casual picture-postcard way.

Look again at his buildings, and the sense of volume and the complex patterns of illumination that he first discovered in Europe are there to see. At the start of his exploratory drawings, Gehry is playing with volumes, either through actual models, or through the practice of intense drawing with pen where he never takes the point from the page until a sketch is completed. In exploring volumes and how to manipulate and express them in buildings, Gehry is not confronting today's problems but those of a millennium ago. The quintessentially 'contemporary' Frank Gehry – he insists he is not a 'modernist' because of his rejection of Mies van der Rohe – would not be the architect he is without these deep roots to the past.

Although involvement with the past is an important feature of many of the 'crossover' artists, it is neither mandatory nor totally consistent. In the case of Richard Serra, his position in relation to a sense of necessary continuity is decidedly ambiguous. (Regrettably, he declined to allow my interview with him to be printed.) As a student painter Serra had two strong beliefs. Once you have left art school, you create your own definitions of activity. And as a would-be sculptor who was trained as a painter, he enjoyed huge freedoms in deciding how he defined his new role.

As a young sculptor Serra worked with many 'unfashionable' materials, among them lead, scrap rubber, old neon tubes, stuffed animals or, as he said to me, anything including 'balls of spit'. Serra, too, knew that he was not – as he put it – 'going to be able to implicate the viewer in the painting in the way Velázquez did, and I'm not going to be able to hang a brush stroke from a fan to a dog's eyelid in one stroke and put a whole cosmology there'. Most of his immediate terms of reference are to the great twentieth-century modernists, sculptors of space such as Brancusi or Giacometti, painters such as Pollock, De Kooning or his great love, Barnett Newman. With such admitted antecedents Serra, with his great leap from 'fine' sculptural materials to the epic, industrial use of rolled steel sculpture, looks a strong candidate for categorising as a 'crossover'. Certainly, he acknowledges important influences from the past but apparently – as noted above – principally from the last century of experience.

Yet closer examination reveals even deeper continuities in Serra's work, with an appropriately 'Janus aspect' to them. His famous series of torqued ellipses are inspired by a shape in Borromini's church in Rome, the Quattro Fontane. The oval space on the floor is matched exactly by the oval in the ceiling, called a 'Borromini ellipse'. Such a startling link between the Renaissance and the outer limits of contemporary sculpture using industrial materials with a classical grace, a humanistic feel – not to mention a romantic passion – surely puts Richard Serra firmly in the ranks of the other artists who speak in this book.

His own definition of the link with the past is revealing: 'You have a sense of continuity,' he told me, 'not in that you want to make what other people have made. You have a sense of historical continuity in that you would like to leave a body of work that's meaningful.' And he summed it up: 'The way that I relate to the tradition is, I guess, in a way Eliot related to the tradition; as soon as you break with it, you're part of it.'

In posing the link in this deliberately paradoxical way, I think Richard Serra puts it well. Past and present are not linked in a single, irreversible, rigidly connected time line. The links go backwards and forwards, carrying different weights at different stages of the transactions. The precise manipulation of those weights and the directions in which they go are up to each individual artist. But the very idea of transaction opens up huge possibilities for innovation. That is one of the characteristics of the 'crossovers' as they look in both directions.

Significantly, that most contemporary-looking of artists, Michael Craig-Martin, with his bold, unmediated colours, his hard-edge outlines, his selected catalogue of everyday objects, finds links for his most recent work in Piero della Francesca and Seurat. In doing so, he is not merely making an *obeisance d'hommage*, he is acknowledging that his approach to the organisation of shapes has a distant, historic but important ancestry, a living connection with his search for expression today.

Many other themes emerge from this very varied group of artists. To begin with, they have an openness of mind towards starting their work that is courageous, even reckless. William Forsythe, the choreographer, begins each new work with a blank sheet. He takes the huge personal risk of starting to work without preconceptions. And if he begins by repeating a previous work, his dancers tell him. The road to innovation and originality is a painstaking and exposed one. Heiner Goebbels, the composer, accumulates his stage pieces through the active involvement of actors, musicians, designers, lighting designers in the creation–rehearsal process. Only once a body of material has been created does he start to pare away at it and nudge it towards its final form.

There is no guarantee that this 'open' process of creation will yield the hoped-for result. As Simon McBurney discovered while creating *The Elephant Vanishes* in Tokyo, there were times when he faced a totally blank wall of nullity. In the event, the finished product was one of the most exhilarating pieces of theatre of recent years.

If I had to risk a summary of the characteristics that inform many of the artists in this volume, I would suggest that they include: deconstructing form in order to discover new ones; learning about and from the properties and potentialities of new materials; being open to the ideas that creation comes from a readiness to take risks in process; working through chaos to a new form of order; using play as a path to discovery; knowing that the most daring kinds of innovation can sometimes emerge from a real engagement with the past. All these activities and processes involve a quality of fearlessness that is shared by many artists but has to be possessed in special degree by the pioneers.

Does any of this represent a systematic checklist or academic definition? Of course not. But I do believe that – through the mouths of the artists themselves – it sets out some significant pointers for how one gathering of the truly innovative actually works.

BERNARDO BERTOLUCCI

Psychoanalysis was like adding a new lens to my camera

In one sense, Bernardo Bertolucci's creative journey is simply expressed: from *Last Tango* to *Last Emperor*. The former, one of the most notorious films of its time, a deeply personal exploration of human despair, still a byword for a certain kind of cinematic sex, has become a classic. This was Bertolucci as a leading exponent of European art house cinema. *The Last Emperor*, made in 1987 just twenty-five years later, showed him making an epic film but with an intimate core.

This has many admirers too and, of course, has won many awards. But the stylistic and aesthetic distance Bertolucci has travelled raises questions and, for some, problems. For one school of critics it was the early art house director, most famously with movies such as *The Spider's Stratagem* and *The Conformist*, who is the master to be revered. For others, his later films, including *Little Buddha* or *Sheltering Sky* or the sentimental Tuscan bitter-sweet romance *Stealing Beauty*, show a resort to international values, a revelling in sheer texture and mood for their own sake, which are seen as less interesting than what he did earlier. Others, though, disagree, still admiring Bertolucci's sensuous composition, his subtle direction of actors, his creation of ambiguous atmospheres. Above all, they like his fierce, personal independence, all seen as consistently admirable. Bertolucci's sixty-five-year journey is not a straight line. Rather, it's marked by a series of major diversions, changes of direction, often involving rejections of his own previous experience. He rejected writing poetry because his father was a poet. He rejected his mentor, Jean-Luc Godard, for being too theoretical and dogmatic; Bertolucci wanted to communicate with his audience. He rejected Marxism and took to Buddhism. He seemed to reject Italy and turned to the international. He is, after all, the man who credits his analyst with his own creative opening-up and put his analyst on the credits of one of his films. Throughout, Bertolucci has remained independent. He has refused to get involved in the big studio system and he has veered from the huge to the small canvas as his creative needs have dictated. He retains a capacity to surprise and to make personal films that many other directors envy.

What sort of films do you think you'd be making now if you had not gone into analysis in your late twenties?

It's a very difficult question because it doesn't involve only the movies that maybe would have been completely different, it involves also my life. My life would have been probably something very, very different. I went first to a Freudian psychoanalyst in 1969, just two or three months before shooting *The Spider's Stratagem*. I didn't go really because I wanted to make bigger, wider, my perspectives or my horizon. I went because I felt in need of a kind of very intimate dialogue, to be able to speak with somebody about things I wasn't able to speak with anybody else. And that was really the beginning of a great discovery, the discovery that psychoanalysis was like adding a new lens, a new objective to my camera. And maybe, the therapeutical effect of psychoanalysis on me came also through my movies. I was so excited as a neophyte about this discovery of the world of Sigmund Freud, for the first six, seven years, I was kind of going around as a PR of psychoanalysis.

And yet Spider's Stratagem *and* Conformist, *the early films, they are not glibly Freudian at all, but they're certainly very free. Was it the freedom to explore character that the analysis gave you?*

I'm very pleased that you say that because I know how important my shrink was during the preparation of these two movies, but I'm very pleased that it's not too obvious when you see the movies. I don't like to see a movie which is too openly influenced by psychoanalysis; it's always a bit embarrassing. I think that this new language, this new instrument of discovery, has to be always very hidden and very discreet. But when you said *Spider's Stratagem* – yes, it comes from a Borges short story called 'The Theme of the Traitor and The Hero', and in Borges, it's a story of a young Irishman who goes and investigates about his ancestor, somebody who lives in the nineteenth century, who was considered a hero. I moved the story to Italy in the thirties during Fascism and I made the story of a man who goes and investigates about whom? Not his ancestor, about his father.

That's the Freudian bit coming out.

But it doesn't seem too heavily Freudian. Same thing with *The Conformist*. The Italian Fascist who goes to France to kill his teacher, his ex-university professor who is an anti-Fascist militant, it's the story again of a young man who goes to kill his father. But what is more important for me is that psychoanalysis came in the transition between the sixties and the seventies; and where I can notice the effects of that is specially that in the sixties, my cinema was very hermetical, very close, very difficult. Very few people could go and enjoy it, just other film makers, or critics, or maybe my relatives!

That's not true of Before the Revolution*?*

But *Before the Revolution* was a very art movie! It was a kind of – what I would call a monologue. After the analysis, the cinema that came afterwards, which is *The Spider, The Conformist, Last Tango in Paris, 1900, La Luna* et cetera, there was a real change in my cinema. I became able to go from monologue to dialogue.

Dialogue with the audience?

With the audience.

And dialogue within the film as well, dialogue between characters?

Especially between the film and the audience. So, I was able to accept feedback. You know, in the sixties we were obsessed with the idea of rigour, severity, and we were thinking that any movie which was successful with the audience would be a horrible compromise with commercial values et cetera. It was also proof of our insecurity. We weren't, or I wasn't, ready to face the audience.

But neither The Spider's Stratagem *nor* The Conformist *is, in many respects, an easy movie. They are complex, what the characters do, what the characters say. So the fact that they are popular, that they are both cult and popular, is quite an achievement. You clearly didn't sell your principles in order to make them popular.*

Not at all, but I think that in comparison with *Before the Revolution* and the movies I made before, they are incredibly readable and there weren't this kind of, I must admit, punishing moments in these movies as in my movies before. Anyway, for me the big thing was to be able to have a dialectic moment with the audience, to accept that somebody could have seen the movies.

Did the Freudian analysis help to liberate you from Marxism? Was there a straight or a gentle switch from the one to the other?

Here, if I can say, when I was listening to what you were saying, describing a bit my work and my life at the beginning, you were talking about rejecting, rejecting, rejecting! Rejecting Marxism, rejecting Godard. I think that is not the right word, if I can dare! I think that I didn't reject any of these things; I accepted it, I stored it in myself. They are there. It's a kind of enrichment. I don't think you have to reject if you move ahead. You just move ahead within your knowledge and in your experience!

You've absorbed it and come to terms with it?

Yes. You know it's extremely good that, for example, what was called real Communism in Soviet Union has finished. I think it's very important for millions and millions of people. But, I'm sure that there are major questions that Communism asked which had not been answered by capitalism. There are still big, big, unanswered questions.

You were incredibly young, as well, when you started making films. You were incredibly inexperienced! What made you think, given that your first instincts were to write poetry, that you were interested in making films and how did you dare to make a film when you knew nothing about it?

It was the unbearable lightness of the hormones when you are twenty or twenty-one.

You can do anything!

You can do anything. I was incredibly determined, nobody could stop me. I didn't know why but there was a kind of call. At that age you feel these calls. There was a call to be a director and to show that I could be as free as a director as I was as a poet.

And, of course, one of your earliest experiences was working with Pasolini, and you've said that Pasolini himself had never made a film before. So there were the two of you: you, his assistant, and he hadn't made a film before. This doesn't happen nowadays, does it?

You know, Pasolini had such a talent and he was such a competent man about literature and critics and poetry; he was very curious about this new film language. And what came out was the first Pasolini movie called *Accattone*, which I think is one of his masterpieces, together with I think the *Saint Matthew Gospel* and *Oedipus* and . . . oh, he did so many good movies. But it was an incredible experience because for me, it wasn't just being physically, for the first time, on the set of a movie. It was physically witnessing the birth of cinema. You rightly said Pasolini hadn't done anything before, and that's why he wasn't following some kind of knowledge; he was just inventing, day after day, cinema. It was like being present at the birth of cinema with him.

Let's move on to Last Tango in Paris. *You've probably said most of the things you're ever going to say about it but I wonder whether it was almost too famous for you. Did you find its success, internationally, a problem and has it ever been a burden to you, because everybody says 'Ah, Bertolucci, the* Last Tango *man'?*

Yes, that kind of success, it can be on one hand a kind of overdose, on the other hand a kind of nightmare. I don't want to sound melodramatic or sentimental, but success can be a nightmare. When you are identified always with a certain title, with a certain movie, especially with a certain sequence in that movie, it becomes a kind of a little nightmare. Meantime, when I say it's an overdose, that's because I said I wanted to go from monologue to dialogue. With *Last Tango in Paris*, the dialogue was global, it was wherever I was going. I remember I found myself in Singapore and people at the hotel organised a kind of dinner, all based on *Last Tango*. And that's why I say it can be a bit of a nightmare, because then you have to really do a big effort to move from there, ahead, forward.

Which you did. Do you accept that your career has a feeling of two halves to it or, as far as you're concerned, is there a linear development? You don't accept it as a sort of early Bertolucci and a late Bertolucci?

I'm not the right person to say there is an itinerary that can be followed, a consistent itinerary. I think that because of this desire to change after I've done a movie. After *The Conformist*, which was a political film about Fascism, comes *Last Tango in Paris*, which is really about the most intimate relationship between a man and a woman. It's a film, I think, which now looks to me quite romantic even if, then, it was considered obscene. I was even condemned to two months of prison in Italy with suspension and then I lost completely my civil rights for five years, and that still hurts! And then after *Last Tango in Paris* comes *1900*, which is a kind of big epic fresco on the birth of Socialism, at the beginning of the twentieth century, in Emilia which is my country in northern Italy, following the lives of two men born on the same day in the year 1900, the son of the landowners and the son of the peasants. I need all the time to abandon a certain field, to go away, to try not to repeat myself. I am really obsessed with that. I am afraid of repeating myself. So, that's why I constantly try to find material which is challenging.

But certain things are constant and you create images in a certain sort of way. Where does your visual instinct come from, the subtlety of the composition, the use of light, the use of shadows? What I love is your cityscapes, your townscapes, long views down receding roads or streets. Where does your visual instinct come from?

That's very difficult to tell. I don't know. I have no idea. My father was not only a poet but he was also an art historian and so, since I was a child, I was taken to see art, churches, museums, exhibitions, and I was very familiar with the world of visual art. I think that has a weight in everything. But when I stopped writing poems and I decided that I wanted to be a film director, there was something, which was, for me, a revelation. I discovered that cinema was able to be together many other languages at the same time. Cinema is theatre, of course, music, literature, poetry, painting, sculpture, dance, architecture even. Some shots, very complicated shots, are built up as something kind of architectural. So, I was feeling that cinema was really the expression of the times I was living in.

And all the things that you were. Because you mentioned music and after all, the sense of the fastidious placing of the music and the way in which, for example, you use Verdi in both Before The Revolution *and in* The Spider, *they are integral parts of the film. I suppose every Italian knows Verdi!*

Yeah, but if you are born in Parma – and Verdi was born in Parma – Verdi is one of our local legends. And in those years I was listening to Verdi and jazz a lot, between the ages of seventeen and eighteen, and I was seeing the countryside where Verdi was living and I was imagining his inspiration coming from the same huge cornfield I was seeing, from the Po river which runs slowly, from all the things that I saw in this Po valley; I was feeling like identifying with that music, it was something physiological, almost. And there is a book called *Il Paese de Melodrama* by Bruno Barelli, *The Country of Melodrama*, about Verdi which is fantastic, which says 'in that enormous mosquito net, which is the Po valley between Parma, Mantova and Cremona', which for me is the beginning; I was seeing the epic side of that Po valley. I was seeing the Po river as if it was like the Mississippi. I think that when you are young, you have the capacity to create mythology.

Is that why, in Before the Revolution, *there is this eulogy for how the Po is going to be destroyed by the bankrupt landowner, the dredgers will come, nobody will look after the trees, nobody will fish for the pike and the machines will come. So even at the age of twenty-three or twenty-four, you had this incredibly deep identification with what the Po stood for.*

Yah, you're right. And I saw that movie, *Before the Revolution*, for the first time since I made it, in Cannes, two or three years ago. And when I saw that sequence you are talking about, the eulogy of the old kind of country aristocrat, it was incredibly pre-ecological. There was a kind of sensibility, like somebody who is in the Green Party today, which I was quite surprised.

Do you feel an exile from Italy?

I felt a bit like that in the early eighties. I decided that Italy was getting so corrupted and cynical. And I wasn't completely wrong because ten years later, you had all these trials in Milano, '*mani puliti*', the clean hands, 'Tangentopolis', about the corruption of the political world. So at the beginning of the eighties, feeling that, I said, 'Enough with this country, I will go away in a kind of voluntary exile,' and I found myself in China, and I did *The Last Emperor*. Then I went to the Sahara, when I did *The Sheltering Sky*, then I had this incredible crush for Buddhism.

You still have it?

Oh yes, but I don't consider myself a Buddhist. I consider myself an amateur Buddhist, a dilettante.

A Catholic who is informed by Buddhism? Still Catholic?

I was born Catholic like every Italian. We are born Catholic. But then, when I was twelve, I decided that I couldn't be a religious person any more and when I think about Buddhism I don't see it as a religion, I see it more as a vision of the world, as a philosophy.

Was that the attraction also of working in China, Morocco and the Himalayas, what enabled you to say something about the world, that you don't want to be imprisoned, even in a culture as rich as the Italian culture?

Right, because I felt a bit rejected by the reality of my country at the beginning of the eighties, being in China and then in Africa and then in India, I really discovered that other cultures can be as interesting as your country, even more sometimes, and is exactly the kind of nodal point of our present, now. If only it could, a little bit, be able to transmit this feeling of love for a different culture, for different values.

Which doesn't threaten your own love of, or connectedness with, your own values?

Of course, not only that, but it makes me more aware of what is my original culture.

And yet, in Besieged *the English protagonist, the young musician, is desperate to have sex with an African woman, who cannot understand his culture. And in the course of the film he slowly gets rid of, or sells, all his Western cultural objects. Now surely you don't believe that you have to reject your cultural past in order to have a sympathy with world culture?*

Not at all. There is a point – and the point is your mind, your spirit – where the values, which are completely in contradiction, can find a system of being organic to each other. And the first time I went to Peking, to Beijing, to do the first recce for *The Last Emperor*, between the airport and the city of Beijing there is a flat landscape with poplar trees, exactly like in the Po valley, and immediately that put me in a kind of good attitude to accept. But there is a moment when you go on these travels, which take you in places completely different from your original places, there is a moment when you do everything to find a point of link and a point of connection. And then you understand that you don't have to have the constant presence of all your education next to you. You don't have to have all the time to be protected by your father, in a way!

Or to protect what you know and what makes you. You can be free about it.

Yes, because it's exactly in you that everything can be recomposed. If you are reaching a point of abandonment, freedom, values which are completely unknown and new, your mind and your body can become the place where so different things can meet that movies can be like that.

I think the word freedom is the one which you have used most consistently and interestingly. Now, what sort of director are you? Because I think Novecento – 1900 – *rejected the idea of the padrone, the boss; and, indeed, the very first scene of* Besieged *shows a young African teacher saying to his class, 'What is the difference between the leader and the boss?' So what sort of director are you?*

And I think that is very important that you accept that film is very, very sensitive; it is much more sensitive than what is written on the box, and the box says '400 Asa', '1,000 Asa'. No, the film is much more sensitive than that!

Those are film speeds, by the by!

Film is able to catch the creative energy which is on the set, which is not only coming from the director. It comes from the person who moves the dolly, it comes from the person who painted the wall; everybody can be creative. For me, a big part of my energy goes in trying to stimulate the creative energy of the people which surround the camera. A movie is done by the communion of many creativities.

Do you talk to them all when you're on location and when you're shooting? Do you actually have the whole team in and say 'This is what I'm looking for, this is the feeling I want'?

You know, there is a way of participating with them, of being with them, which is not only talking. There are other ways. Maybe just one phrase without making long speeches, in the right moment, can really explain to everybody and reassure everybody on the fact that they are there not only to do their little piece of job – which is essential – but they are there also to bring their emotions. So it's like becoming a bridge between the film and the crew.

And as you're shooting – and presumably at the same time you are mentally layering in the music as well and beginning to think how it will all cut together – do you have any idea by the time you've shot a sequence how it is cut? How much do you leave for the cutting room itself?

I'd like to tell you a bit my relationship with cutting. At the beginning, during the sixties, I was considering cutting as a kind of moment where this strong material, the rushes that you see the day after you've shot, which contains a kind of wild strength, it then goes to the cutting room, which makes everything consistent to a story; this strength disappears or is contained. So, in the sixties, I was considering the moment of the editing a bit like, let's say the editing room to me looked like a slaughterhouse, where the best in the material that I've shot, the most wild things, the most unpredictable things were cut off and so you could see the blood on the floor of the cutting room. Then, with *The Conformist*, I met Kim [Franco] Arcalli, who has been very important in my life. It was between 1970 and 1978 when he died, too early, too young. But in these eight years, he did the editing of *The Conformist* with me, he wrote with me *Last Tango in Paris* and he edited it, and he wrote with me *1900*, *Novecento*, and he edited it. He made me change my opinion on the editing. In the sixties we are doing long shots, in order also to avoid the editing. We were doing long shots which refused to be cut in order to avoid these moments, which for us – we were also very politically engaged – was like a moment of law and order, a moment of an operation of police.

This is when you imposed yourself on the action?

Yeah, in a way. And so, it was like with Kim, I said 'OK, show me that the editing can be a moment also as creative as the shooting! Show me that there is something unpredictable in the editing!' And he did. He showed me that he was going into the editing room like going into a mine, like a miner goes into a mine, looking for hidden, precious things; things that I was in fact ignoring, they were there. Things that were existing when you put two shots – not supposed to get together – but you put them together, you discover something new. So I discovered that also in the editing, there was a completely new thing for me. There was the unpredictability that you can have when you shoot.

And it wasn't just a question of restoring what you call the wilder moments, it was more subtle than that.

No, it was something new. It's like saying that one plus one doesn't make two. One plus one plus one doesn't make that something else. You have a kind of gestalt effect.

And did that change the way you shot?

Made my way of shooting even more against the editing because I wanted to challenge more the editor, which was extraordinary. You know, if you live for cinema, something like what we are talking about now, it can really fill up your life as an incredible gift. I love directors who are still reinventing cinema, who are still asking the question, 'What is cinema, why do I do cinema?'

How do you answer that question, apart from loving doing it and it clearly releases all your creative energies?

Yeah, it's very simple because I didn't know how to do anything else.

It matters to you that it matters to us, the audience. So, what is the effect that cinema has on audiences?

For many years in the sixties till the late seventies, I thought that cinema could have a kind of didactical effect, a kind of pedagogical effect on the audience. I thought that if you were doing a politically correct – in that sense of those years – a good political movie, you could in some way change the mentality of many people. I don't think this is true. I think that there was an illusion. I'm afraid that the effect on the audiences of movies, seeing it in retrospect, has been more negative than positive.

Well, you can't be Messianic about it, you can't see yourself as a prophet and people will follow you to a new way of life?

No, you maybe thought that, you maybe hoped that, when you were young and maybe even too idealistic, but in fact it's a complete illusion. What I think can change the mentality of big, big audiences is television. Television is a presence in the life of people and that's why, in our country, the Prime Minister, Berlusconi, has done everything he could to avoid becoming Prime Minister, to give up his own private three national big channels, because he knows the value and importance of television. I think that if in this very moment we have a kind of a big cultural problem in Italy, because I think that the fact that the elections last year went as they went, this is a cultural problem.

Which reflects television?

Television is the major vehicle for culture, let's say, or sub-culture. Television has created people, especially young people I'm afraid, who are watching without seeing, who are listening without understanding. Because something has been communicated through television, people are reassured in a way: everything happens in the distance, and everything is just in the box and you are safe. Now, this is completely wrong!

It's an illusion?

It's a complete illusion. In *The Conformist*, at a certain moment, the conformist goes to Paris and he goes to meet his ex-teacher of philosophy from Rome University. In fact, he has been asked to kill him by the Fascist secret service. He goes to see him and they recall when the professor was teaching Plato's *Republic* – 'The Myth of the Cave'. When I was shooting *The Conformist*, I was preparing a dialogue between this professor of philosophy and the conformist, the student. I went to read a bit of philosophy, I read 'The Myth of the Cave' of Plato, and immediately I couldn't help but put it in the movie. Because Plato says, here you have a cave, you have a group of prisoners in chains sitting at the entrance of the cave, turned towards the bottom of the cave, the interior of the cave. Behind them, there is a fire. People pass with statues, between the fire and prisoners sitting down and the cave. The fire projects the shadows of the statues on the bottom of the cave. So, I was thinking this is exactly – after all, Plato is about 500 BC! – this is cinema! The fire is the projector with the lamp and the sculptures are like the film passing and the prisoners sitting is the audience and the bottom of the cave is the screen. And what Plato says, the prisoners are not seeing the statues, they are seeing the shadow of the statues. And the professor says, 'Like you Italians' – he is an Italian exiled in Paris in the late thirties, anti-Fascist – 'You Italians now, you are not seeing the reality, you are seeing the shadow of the reality.'

And that's even truer today than it was when you made the film.

And I think that a period film for me, it's an achievement when it talks not only about that period, but it talks also about the present.

Well, having seen a screening, very recently, and the audience, a lot of whom weren't born when The Conformist *was made, clearly recognised its topicality and its immediacy. I want to ask you another political question and that is your view of Hollywood. Because, if you're talking about expression, if you're talking about freedom, if you're talking about giving something to the audience, the Hollywood system doesn't do that, does it?*

You know, Hollywood, a long time ago, was a fantastic factory of movies.

A dream factory.

A dream factory. But there were great directors able to find their freedom in Hollywood. There were fantastic movies coming from Hollywood. In the last ten or fifteen years, it's like if Wall Street had taken over Hollywood. What there used to be was this kind of sometimes not very cultivated producers, but with great taste, adventurers maybe. Now, they're all these executives, very often like bankers or like businessmen. Their relationship with the movies they produce, it's purely based on market researchers, the complete elimination of risk. That makes Hollywood movies more and more uninteresting.

And what does it do to us, to our culture? You've used a striking phrase, you regard it as 'like the military occupation of the multiplexes'.

Yeah, I'm smiling but there's very little to smile. The situation at the moment is that almost all theatres all over the world are occupied by Hollywood movies and it's very difficult for independent movies who are not in the chain of Hollywood distributions to be able to be shown to an audience. A movie which is not shown is like a baby who is not born. It does exist, but the proof of a movie is to be seen by the eyes of an audience. It's an old, terrible question, it goes beyond the Hollywood superpower of this moment. Half of the masterpieces we love, obviously of cinema, have been seen very, very little. How many people have seen Bresson movies, how many people have seen, in the West at least, Mizoguchi movies or Dreyer movies?

But they're part of the collective subconscious; they are seen and they are shown and they are there. They're an available, imaginative resource!

You're right, it's true. But, in fact, it's a kind of reason of sadness for a director, the fact that his movie is being seen in a very, very, very reduced milieu.

But your movies are still going to be shown, and nothing will stop you, even the power of Hollywood, from making the films you want to make?

So far, I was able to do more or less what I wanted. Let's see if it goes on like that, now that the cinema is in one of its big moments of mutation. Mutation is what's going on now and that makes me very excited. The new technologies, the digital technologies, and also the chance that everybody has to do a little movie and to show it through the Net, it's something completely new, something that has not been analysed and studied, but that will change the way of the language of cinema. It will change because it's such a structural mutation that it will have a dramatic effect on style, language, structure, the way of telling a plot, the way the actors will act. Everything will be very different in ten or fifteen years' time, and thank God for that because there were other big mutations in cinema, from the silent to the sound, from the black and white to the colour and this is another of these great moments. So, I think that we all should be excited about that.

MICHAEL CRAIG-MARTIN

I'm my own ideal audience

The interesting thing about Michael Craig-Martin is that you can't pigeon-hole him. He was a sculptor and he is a painter. Those paintings where everyday objects outlined in black tape float at you out of bright red, green or blue backgrounds; that's Craig-Martin. Or entire rooms in galleries where the assault of intense colour and artfully distanced objects create a whole environment for experience and looking; that's Craig-Martin too. Further back in time there's the famous, or infamous, *An Oak Tree*, a glass filled with water on a glass bathroom shelf with an accompanying text, where Craig-Martin answers questions from himself about how the apparent glass can be a real oak tree. But Michael Craig-Martin is famous, or infamous, as a teacher of art students too. More than once in these interviews, major visual artists have praised his teaching at Goldsmiths College; others blame him personally for undermining quality, whatever that is, in British art. If you want to know who spawned the Brit Art Brat Pack, say his critics, that's Craig-Martin as well. And the trouble is that there's something elusive about him. Born in Dublin, educated in the United States, he carries a slightly detached mid-Atlanticism around with him, which only makes him harder to pigeon-hole. That detachment is ringed by a rather British coolness and capacity for irony that leaves many of his critics guessing.

Let's get the teaching out of the way, because you sometimes tend to be labelled just with the title 'teacher'. It mustn't be overplayed, but it shouldn't be underplayed either?

No, I wouldn't want it to be underplayed. I've devoted a great deal of my life to it, far more than I ever intended. When I started, when I left art school, I started teaching immediately, and it was really just a way for me to make a living and to provide for myself as an artist. But I have to say that I got very interested in the whole question about what art education might be, and it fitted in with things that I was thinking about art. And then there were things that I learned from the question of what does somebody bring to art in those first moments when they decide to study it, and I got interested in how you move a person from that position into a more sophisticated position.

But you didn't come with any professional experience about what an art teacher should do and what relationship he should have with the students?

I was very fortunate, because I had a very good art education myself. I went to the Yale University School of Art, and when I first got there Josef Albers had left but his teaching remained and the basis of my art education was Albers' teaching. And Albers was extraordinary because he created a very intellectually coherent package of ideas about the nature of art and art teaching, what could be taught. Subsequently I came to feel that it was a certain view of art, but it didn't cover everything and in some ways it didn't cover certain things that I came to consider more important. But what was impressive about it was its intellectual coherence.

And he insisted, I think, on a certain coolness, a very rational way of looking at things and expressing what you saw.

His idea was that art was essentially a perceptual activity, that you had to understand what it was to look at things, how to describe things. And essentially you could only really understand by experience, to be better at something was to have experienced more of it, and I certainly think that remains true.

Some people have said this is so rational, so detached, where is the room for feeling, for emotion in painting?

Well, Albers' view was that there were things that could be taught and things that couldn't, and the most important things were the things that couldn't. But it didn't mean that there weren't things that could be taught, and so what you should concentrate on was trying to teach those things. He never considered what you were doing to be art itself; they were exercises, they were studies, they were things that you did to prepare certain aspects of your own understanding, perception, skills, in order to be able to be an artist.

You had experienced abstract expressionism in New York very close up, minimalism and I think the start of conceptualism. So, by English teaching standards, you came with a lot of first-hand information from the very front line of art. Did you feel that was what you were passing on, or were you passing on the things you've just been describing?

It's an interesting question. When I arrived in 1966, and I had just finished a Masters course at Yale, I was very attuned to what was going on in New York, in America at that time. It was a very critical moment in art, a very exciting moment, and when I arrived in Britain I met incredibly interesting people, but almost nobody knew about the things that I was most interested in. And in retrospect I think that I misunderstood one's cultural background and how much a part it plays in one's development, in one's understanding of what it is that art can be.

Did you try to proselytise about all these exciting new movements which were slowly coming over to Great Britain?

I don't ever think of myself as proselytising in that way, and never in teaching. My idea of teaching right from the beginning was that I would never try to get somebody else to do something that I wouldn't have been prepared to do myself as a student. I tried to make the teaching what I wanted it to be, to a certain extent what it had been for me; but also to bring to teaching the thing that had been missing for myself, the thing I had wanted. The thing that intrigued me from the beginning was how different people were, how complex the situation is and how much people bring individually to what they do, and that the start of what people do as students always comes from that individual experience.

So leaping forward about twenty years, when the people who are loosely called the Brit Artists started to emerge and a lot of them passed through your hands, was what they did a surprise to you?

By that point my ideas about teaching had become very, very much more complicated, very much more worked out, and in a sense Goldsmiths, which is where most of those people were educated, had become a school where I felt very comfortable in my own approach to teaching. And the idea at Goldsmiths was to allow students to follow their own instincts and for the teaching essentially to be retrospective; the students were expected to act and the teaching would then become a commentary on their actions, which would provide them with an understanding of how to proceed. But always the initial thing of what they did was expected to come from them.

Were you indicating that painting was not just about the line, the canvas, the oil or the materials, that any materials were a part of the subject of art? Was that a crucial part of what you were conveying?

That was certainly something that had always been very crucial to me. There are certain periods in the history of art where there's the history of art teaching; and the art teaching that I came from, and that preceded the art teaching that to a certain extent I've been a part of, was a teaching based on the materiality of the subject. So that painting was defined in terms of the physical act of painting; sculpture, there were ideas about what was sculpture; there were proper materials, there were proper techniques. So what the teaching focused on was teaching art through the techniques of the making, as though the techniques of the making would somehow produce the creative understanding.

The craft underpinned the art?

It's essentially an idea about craft underpinning art. And my generation questioned whether, not as many people think, that there should be no craft, but whether this should be seen as the central question either in art or in teaching.

It comes out in the sort of comment that one hears, 'That Picasso may do peculiar things, but he can certainly draw!' And the fact that he can draw makes this all right!

Yes, it makes it all right. My view of craft has always been that people underestimate how much skill and craft is involved in various kinds of activities. Some activities for some reason are seen to accrue greater kudos than other creative activities, and a creative activity is what is appropriate, partly what's appropriate to what you're doing, and partly what is within the temperament and the skill range of the artist in question. Many of the most original things that have been done in my lifetime have been by people who have taken what in a standardised situation was a weakness and turned it into a strength. What constitutes the success is the focusing on the thing that is theirs. So that for somebody who is not good at drawing the figure, it is a very good idea to abandon this as an area of activity; they will more than likely move into something else. On the other hand, there are people who are not good at drawing the figure but who stay with that precisely because of their own inabilities with it, force it to become something, and very often that's what becomes original. You could say Lucien Freud is like this. There's awkwardness in Lucien Freud, he's not the most natural draftsman, he's not the easiest person. But he stayed with it for so long, he stuck with this thing, he's turned the whole question of this art into something that is his.

Now you began with craft, by making wooden boxes which looked like wooden boxes and then when they were opened up, turned out not to be wooden boxes. And to start with you made them as a craftsman, because you've written about the joys of plywood and the power drill.

I'm a person who likes making things; I've always liked making things. And it's interesting, when I look back, that almost every time I tried to do something, I was interfering with something which was already satisfactory before I did it. And in a way *The Oak Tree* is the culmination of that period of work, where in essence I don't do anything at all. So somehow that is to me the point at which I've brought to fulfilment a certain kind of train of thought.

Let's stick with The Oak Tree, *as it's such an important piece. It's a normal water glass with normal water in it on a glass bathroom shelf and in exhibitions it is always positioned fairly high. Then there is this text about why it is, in fact, an oak tree; you play games with yourself in the text and every question that you throw at yourself about its nature, you deflect immensely ingeniously. I've read that a number of times, I thought there must be an answer to this and I haven't found it somehow. Now what's the element of provocation or of humour in this?*

I see myself as an artist of a generation of the sixties, early seventies, that's essentially where my thinking is based and the experience that's the root of what I do. We were very interested in the question of what essentially is a work of art, how does one define it, what is the baseline? Do you need to do something or don't you need to do something, what is it? And that was going back to the question, 'Is it the paint that makes a painting a painting, or is it something else?' So these were questions that interested us a great deal. So in *The Oak Tree* it's really my exercise in trying to think about what is the absolute essence of a work of art. So I came to this idea that it had really to do with belief; both the belief on the part of the artist in the genuineness of the activity that they were engaged in, but also the suspension of disbelief which is called upon with a viewer. Everybody understands that in the theatre but people have to do that in an art gallery too. So what I tried to do with *The Oak Tree* was to play on the relationship between the artist, the object and the viewer, and all three of them are engaged. The text is in the form of an auto interview; there's the half of me that's the artist and there's the other half that's the audience; there's the part of me that believes it and there's a part of me that's sceptical. So all of these things are played out in the one, and the work has been surprisingly successful and long lasting. And I think it's because people recognise in it something about what it is that happens in all works of art.

You said at one stage that it would continue to be an oak tree until such time as you changed it. So I thought, maybe you've decided to change it in the meantime but you haven't told us?

No, I've never decided against it. I might have done so if I thought it had lost its capacity to engage people, but it doesn't seem to have done that!

Would it be less interesting now, given what you said about The Oak Tree *only being an oak tree because you say it is, and we have to believe in it, if you change it back and say I've now decided to change it either into a glass or into another object? Would you think that would make it less interesting as a work of art?*

I don't think so, because I think the essence of *The Oak Tree* is that the proof that it is what it claims to be is exactly the same as the proof that it isn't. It remains that it looks exactly like a glass of water no matter what I say or what anybody says. And nobody can prove that I haven't done it, just as I can't actually prove that I have done it; so therefore even if I was to disclaim it, I might actually be wrong, mightn't I?

So you can assure me that you haven't changed it without telling us?

I haven't changed it, no, no!

Now, you began with everyday physical objects. What was it about the buckets, the milk bottles, the stepladders, what was it about the pure unvarnished object that attracted you?

For some reason, one of those instinctive things that I don't really understand, I was from very early on drawn to simple objects. Partly because I'm very interested in why if you take a pile of wood and assemble it in a certain way it becomes a table, and if you assemble the same pile of wood in a different way it becomes a chair; or you can just leave it as a pile of wood. Why something configures into something and about the relationship between those objects which we think of as art and those objects which we think of as not art. And I came to feel that the objects around us, particularly the ones that we value the least because they were the most ubiquitous, were actually the most interesting; these seem to me incredibly complex and extraordinary things.

Because nobody had invested them with an excess of meaning? The milk bottle may be well or badly designed, that wouldn't have concerned you, would it?

Ordinary objects, particularly in the beginning when they are first designed, have tended to look rather old-fashioned. That's partly because there's something wonderful that happens at the time when an object is first realised, because it's always done in the most economical manner possible. Nobody produces that first object without wishing it to be simple; they will use as little material as possible, they want it to do exactly the correct function. It's a certain size because of what it has to do.

Yes, a zinc bucket isn't designed but I suppose when we look at it, it's quite a graceful object.

It's a very graceful object and the reason why they're not twice the size is because if you filled it up, it would be too heavy to carry. The reason the handle is in a certain place is because if it was bigger, the side would always hit the side of your leg! So they're designed a certain size. All tools are designed to fit in your hand, that's why they are like what they are. And I got interested in the question of how function defined the nature of objects, because people talked about art as being functionalist objects. Well, what's function and are they truly functionalist and what is that difference?

Would you have been interested in them even if they hadn't worked as objects? They might have been much clumsier but still been the ubiquitous, everyday bucket? Its ubiquity and universality was the important thing?

The thing that interested me was its universality and also I never used objects which were unique or had history to them, or that had aged nicely, had a good pattern of some familiar thing of ageing.

Is that a conscious rejection of the process of the history, accretion, of association?

What interested me was the idea that there were lots more of these things, that a milk bottle is a wonderful object because there are thousands of them – or at least there were, I don't know how many there are left any more – but there are thousands of them. And the most wonderful thing, the sign of how absolutely worthless the one that you've got is, is that you leave it outside and you get another one! And I think there's something very interesting to me about an object where every object is the same and every one is unique.

But my generation was brought up in the unique value of the work of art: everything had to be special, everything had to be meant, everything had to have a transcendent quality. So faced with your propositions, the first reaction always is, 'I can see it's quite interesting, I can see it's well put together; but how can it be art when it is so common?'

Of course, that was the question that exercised me as well. What intrigued me is what happens if one pursues a course that is engaged with that thing which seems most resistant to being easily absorbed into one's understanding of the work of art. I wasn't sure where it would take me or whether it would work, but it was what intrigued me.

Are you satisfied now with the answers that you gave then?

Well, of course, I'm delighted with the things that I did then. One of the things that you learn as an artist is that at each stage of your life, of your work, there are things that you do and there's things you think about doing and you don't do them. The ones that you do, it's not just that they exist in the world, they become part of you in the world, something that has something extraordinary about them. The ones you didn't do don't exist at all, don't matter, they exist in some entirely different way.

You don't even recollect them as 'I wish I'd gone down that particular route', or 'That was a marvellous idea but I can't get back to it now'?

The amazing thing is that I do have things that I should have done that I think about, but there's no way of going back. I couldn't do them now, it would be absolutely meaningless and I couldn't bring myself to do it even though there is absolutely no technical or financial reason not to. They are lost. That's very interesting; things become lost, you can't go on doing them.

Now, you then moved on to painting objects flat on the wall and you have this catalogue, stored on the computer, I think two hundred objects; and they're the routine things, filing cabinets, sardine tins, chairs, ladders, light bulbs. How did this collection of objects, apart from their everyday quality, how do you think that you accumulated them?

After *The Oak Tree*, where all the things I'd done prior to that had not involved the making of images of things, it involved the use of real things. I started to wonder about the question of the representation of things, and I realised that artists of my kind of thinking tended not to make representations of thinking. People who thought differently did representations and they took it for granted; whereas I was interested in the whole extraordinariness of what it is to make an image of something. So I thought what would happen if I took the way I think and I thought about images in the same way I've been thinking about objects. So I made the images of the objects that I had previously been using as real things, and since that time virtually all of my work has involved the use of images because images do this amazing thing of having this double life. They recall, they bring into presence an object which isn't actually there at all, and at the same time they have a kind of life of their own as images. If you do a drawing of a bucket you can make it really tiny, it can be half an inch high, or it could be thirty feet high and I've done both. And if it's a metal bucket, it's going to be a silver zinc colour, but when I make a painting of a bucket I can make it pink, yellow, and it doesn't matter.

Were you in some sense, by going back to painting at about the time when painting was officially declared dead, especially by people of your radical persuasion, taking quite a radical step?

This may be perversely me, but I've always thought that when there's a lot of people operating in a certain area in art, it's probably best to go to another one. I think my generation turned away from painting not simply because painting was seen to have failed in some way or to not address everything, but because there were so many people doing it at the time. Ten years later there are very many fewer really interesting people doing it. It creates an opening, doesn't it?

Yeah, a nice piece of opportunism. Now, when I read that you had two hundred images stored on computer my first reaction was 'Only two hundred?', and then I thought 'How many images does Cézanne use in his still lifes?' So is this a collection that is growing, your two hundred?

It's had different spurts of growth over the years. I've been doing it for over twenty years, adding to this collection of things. It's also important to understand that when I do a drawing of a book I never draw a book again. I have two drawings of a book, one is a book closed and the other is a book open, and I drew both of them in the late seventies and I haven't drawn another book since. I've used that drawing this week in a work. I treat the vocabulary as an existing vocabulary. Now if you do that, I have to admit when I started becoming involved in this idea of making these images I thought that there was going to be thousands of them by now. The reality is that there are comparatively limited numbers of simple objects which are truly simple and ubiquitous objects. Many things are variations on those things.

Well, either they're round or they're square.

Yeah, well, and there's something else that's very extraordinary that's happened, which may say something about a very profound change in the nature of things; that the difference between a bucket and a light bulb and a chair and a hat, these are big differences, but now nearly all the objects that are invented today look exactly alike.

How do you mean?

Well, the portable telephone doesn't look like the telephone used to do. The telephone used to have a handle and had a part that you spoke into and a part that you listened into, and it looked like what you did with it. My mobile phone looks like it might have been a cigarette lighter some years ago; or now it looks exactly the same as a Walkman; the Walkman looks exactly the same as something else; the computer looks like the microwave; the microwave looks like the television. So the way in which different objects are defined by how they look is disappearing, and more and more things look almost identical.

So do you feel that almost forces you back into a sort of archaic language of objects at a time when they were more distinctive?

One of the things that I have to say about the things I use is that I find very little reason to add things. I do occasionally add things; you know in the past year or so I added a pitchfork, well, pitchforks have been around for a long time and it was the first time that I thought of using one. It's not that I have drawn everything that I could, but I don't have an interest in drawing a stereo because one box is pretty much the same as another.

And you've never wanted, as it were, to collect archetypical human images, so that you have a vocabulary of human images? They might be historic statues or they might be great figures like Napoleon or something like that. Putting the human into this sort of vocabulary has never interested you?

Well, I've always considered that all of the images that I use have to do with some play between presence and absence. I mean all of the objects, because each object is seen individually, it always needs another object in order to be completed. The pitchfork needs earth or it isn't really a pitchfork. It needs something else in order to be activated. The light bulb needs electricity, it needs a socket to go into. All the different things need something. And the other thing that's present and also absent in all of them is human presence; they are all the most human of objects. No one looks at these things without thinking of their own life, these things mean something to absolutely everybody.

So you're not saying something about dehumanisation?

I would say I would think of myself as doing something to the contrary: I think that they are essentially positive. You know, I grew up in America in the fifties, and it made one an optimist and I've tended to keep that, which I'm very grateful for.

But it has been noticed that there's never a picture on the screen on your television sets, there's nothing in the microwave oven, the light bulb is not on. From that point of view these images are all empty and incomplete. Now, that has to have some personal resonance from you, doesn't it?

I've always thought of them as latent in the sense of latent energy. I'm doing something that on the one hand I'm trying to make it explicit; you see I never draw, say, a funny bit of plumbing that might make a very interesting drawing, but you wouldn't know what it was because you wouldn't know what it was for. So I'm not going to draw that. And I want, when you look at it, you know instantly. I don't want you to think for a split second about what it is. I don't want you to speculate, I want you to know when you see the thing; but I don't want to answer all the questions either, and so I'm trying to locate some area of mystery and something unknown in a general sense but also something that's unknown in a personal sense, to do with how one understands these objects or this accumulation of objects.

Do you mind when people invest them with the symbolic overtones and read non-realistic things into them?

No, I love it, and I try to add as many false trails of that kind as I possibly can myself.

Because I remember when you did that piece for the British Embassy in Moscow, and it has a torch and it has a chair and a globe and a filing cabinet. And I remember some Russians saying to me at the time, 'Ah, the filing cabinet; this is very significant because all the secrets of the KGB were kept in filing cabinets!' And I think the Russians read a symbol, and a political one, into every single one of those images.

It seems to me part of the richness of an object that it can be understood in that way. The filing cabinet is understood in that way because this is in a painting, the painting is in the British Embassy, the British Embassy is in Moscow. So it's not just because a filing cabinet has a meaning, its meaning is changed by the context of what I've done and where it is. And I try as much as possible to draw upon the richness of what it is that these objects can contain. People bring a fantastic amount of understanding to the things that I draw. If I draw a safety pin, I can make the safety pin twenty feet high and make it pink and green . . .

And some of them do look very threatening!

Some of them at that scale they become architectural. But everybody knows the real safety pin is metal, it's tiny and it's essentially an old-fashioned thing for keeping babies' nappies on. So there's a very wide range of understanding information that people bring to these things which is then released in these other things.

I don't know whether this is why you do it, but is it that you really want the viewer to do much more work themselves when they look at a painting? You actually want the viewer to look at the object and bring more of their experience to that object?

Yes, that's exactly what I want and sometimes I'm sure that people feel that some of the work that I do is too simple, a painting of a single object. But my feeling is that these things are so extraordinarily rich in their associative power that I don't need to do very much in order to create an ambience of speculation. I'm trying to create something, I'm not trying to answer something, I don't have a message, I'm not trying to express something in some elaborate way; but I am trying to touch the imagination of somebody who looks at it so that it releases something in them.

You call yourself a radical and I'm sure you are, and you certainly are a modernist. The way you use colours – brilliant, vibrant colours, vermilions – it is certainly sensuous. I think they're romantic, aren't they?

There's colour in what are apparently colourless things. There's beautiful colour in the buckets and the milk bottles and all of those things, they are quite wonderful. But obviously it's not in the foreground of things. And then I used colour a little bit in the eighties in a kind of slightly tentative way, and then I did a room installation. I'd been doing lots of wall drawings for many years and then at one point in the early nineties in a project in Rome, I painted the walls of the room for the first time, and I've never not painted the walls of the room ever since; that was it, that just changed everything.

That happened largely by accident, did it?

Well, nearly everything I've ever done, I've thought about doing for about ten years before I actually got round to doing it. But it released something and suddenly I had a way of knowing how to use colour. I didn't know how to use it before, and what's happened is that I found a way to use colour – it's exactly the way that I was told as a student you shouldn't – which is to use every single colour in every single painting. And I decided to use colour in a way that was similar to the objects, so actually I only use twelve or fourteen colours, they're always exactly the same colours.

They're never mixed?

They are mixed but they're mixed in order to create a colour that doesn't look mixed.

Which is then put on flat?

Which is then put on flat. There's no modulation in the colour at all, and so I have the images which come from one vocabulary, I have the colours that come from another vocabulary. They're both comparatively limited: twelve colours; out of the couple of hundred images I actively at any time am using about fifty. It's to do with bringing together these very limited things that I am trying to find as complex a realm of things to do that I can.

Is that one of the key things: the tension between the limited nature of the means and then the final richness of the outcome?

Yes, but I would say that this has been true of art through the ages. What one does essentially as an artist is that you create a highly limited situation in which to operate and then you use it in such a way that people don't think it's limited at all.

Now, these room installations: the last one you did in Britain was in Manchester for the very large room at Manchester City Art Gallery. Did you know before you started work with your assistants exactly where everything was going, what object was going where and in what scale?

Yes, I'm a constructor. I am a person who puts things together, and just like when I was putting together bits of plywood to make boxes, now I put together images in order to make compositions, in order to make certain associations occur between things.

And most of these rooms, they're up for a certain time, they're a commission for a specific place at a specific time, and then at the end of it they're gone!

This seems to trouble other people more than it does me. My attitude has been that since I started doing these things I have been asked to do work in the most incredibly wonderful spaces. If the people thought that the thing was going to be there for ever, of course I'd never have been asked, I'd never have been offered these wonderful places to do them. The rooms are works of public art. They are intended to be public works. It seems to me that in our time the idea of a public work which is temporary makes more sense to me than a public work which is permanent. I like the idea of works that change. You know, I still think my favourite work of Rachel Whiteread was the house, the cast of the house.

But it should have stayed, shouldn't it?

No, I don't think it should, you see. I think it would be an absolute mess now, it would be covered in graffiti and it would be terrible and it would have deteriorated and it would have lost that vibrancy. What I think was wonderful was it captured a moment, the moment gets recorded – we're very good at that in the modern world – and then it's gone.

Do you work hard?

I suppose you'd say I work hard. I'm very driven and I'm at my happiest when I'm working.

What's your daily schedule?

I get to the studio about nine in the morning and I used to leave around six, I've been leaving about nine at the moment because I have a very big exhibition coming up and so it depends on the demands. But I like being in the studio. I like working. I like making things and one of the things that drives me is I'm very intrigued to see the thing that I want to see. And the only way to see it is for me to do it, it has to be made so I can see it.

You've said that many of your works of art, not all, don't exist if a viewer isn't looking at them. That suggests that making them in the first place, you are making them for a viewer rather than just for yourself. Is that right?

It's a complicated question because I do make the things for myself and I make them because, as I said, I want to see them. But I see myself in the way that *The Oak Tree* does; I'm my own ideal audience. I am the audience as well as the viewer. I believe that art is a social activity and that without the viewer, it isn't really art. There are lots of things that are called art. I'm not against people doing a very private activity that they do as a pastime or something like that. It seems to be perfectly reasonable for people to do. But to me that's not what I mean by art, for me art is something that does seek to engage with an audience. It seems very important to me that it should do that.

Do you seek to do anything to that audience as a social, political, purpose?

No, but I do have a sense that art has an ethical dimension, and that what one is doing with a work of art is one is presenting values. I consider that all works of art essentially represent values. When you look at what I do, in the most simple way I'm saying to me, this is what is the most important thing. I could do something else. I could do other things; but this way of looking at the world, this way of acting in the world represents what I most value. And that seems to me to have very profound implications. The difference between what I do and what Richard Long does, it can be very simply understood that I'm interested in value. We know each other and respect each other's work, but the things that animate him as an artist, that he values most, are very different from the things that animate me. And if you want to understand the difference, it's very simple: just look at our works and it tells you exactly what the difference is between him and me.

But therefore you don't have to have an ethical dimension in order to be a good artist?

I don't think that one can be an artist without having an ethical dimension. I think it's part of the territory of what one does.

Is that what society needs from art?

One of the things that I feel about art is that its function is essentially speculative. It's on the border of things, and the reason why people often reject new things in art is usually because it's presenting as valuable something which has previously been considered to be without value. If you look back over the last couple of hundred years and you look at every phase at which something has been considered outrageous, it's because the artist has said in their work something that we've always thought before didn't matter. Well, to me it actually matters, and not only that, it matters more than other things. I'm foregrounding this thing which has previously been thought of as not important. When we talked about common objects, I was trying to pull those things into a different kind of focus.

So there is a kind of, in the loosest sense, a democratic impulse behind it?

Well, as a teacher my belief has been that essentially everybody is creative. I don't mean that everybody can be an artist, but that all the creative functions that make somebody able to be an artist, those things exist in everybody. Some people wish to turn this into an activity that engages their lives. But I don't think there's anything that's fundamentally different between the people who are called artists and everybody else; and we all know that there are people who are clearly not artists who are extraordinarily creative within their fields, and there's some people who are much less so.

It sounds like a democratic impulse to me.

It's a democratic impulse.

MERCE CUNNINGHAM

In Paris they threw things at us, but their aim wasn't very good

He was born Mercier Philip, he is universally known as Merce, you don't usually have to add his surname, Cunningham. Merce Cunningham, choreographer, that's all. That's enough. The world's greatest, they say; few would bother to argue. Fewer still would dare to challenge the idea that, for innovation, daring, imagination, originality, Merce Cunningham has worked at the highest level for more than fifty years. He's now eighty-six and if there is any waning in his powers it is hard to see. In New York, in the autumn of 2003, his new work *Split Sides* involved the random selection on the night of the order in which two rock bands would perform, which costumes would be worn, which of two backdrops, and different lighting schemes. And of course the order of the dances was similarly chosen. The result: performances built out of thirty-two possible permutations. Typical Cunningham, who has worked on the element of chance in performance since the composer John Cage introduced it to him some fifty years ago. More recently Merce produced a forty-minute piece in the Turbine Hall of Tate Modern where dancers mingle with, relate to, dance in three separate performance areas within the huge, magical *Weather Project* installation by Olafur Eliasson. It was entrancing, lyrical and magical. Merce was taught by Martha Graham, influenced by people like John Cage and visual artists such as Robert Rauschenberg, and his trademarks include the separate development of movement and music, the absolute commitment to pure dance and, of course, the use of chance elements in work. All of which is a hopelessly inadequate way of even hinting at the complexity of the man and his work.

For fifty years he has fought through early periods of incomprehension and downright hostility, embracing en route opportunities offered by everything that came his way, right up to the recent use of computer technology in the creation of his latest works.

I'm going to wind you back many years to when you were twenty, and you were introduced to Martha Graham. You knew then that you were going to be a dancer, did you?

Well, I had been a student at the Cornish School in Seattle, Washington, which was a school for the arts, and I had gone to study drama, actually, and dance. But the woman who ran the school, a Miss Nellie Cornish, this remarkable lady thought that if you wanted to be in the arts, you should just as well know something about all of them. So we had, as well as the dance and the drama, we had music and visual training in drawing and diction, for which I've been grateful all my life.

But it was the dance even then which attracted you?

Well, actually, I went to be in drama, in the theatre. But I had had tap-dancing as an adolescent and was under its spell, and when I went to the school I of course wanted to study dance and Miss Cornish suggested the modern dance, taught by Bonnie Bird who had been in the Martha Graham company. So this was all new to me, I knew nothing about serious, so to speak, dancing at all. But I said all right, I'll do that, and I spent two years at the school.

And then you went to this class at which Martha Graham appeared?

Well, after the two years of summer school in Mills College in Oakland, California there were a number of modern-dance people. Of course, since my work had been with the Graham work I naturally took that there and Graham came at some point to be the teacher for the last part of the session and she said at one point near the end of all this, 'If you come to New York, I'll put you in a piece.' I said, 'I will.'

And when you joined the Graham company she was quite surprised that you turned up, I gather.

Well, she said, 'I didn't think you'd come.' And all I could think of was, 'Lady, you don't know me.'

But you knew that she was the person that you wanted to work with. There was something about her that attracted you?

Oh yes. I think she was extraordinary, certainly in the theatre, and to perform with her, to be on the stage with her was a remarkable experience.

How much did she teach you about dancing and movement?

We had the technique class every day, five days a week, and then when there were to be performances, we would have rehearsals naturally, working on the piece. So there was in that sense daily contact, but we were members of the company and I was the youngest then. And, frankly, being in New York was so superb for me. I stepped on the pavement in New York for the first time and knew this was where I was going to be.

But your technique as a dancer came from Martha Graham?

I had, naturally, her work for several years in the time I was with her company and I also had infrequently ballet training at the School of American Ballet.

Classical ballet training.

Classical ballet – the Balanchine School, of course it is. And I went once or twice a week, that's all the time I would have, but it was strictly classical work.

But were you then in a state that you thought 'I'm not interested in the classical tradition' or did you just see what you could do with and beyond the classical tradition?

Well, I wanted to learn as a dancer as much about dancing as I could get. And the Graham experience, not only the technique, but working in her company and performing when there were performances, all of that. But I also went to see all kinds of dancing, I didn't have any prejudice that way. Because I was simply interested in the way people moved.

I mean it sounds as if there was a kind of, sort of blank sheet. You were a kind of tabula rasa ready to take anything in.

Yes, I even attempted at one point to study, very briefly, Bharata Natyam, the Indian dance, because when I first saw it I was so fascinated by the rhythmic thing of it and, of course, the skill with which it was done. I wanted to know what was underneath all that. I didn't last very long, but it was a marvellous experience.

Now it's said that quite early on you decided that although Graham was wonderful, the narrative approach to dance was not something that you were interested in. How quickly did this evolve and is that the correct way to describe it?

Yes. I think it was the third year, perhaps the fourth, that I began to think that I wanted to do something else. I didn't know what it was, but that this was not what I wanted to do. And you have to realise in that time, in the forties and even into the fifties, there was not a great deal of dancing in New York, serious dancing. There were people teaching it and they would have, say, as Graham did, one or two programmes a year, and it increased, naturally. So that if one didn't have that, what did one have? And it seemed to be the only two possibilities then for earning your living at dancing was in the ballet company (the ballet was the Monte Carlo) or in Broadway shows. And I tried a Broadway show. It was amazing to have a salary once a week. But I didn't like it.

What was the show?

The show was *One Touch of Venus* and it had choreography by Agnes de Mille.

That wasn't bad.

And I rehearsed for a week and then went to Boston to perform in it. And I lasted a week and I knew whatever else, this isn't what I wanted. So I went back to my cold-water flat.

So you began thinking about making your own dance, almost for economic reasons?

No, because I wouldn't have made any money from it. No, but John Cage came to be in New York because he was interested in furthering the compositional part of him and he suggested we give a programme together, and that would be about 1944, I think. And I made six solos and Cage made music for each of them and we presented it in a very small theatre in New York. It was like a dance studio, but it was adequate enough for this kind of performance.

But you felt deeply that you wanted to be in charge, so to say, of the movements that you danced. Because it's a big step from being a dancer to a choreographer.

Oh, yes. Yes. And I worked terribly hard, and it was one performance, of course, but it was a way to begin. And then from it I just continued.

But you knew that that was how you wanted to express yourself, that dancing by itself wasn't enough.

Right. Yes. Also I wasn't interested, as you might gather since I had left the Graham situation, I wasn't interested in the narration or expressing some particular emotional situation. I was interested in movement. It's at that time that we began to separate the music and the dance and that was so interesting to me.

Was that his suggestion? Cage's suggestion?

Well, his feeling was that one of the two elements should not support the other or be in charge, that they should be equal but separate. And I liked that idea.

Yes, the idea of going rumpety, tumpety tump and, and matching the music was awful.

Yes; well, as he said, it's a form of slavery and so those first solos, about three or four of them, were made, we were given a kind of time structure between us as to how long, and certain divisions; then we separated and he made the music to the structure and I made the dance.

So there was a fairly tight structure, there were a certain number of milestones at that stage?

Yes. They were quite strict in one way but in between there was this incredible freedom. Because you didn't have to follow music, he didn't have to follow the dance. So when the elements got together they produced something that neither one of us alone could have imagined.

Why didn't this come out as a mess? That's still a question?

No. Because Cage, regardless of what anybody thinks about what he did, was very clear about structures. And these were structures in time. As he said when asked this question, 'Why do you separate the music and the dance?' once Cage replied, 'Well, you see, Merce does his thing and I do mine, and for your convenience we put it together.'

Extremely clever elliptical answer.

Yes.

Now you were only thirty-four when you took this huge leap, and did you know then that of course the separation of music and dance was one principle, absence of narrative was another principle. Was this clear, that this was the basic philosophy of the Merce Cunningham Dance Company?

Well, I wouldn't say I put it that way, I'm not a philosopher. But it's the way I work and I enjoyed working that way.

Was it difficult finding dancers who would work in this way or . . . ?

Well, there were very few, naturally. The original company at Black Mountain was seven, actually, and then for a number of years after that I continued to make dances and I would give classes like a small studio situation and we gradually began to tour. Not vast tours but to go out and play something, present something in a situation where it wouldn't be just New York that wanted to see it, but we might have to capture some strangers.

But they were pretty tough, weren't they, the reviews were very hostile, weren't they?

Oh, yeah, terribly. But I really thought, 'I don't think they're right. I may not be doing this very well, but I think the ideas involved in it are interesting enough to continue them.'

That took a huge act of courage, didn't it, because people must have said that you and Cage were, were pretty well mad. You were going so against what was done in dance.

Yes, but certainly I am stubborn.

But you could have been wrong.

Of course I could. But I didn't think the ideas were wrong. I knew there was something there that was interesting about how to put things together. Whether it was in time, or as later with the visual artists, with visuals, sets, with the visual activity. Again there was the same principle: we did not ask the visual artist or tell him what to do in any sense. If he wanted information I was delighted to give it, but I didn't force anything because we wanted the same principle of three separate things which could come together and produce something which otherwise we couldn't have imagined.

When you say that an artist, like Rauschenberg or Warhol and many others you worked with, would come and ask for information, what sort of information could you give them?

Well, whatever they wanted. If they wanted to know how long it was going to be, or if they wanted to see it. I wasn't objecting to all this. It's just to leave the other artists working this way as free as one could possibly do. Certainly one of the things that one would have to make clear to the visual artist is that if he put something in the space, then there wouldn't be space for the dance. So that might make them think another way.

But would they ask even for indications of mood?

No, no, no. They would ask often, and they would sometimes come and watch, for any number of reasons, simply to see what we were doing. Or if they wanted more practical things, I was always happy to give whatever, but not to put something in their way.

And you wouldn't say, 'Please bring me back your sketches and I'll see if I like them.'

No. I would wait. Very often in the course of this kind of working, the day of the performance is the first day we hear the music. Well, with the costumes it's a little different because they often have to fit them on to the dancers, but we wouldn't see them complete. In other words, what I'm trying to say is – it's not to make anything mysterious about this – it was a way of really working which allowed the individual artist to think in his or her way. And then when it came together, if there were things that had to be adjusted, for example, about the costumes that we both could agree on . . . But not something where I told him 'this should or should not be'.

Ah. I just want to take you through to the point of acceptance and recognition, so to say, which was in 1964 in London. Before that you'd had a torrid time in Paris where they'd thrown tomatoes at you.

Well, they threw things at us, but as I said then, their aim wasn't very good so it was all right.

But even then when you came to London, 1964 – and I saw the show at the Phoenix, and I remember Lamont Young's music with the tin lids scratched over the exit signs and things.

Yes. Yes.

I can't say for a moment I understood it, but my God, I never, I never forgot it. But that was when the company was recognised as a force in world dance, wasn't it?

I think that tour, London certainly, because I was amazed that we even played a week and then when we stayed for three more weeks it was a marvellous experience. I wouldn't say it was easy.

I don't mean in terms of the public, but just for our way of working, but still it was a remarkable experience.

Did that reception and the recognition make you feel different about yourselves?

Yes, I realised first of all that European audiences, London for example, were seeing this in a different way than the Americans. And the same thing even when they threw things in France, because one of the women who had helped us there was Benedicte Pesle, who is still our presenter in Paris, our agent. When they threw things, I was sitting in my dressing room thinking 'Well, it's very sad because I always wanted to play Paris' naturally and then when this happened, this was it, it was the end of it. But Benedicte Pesle came in and looked at me and she said, 'Now Merce, we must prepare for the next time.' And she's been doing it ever since.

When you say that European audiences looked or saw differently, can you express what you think it was that was different?

Well, for instance, we played Germany and not so much about the dancing, but there were situations there where the contemporary composers had some connection with the way Cage composed – and David Tudor was with us, in those programmes also – and the way they thought about contemporary music. So they could perhaps accept the sound and the way it was put together in ways that other places were not at all familiar with.

Does the word 'control', when it comes to how you work with your pieces, does the word 'control' play any part in what you do?

Oh yes. It's control, not in the sense of guiding it towards some particular expression, but how the movement is done. How far can we go, given our ideas about moving, how far can we push that? Not to gain something about expression, but to gain simply a wider range of movement even. *Winter Branch*, for example, was comprised physically of falls, of people falling on the ground, getting up and then walking off and then other people coming in and doing falls. The falls are very physically complicated and have to be taught, it isn't just you drop to the ground, because in dancing it involves how long it takes you.

You mean there are quick falls and short falls?

Yes, oh absolutely. So how do you train for that? So that comes into the technique class. And the same thing happens with most of what we do. In recent years I've pushed things because of using the computer, the dance forms. I've seen possibilities that I hadn't seen before and I try them out in the technique classes to see if we can push movement further.

You've often talked about chance and I don't want you to repeat yourself endlessly, but you've said that the point about using the random and relying on chance in your work is that it helps you to eliminate clichés.

Yes, because your physical memory is, you remember how to do things certain ways; like it goes in this direction, or it takes this amount of time. But what if using chance means it comes up that you don't go in that direction but another one and the movement may take instead of this amount of time, through chance it indicates you might try doing it quicker. OK, then you have to figure out a way to do that. I have to, or the dancers, we have to figure out a way which changes, or adds to, our physical memories of how movements are done.

Because otherwise the physical memory would keep the body kind of stuck in the way it's always done it before.

Yes, well, I don't see programmes very often but if I do watch young dancers, and say they've found an interesting idea, they do a certain phrase which they like, so they always repeat it exactly the same, and always through the same space and always in the same time. Now what if they tried to do that phrase, exactly as it is, but in half the time? Or double the time? This way of looking came from working with film and video with Charles Atlas and Elliott Caplin.

How?

When we made dance films together, and I'd never had anything to do with a camera and Charles Atlas was our stage manager. And he said, 'You should look through the camera.' I'd listened to dancers who'd worked in television and I'd say, 'Well, how did you feel about it?' or something. They would say, 'Well, I didn't like it because it didn't look like what I thought it should' or 'The space was too small' or something. So I looked through a camera, Charlie showed me how to do it and I thought, 'Oh, it's marvellous. It's totally different from the stage!' So you don't have to do the same thing. You could do something else.

And that then introduced new ideas?

Oh yes. For instance if you notice on television, if you repeat too often they turn the channel. So if you shifted the camera each time you repeat it, you saw something different. And you can shift with the camera, you can make small differences which are noticeable through the TV camera but which are not necessarily noticeable on stage. So it just gives another thing; it's not that one is wrong, it's just you have a chance to shift the way you think and work. It's not easy, it was terribly difficult.

I want to go back to you as a dancer, because everybody says you were a wonderful dancer, a very athletic dancer. Was there just the physical, animal side to it, or did you feel you were expressing something, communicating something?

No, well, I think movement by itself – regardless of somebody saying 'This is how I'm sad' or whatever – I think movement by itself is what absolutely touches me. Not something where the movement is to describe something, but where the movement itself has a life. Now, using these things the way I have – chance and the film, separating the music and the dance – broke up any ideas I might think of 'Oh it has to go this way', because there were these other possibilities. And so you try them out, or I did, and would find that they were often in the end more interesting to do because you were pushed into a way of moving that you had to learn about.

So it didn't take away from what I assume is the physical exhilaration of dance from time to time?

No, not at all. I think it added; for myself it did.

Somebody described you, as a young dancer, like a gazelle, or like a lily blowing in the field; they seem to me two pretty extreme options. But did you have a self-image of yourself as a dancer, because you were obviously very striking on the stage?

Well, to start with, I absolutely loved to dance. I don't know how else to put it. From the time I did the tap-dancing, ever since. And it was something I just do, want to do. Well, then you can leave it at that, or you can further it by training or all kinds of other ways. And each thing that I would do, I could see 'Oh this is something I don't know about'; not about how you feel about it, but even movements that might remain what one would call awkward. But even that I would try out because it furthered the physical range.

Did you reject it because it was awkward?

No, I would try to figure out how to do it.

You used the word 'pushing', I think, a number of times, and you are obviously famous for pushing yourself, pushing your body to extremes. Was that conscious inside you that you knew you were taking risks?

Oh yes. Yes, I've had enough injuries but not purposely in any way. And if something might cause injury, I would not do it.

But were you testing yourself?

Yes. Oh yes, how can you go a little further? How can you do a movement that you've done over and over again and think you have it perfect? How can you do it in a way that it becomes awkward again, so you have to find it all over again?

That word 'awkward'.

Yes.

That's interesting.

Yes. Well, I think that brilliant dancing always looks to me – really brilliant dancing, not just somebody who has a technical range which is extraordinary, but beyond that – there's always flaws and I'm delighted. It's again John Cage who had a small percussion group and he told one of the players that she had played everything absolutely accurately: 'Now just go a little further and make a few mistakes.' And that's to me, always has been, you have to go further and make some mistakes. So you don't settle it in a mould of some kind, thinking that that's perfect.

I just want to stay with the word 'awkward' for a moment. This is your category recognising that there is something at first sight which is original, unexpected, unorthodox.

Yes, yes, yes. And how can I or with the dancers find a way to make this work, physically. You're doing something that at first glance you might say is impossible, and often it is. But if you try it out you'll find something else that you didn't know about.

But dancing as you did finally gave you arthritis, yes?

Yes, yes. But I don't think that that's necessarily the work. I don't think it didn't contribute; but you see I had to often dance on stages which were cement. So that's one of the causes and I know a number of dancers who have the same experience.

But you resent that? Do you ever think back and say, 'Why the hell did I end up with arthritis?'

No, I don't resent it. No, no, no.

'If I'd been more careful'?

I'm sorry I have it. But no, I don't resent it, I can see that it's part of life, so I'm attempting to deal with it.

And even the limitations when you had to stop working directly with dancers. I know you went into using computers, which we'll discuss later, but withdrawal from the physical contact with the dancers, that must have been painful.

Yes, and I still don't like it, I still get up and try and show them, or help them, certainly. But now I do more talking. I don't think I talked very much when I taught, for example. When I could physically move easily I would just do it, and then I could explain something: 'Well, if you did this with your leg it would be easier to do that movement.' But now I talk more.

Your artistic relationship with John Cage over fifty years, and you've never talked about your personal relationship and that's fine. Who learned more from whom in that relationship?

Well, I think that I learned more from Cage; very often primarily his musical composition of course, but also about painting in later years. He took up painting and making drawings and paintings, and those were done very often with chance operations.

So it was that idea of allowing chance to add a dimension to your work that was the most important thing.

Yes. Well, I think the chance thing came about between us

both, really, because it was the early fifties and it was the time they published the *Chinese Book of Changes*, the first publication which was so fascinating of course. And it had that extraordinary introduction by Carl Jung, where he asks the I-Ching, casts it to see what the I-Ching thinks about being presented in a new language; it had never been translated before, I gathered that. And the book's answer is this astonishing thing of going forward, or something, that was the way they phrased it. And then there was an Institute of Random Numbers, where they said they found the use of random or chance operations in digging up numbers was just as good as logic. And so I thought I would like to try this on simple levels. So I tried it, just in very simple ways, but in class, where I would make a phrase to give to the students, using pennies, at that time, see if by chance how the phrase would come up differently. And then having done that, how do you get that across to the student? And it was so fascinating and some of them were impossible of course, but so fascinating the way it broadens your mind, certainly my thinking.

So digging deep into the non-rational side of your understanding.

Yes. And then, that's when I applied this to making movement phrases and to time. But it was the statement of Einstein's which I read at that time, where he said, 'There are no fixed points in space.' And it was like a flash of lightning; I felt, Well, that's marvellous for the stage. Instead of thinking it's front and centre, to allow any point, very Buddhist, any point in the space to be as important as any other. It opened the way one could think. Not just that you face the way that you might think is unfamiliar, but how do you get to that? How do you get from wherever you were before instead of using ways that are familiar to your physical behaviour, you know. You have to really find out how to get the dancer, in beginning cases, myself, how do I get from here to here.

So even coming on to the stage you use the roll of chance as a way of finding out how you get on to the stage and to a particular point of the stage.

That's right. And about anything, whether you exited, or

whether you entered. So it just opened, at least for my way of thinking, it opened up possibilities, that I could have said, 'Well, I don't want to deal with it.' But I was stubborn.

When you work, you've been described as sitting at the back of a room dreaming up steps. Is that word 'dreaming' right?

No. No. No. I make them up. I don't dream them up, I make them up. I'm sitting there – and I used to not sit, I'd be up doing it – sitting there thinking, 'How do you put this together with this and make it work for the dancer?' So I don't think . . . well, you can call it dreaming, but I don't.

It doesn't sound like it.

No. It's really, it's really practical, odd as it sounds.

And how do you avoid repeating yourself, because you must find yourself saying, 'Oh no, I've done that so many times before'?

Yes. Say with two dancers together, if I've had them move, do certain kinds of things before . . . I try to avoid those, because I always know there's something else, there always is. But how do you find it? How do you instead of accepting a certain way say that, if the man is dancing with the woman, how he lifts her for example, or how he holds her. There are limitations about this, naturally, but one gets into habits, as you do in life, in everyday life. And so if I caught myself that way, then I would, using chance means, find another way.

And you said that dancing is looking.

Yes, I think you have to watch. You have to watch how steps are put together, where are your feet in this; and, in recent years, I've added action in the upper torso and the arms, in the way they're used.

Which you didn't do before?

Earlier on in the dances, if you look at the arms, their arms are held usually quite to the side, or rather, to my eye now, simple arm positions. They weren't then, I didn't think of it that way. But this way, there's a complication in the arms which when we began to use it, I had seen it on the computer, and I wondered if this was possible to get to the dancers. So I would bring it and try to show them and I can't describe it except it involved being able to change each arm to different kinds of positions and not think that there were limits to that.

Because this takes us back to the arthritis and the computer. Did you ever have any doubts about the use of the computer, because I think it has turned out to be something which has given you huge liberation and discovered new things.

No. No. No, I had no doubts at all. The first day I saw it, Life Forms, they came and showed me a film, I said yes immediately. Because although it could do very few things then, that's ten years ago or more, everything that was in the computer looked useful to me. For a teacher of dance, you could put in the way an exercise is done, and then slow it down so that the pupil could see the exact construction. Even though when they did it, they could not do it that slow, they would have a wider knowledge of what made it up.

It must be a very hard business, and you wrote in your notebook in 1998, 'We're beginning the rehearsals again, the same old routes. Can we find a variation?' This is the constant question, is it?

Yes. Yes. Every time I go to make a new piece the first thing I try to do is get at something I don't know about.

And do you feel tired sometimes, when you think, 'I'm damned if I know what I'm going to do with something which is original.'

Oh yes. Always.

Because there's another piece in your notebook from the previous year and you've drawn a picture of an ugly giraffe on a hot tin roof; what you say in the text, you say, 'like the mind on a weary day'.

Yes. Well, it's when you're tired.

So how do you get out of that?

Well, I don't do that any more, but I used to get up and try something, I'd go to the barre, or go out on the studio floor and try something. And then I would, using chance means, throw pennies or whatever, so the order would be different, and then I would have to figure it out all over again. So that my mind, instead of lamenting 'Oh, this is dreary', by using this, I see something different, then I try it. Well, now I have to tell the dancers to. And more often than not they've been helpful, shall we say.

So you work through problems?

Oh yes. I think I always have. Well, you have the drawing books so you know, I began to draw about twenty years ago.

You draw animals and things.

Well, animals, and I like nature, insects and things like that. Somehow I've an affinity to that. I can't draw straight lines, so I don't bother about those things.

But does that help you with making dances?

Oh yes, I'm sure it does. But what it does do if I'm feeling I'm not doing very well, if I start to make a drawing, it puts my mind someplace else and it takes it off of all this thing about 'oh how sad it is', or whatever. I get very interested in drawing the eye of a lizard, so it takes your attention that way and then very often it ends up helping me to think about movement.

You once said that dance is not for unsteady souls. What did that mean?

It simply means that if you're crazy enough to be a dancer, and you love dancing you'll stay with it, but it's rocky.

There are no easy satisfactions?

Well, there is satisfaction.

But not easy?

Oh no. But if you do something, anything in life, you can say it's not easy, but it may be satisfying in one way or another.

You're pretty resilient, aren't you? You overcame the inability to work directly with your dancers. On the day after John Cage's death, after a fifty-year relationship, you were back in the studio working. How difficult was that?

Well, I came in the studio the day after John died and there was David Tudor, the musician with whom we'd all worked for so many years, and we talked about John for a few minutes, and then I said to David, 'Well, David, I think I'm just going to start rehearsal.' And David Tudor said, 'I'm glad to see you're going back to work.'

But you also said that from the time of John Cage's death you had to start to speak for yourself. So it changed you in all sorts of ways?

Oh yes. Well, when I had to make the decisions and, perhaps, we'd make them together, or he would make them, but now I did it. And I remember thinking that they have to be done, so I'll do it. So it was not a question that I was going to fail. You can fail anyway, but the decisions have to be made so you do it.

So it was a pretty late age to have to accept that full responsibility?

Well, perhaps it was, I guess.

Again in one of your sketchbooks you say – this is after you've heard an English drama director talking about making Shakespeare relevant to modern times – 'I wonder if we have moved from word description to picture description, with the eye taking precedence over the ear and mind.' Do you feel that is the appeal of your work, that it engages us in picture description?

I think that's part of it. You see we, certainly America, and I think other countries also, we are so addicted to the television that our whole experience, or a great part of our experience comes through that, and that's primarily visual. One may not like the visual or whatever, that's something else, but the way of carrying something on, instead of through words, is so much through visual activity. On a sort of movie level, years ago, in old movies, the conversation was often interesting to hear. But now they say something and then they blow up a car! That kind of thing, but that's visual. Well, you may not like it, but it's visual. And I do think that's very much a part of our experience now.

Does that make our acceptance of your work that much easier, that the culture and our physical surroundings have changed?

Well, I think it's one of the things. I don't mean to say that what we did caused that, for heaven's sakes, but I think that working with Cage and Rauschenberg and Jasper Johns and Andy Warhol, those painters seeing things the way they see things, through that kind of eye, has added to my experience enormously.

Do you think that there will be a Cunningham School of Choreography and that your works will be done as Balanchine is done now?

Well, I don't know about that. My belief is, in order to do the kind of work we do and do it really well, you have to have studied our technique. But it would take a lot of effort on people's parts – and maybe they're looking at something else!

ATOM EGOYAN

I'm fascinated by the inherent mystery of any meeting between two people

Ask a film critic or those who go to film festivals or movie art houses and all will instantly recognise the name and know the work of Atom Egoyan. Ask the average movie-goer to a cinema multiplex and they might look more puzzled, which is odd in one way. Egoyan has made more than twenty films, of which at least five have won recognition and prizes around the world. Films such as *Exotica*, *Felicia's Journey*, *The Sweet Hereafter*, *Ararat*. He has made installations at the Venice Biennale and at Burlington House in London. He has directed opera – Gavin Bryars's *Doctor Ox's Experiment* at English National Opera – and he is about to direct one of the operas in the first Canadian Ring cycle. And he's only forty-four. Born in Cairo of Armenian parents and living in Canada, Egoyan's trademark features include a search for memory, truth, understanding, often seen through, or mediated by video, television, and driven by the relentless twistings of the curiosity of the mind. His films aren't obscure, but neither are they easy. That's how he makes them, that's how he likes them.

Let's begin, though, with your origins. You're a migrant, an immigrant in a country of immigrants. How important is that to you as an artist and a person?

I think it was very important in my formation. My parents made the curious decision when they came to Canada to move to the west coast, Victoria, which was at the time a very isolated community. We were the only Armenian family there as I was being raised and it meant that I became very aware at an early age of the notion of identity as being something of a construction. English is not my mother tongue and I remember very clearly not being able to communicate, going to school and wanting nothing more than to be like everyone else. That was a very important part of my upbringing, this idea of shedding an identity and embracing another one. My parents, they didn't want to keep Armenian in the house; they didn't feel that it was important for me to hold on to something which they themselves had rejected obviously. If it was important, they would have moved to Toronto or Montreal where all of our other relatives settled when we came to Canada.

They wanted to give you the chance to be Canadian, but the idea of alienation clearly hung around in the background.

It was important to me because I was aware of this idea of letting go of something to become something else. I had a very strong relationship to my grandmother, who didn't speak a word of English and while she was living with us in Victoria, that was my only connection to this other culture. And when she left, when I was about seven, that was quite traumatic for me and I felt that there was a gap. There was something that even though, by the time I was eighteen, I could say I was completely assimilated, when I moved to Toronto and I became aware of a community, I tried to catch up. I relearned the language as well as I could and I became very immersed in notions of what that identify meant.

I want to go back a bit. I'm struck by the number of times in at least three films, Ararat, Felicia's Journey, Exotica, *the point of entry into a culture is the focus of the work. The actual Customs and Immigration procedures, these are key scenes in your films. Is there something about the physical entry into a country and a culture that matters to you?*

Oh, absolutely. I think that there are a number of rules and customs that you are expected to embrace. There is this point at which you are expected to declare what you have. Now, in a Customs inspection that's quite literal. But this idea of the baggage that we arrive with in any situation and the right that we give to someone else to inspect that, to make an assessment, and notions of honesty and exchange and what we expect back; there's a point at which you can break down the constituent elements of what constitutes an identity, but that's rather cold and quite clinical. But as we all know, the things that make one attach oneself to someone else, or to a country or to a place, are mysterious and can't be defined.

But that is a process which takes place at the point of Customs and Immigration. It's as if they're saying, 'Well, you look Armenian, but can you convince us that you are really Canadian?'

Well, it's interesting because the Customs inspection in *Ararat* is based on a very strange experience I had a number of years ago. I'd shot a very low-budget film in Armenia called *Calendar* and I was returning into the country with cans of unexposed film and I was stopped. And the customs officer wanted to know for taxation purposes what the value of the film was. So I said, 'Well, the material value is a few hundred dollars of the raw footage'; and he said, 'No, what will be the value of the finished film?' And I said, 'Well, that's a very curious question; I mean if the film is successful it might be worth millions of dollars and if no one sees it it's valueless.' And at that point he asked, 'Well, what's the story about in your film?' as though he could make at that point an assessment as to what its commercial value might be, based on my ability to tell the story. And about halfway through he sort of stopped and realised that it was far too convoluted to be a commercial success and he just waved me on. But I thought that was quite an interesting situation where, as one is often expected to do at a Customs inspection, you are there to answer questions as honestly as possible, and yet perform the role of being honest in such a way that someone else will assess your sincerity. I'm fascinated by the inherent mystery of any meeting between two people and what are the points of entry that we allow. There is a great degree of formality and there are rules and there are clichés that allow conversation to continue. But how vulnerable we allow ourselves to be, and what we reveal of ourselves is, I think, the stuff of any drama.

Let me take up one other previous thing. Your parents were both artists; what sort of artistic background at home did they bring you up in? Was there one particular kind of art that was particularly dominant?

They were painters. They had met at art school in Egypt. My father had his first one-man show in Cairo when he was sixteen and it was a huge success, and on the basis of that he received a full scholarship to study at the Chicago Art Institute. He was the first person from the Middle East to receive that type of scholarship and at that time Abstract Expressionism was very important in American art culture, and he came back with this excitement but a body of work that no one could understand! He had his second one-man show at the age of twenty and while his first show had been very successful, his second show in Cairo was a complete disaster and I think that really changed him. When they moved to Canada he understood that to raise a family he really probably couldn't continue just painting, so he had a gallery and then that transmogrified into some sort of a furniture design store. And I was aware that my parents had made compromises and that they needed to not do what they loved doing most in order to raise us. But they were happiest when they were painting, and the feeling of creativity in the studio was something that I think had a strong impact on both my sister and me. My sister is a musician and we understood that when people were making things they were in touch with something else.

Has that had an effect on you, in that there's undoubtedly a strong strain of refusal to compromise in your own work? Do you think that is explicitly connected with what your father in particular did?

Yes, I think so. I think that I've tried to fight for structures that allowed me not to have to compromise. My film-making practice started off quite marginally because I think in that industry, the higher the budget the more responsible you are to an audience. And I really tested those grounds very, very delicately as to how much of an audience there is for the type of film I'm doing. It's been very gratifying because the audiences have grown, but I've never wanted to put myself into a situation where someone else was in control, and I think that's difficult to do. Mind you, we are now in a time when the technology allows us to make films for minuscule budgets that are completely uncompromised. I think that the digital revolution has been really liberating for a lot of film makers.

And to distribute them much more freely, and not have to go through the gateway of tyrannical distributors who only want a certain kind of movie.

That's so true and so we are now at a juncture that when I look at the budgets of my first features, which were minuscule, those would now be considered quite healthy. And that's just as a result of this huge technological change.

Now I'm going to start, not with your very first movie, but 1987, with a film called Family Viewing. *That was the one which is particularly famous in film history because Wim Wenders, the German director, gave you his prize money at a festival, because he thought yours was such a marvellous film. It's about an alienated son, at odds with an apparently conventional but dominating family. The father uses video both to record and to destroy the family story. And then, when they all end up with the psychotherapist, he uses multi-camera video to try to help the family interact, to heal their problems. How did video, as an adjunct to living and its interrelationship with living, come up in your mind, because this is such a constant theme of yours?*

What's very powerful about the video medium to me and the texture of video is that it is spontaneous. Unlike film, which involves a degree of consideration and actually involves a number of people to execute, video is something that can be generated at a very personal level. It therefore allows us to archive our experience and perhaps even to surrender notions of memory to a piece of technology. That is both very liberating and also quite frightening, because when you surrender your experience to a piece of technology, while that means that it is fixed, it also means that it can come back to haunt you in unexpected ways. And if someone else gains access and control to that stored technology, that could be something which can be used to victimise and even to torture one. So my relationship to video was something that excited me because I'm fascinated by characters who have to make decisions which approximate to decisions that I have to make myself.

About life or about art?

About life and art and about direction and choreography. I think that one of the imperatives of any act of direction is that you are doing something quite neurotic by definition; you are asking people to do things that they wouldn't be doing otherwise. You're organising people's behaviour and you're putting them into situations that are by definition artificial. So that when that happens within a family, when Dad is choreographing a home video or a home movie, those are very interesting pieces of family archaeology, as to how those decisions are made.

It's intrusive.

It is intrusive and yet it is a medium which can be used to allow one a degree of objectification, that you can objectify your own behaviour, the behaviour of others that are close to you with a degree of distance. And certainly in that therapy which is based on what was a very popular form of therapy at the time, where families would be videotaped and therapists would try to activate certain responses, which the participants would then go and look at later on and try to better understand themselves. What happens in *Family Viewing*, though, is that I integrate the texture of video into the very format of the film. So there are scenes with the boy's, the protagonist's current family, which are shot very much like a soap opera. They're shot on videotape, using live cutting techniques, live switching. So that texture fascinated me because there's something very ephemeral about it. There's this sense that there's something unstable about the look of video, and I wanted to use that dramatically as a texture. And I thought metaphorically, since the film is about different generations within a family, it was interesting to use different generations of the film stock itself; and to weave those together and to use the texture in quite a formalist way to allow a degree of access and entry.

Before that, in your very early movies, Calendar, Adjuster *and so on, you are the personification of the 'indie' film maker. But you must have known that you didn't just want to be an 'indie' film maker, you wanted to keep your independence, but you didn't want to be in that very small group of people who are viewed and appreciated only by movie buffs. Wat was in your mind as to where you wanted to go and where you wanted to end up?*

Well, one of the things I'm really grateful for is that when I began film-making the whole notion of an independent film scene was non-existent. There wasn't really any glamour attached to it. Certainly in the eighties and early nineties there was no idea in my mind that this was an entrée into another world. That only really happened with *Exotica*, which was again made for a tiny budget. There wasn't really an audience in mind as I was making it, but for the first time – and this was my sixth feature – I found that a film could cross over into that other world. I look back at those early features and they were very much the product of an Arts Council system here. They were made for a very select audience and were not really intended for commercial distribution.

So it wasn't that you'd put yourself in that particular world intentionally? You wanted to get into the real movie world and in fact Exotica *was distributed by Miramax.*

Yes. It ended up being distributed by Miramax, and that's an interesting story in itself, because I remember when they showed me their marketing plan and the trailer and the poster and I was aghast. I thought, 'This has got nothing to do with the film!'

It had strippers, nudes, everything like that, and a pretty lurid description. I have to say when I picked the DVD up and I read it, I said 'Oh well, all right, if that's the sort of film it's going to be . . .' And it's not.

Now it seems a little naïve, to think that I'd made a film, a murder mystery set in a strip club, and I wasn't really thinking of how it might be marketed. It just seems really unbelievable that I tried to actually block the marketing of the film, because I felt that it was misrepresenting what I'd done. But that was a fascinating experience for me. I'll never forget a conversation I had with the head of marketing at Miramax at the time and he said, 'Look, it's very simple; yes, we are not representing the spirit of the film. But that's not what marketing is about. Marketing is about trying to get as many people to see something as possible. Now if you are disappointing half the people that you are bringing into the theatre, there's also the chance that you are allowing people that would never have gone to see that film otherwise, to be exposed to something that might have an effect on them.'

I'd like you to talk more about Exotica, *and I'm going to try to put its themes into a wholly inadequate nutshell! It concerns a middle-aged man whose daughter was murdered, and who seeks comfort in a particular stripper in a nightclub. She seems to remind him of his daughter's babysitter. There's a voyeuristic nightclub master of ceremonies, a gay smuggler of protected animal species. It looks like a sex revenge thriller and it ends as a film about understanding and reconciliation. The way it is made is through an intense concern with the business of observing people. Everybody's watching someone else. The sinister nightclub master of ceremonies is observing the people at the club and giving a running commentary on their behaviour. What is this appeal in observation and voyeurism? Or rather in being and observing voyeurism?*

The whole film, *Exotica*, seems to be a lurid and quite exploitative piece of drama, until such time as you understand what the motivations and reasons for those people being there actually are. Even though it's set out at the very beginning with the Customs inspection where the Customs officer is teaching a novice that you must always try and look beyond what is there, to try and determine what the story is really about. I think that the viewers are put into that situation, the moment you're in that nightclub. And it's a very exciting place to be visually. People came to Toronto looking for that club and, as we all know, for the most part strip clubs are depressing and really quite unpleasant places, so the idea of a club which is full of that type of visual tantalisation and colour is irresistible.

But you weren't shooting it as something which was supposed to be resistible, were you?

It's supposed to draw you in, but for reasons other than what you think. That notion of seduction is very important in all the films. You set up a visual scene and an atmosphere through the alchemy of visual and music elements that draws the viewer in. What they're actually having to encounter may be something that would repel them otherwise, that they wouldn't want to have any part of, but at that point it's too late, and your curiosity and your sense of exploration is peaked. I love that place; that's the most exciting place for anyone to be in when they're encountering a work of art, that they have to be at once very self-conscious of their presence and their placement, but also drawn inexorably towards finding out what the logic and the circumstance is that places them there.

Are you reminding us also that we the audience are watching; you make the audience self-aware of what it's doing; and at least initially, to put a distance between us and events? Because by the end of all the films of yours that I've seen, there is no distance between the viewer and events – you are drawn in. But initially, are you deliberately creating that sense of distance?

I am. I've always been very envious of novelists because it seems to me that so many novels that I admire present the story to the reader as something which is a story. And you're very aware of the artefact of the book, and your role as a reader. I think that there's always been a split between the ability of film to allow the viewer to get lost in a reality, and the practice which ascertains that there is an act of witnessing. There is a voyeuristic element, so the films that I'm drawn to, let's say a film like *Vertigo*, you are so aware of your position as a viewer. And that creates a particular tension which I find really thrilling.

Let's just stick for a moment to the voyeurism and the use of video in Felicia's Journey, *where a young Irish girl who's pregnant by her lover, comes to England, to Birmingham, to try to find him. She falls in with a middle-aged obsessive loner, who has a record of exploiting other lost young women; he recalls his experiences with these other young women as if they've been recorded. Now he may have a video recorder in his Morris Minor, or it's just that his memory sees his previous experiences in terms of a video recording. And then he lives most of his life through old video recordings of his mother as a famous TV cook. This is the most thoroughgoing exploitation or exposure of a character through video.*

Well, it was an interesting dilemma I had because when I read the William Trevor novel, the key scene in that book was to do with a moment that would have been very reductive if I'd filmed it. William Trevor was able to use his prose to make this moment – which made the relationship between the mother and the son quite explicit – he was able to shroud it in a language which wasn't pointed and was elusive. When you film something, though, you don't have that privilege very often. So I had to completely refigure what that relationship was about. And I became very interested in this figure of a minor celebrity in English culture, Fanny Craddock, the first TV celebrity cook. Fanny Craddock in some ways was the portal through which English cuisine was suddenly transformed. Now she's a forgotten figure.

Not by some!

Not by some. But I watched those old shows and I thought it would have been very interesting to have been the child of someone like that. Because Craddock herself was a force of nature and she had a personality which was larger than life. And this idea – and of course I was imagining this – but this idea of a child who had no contact to his mother, except through the television shows that she made, and at that time she was far too busy to pay him any attention; but now, twenty years after the fact, after those shows are long forgotten, the boy finally gets to have this contact in relationship with the mother that he never had at that time.

And he's humiliated by being forced by his mother on screen to stuff a turkey in the most overtly sexual way, which for him is the equivalent of having sex with his mother on screen. Which is both funny and revolting!

Right. But in the book that scene is actually quite literal, where he does have sexual relations with his mother! But I found that that would just be unwatchable and in a way it was very reductive, it wouldn't have been that interesting. But to find another way of formatting that, also to use the medium, to use the video texture, to raise issues of whether or not this is a literal event, or whether it's how someone reformats or reimagines what might have happened. And one of the liberating aspects of the video texture for me is that it is an alternative way of recording personal history. Inasmuch as the idea of having any scene in one's background replayed is both something which can be done literally, or as a mental process.

But the thing about video is the replay is always the same. You're imprisoned in that version of events. The thing about memory, and I take it that what you're playing with the whole time is memory – recalled through the mind, or memory recalled through mechanical means – the thing about memory is that it at least offers you a chance of learning something from it. Am I imposing this on you or is this how you approach video and its relationship to memory?

Well, to an extent, because that's what the boy is doing in *Family Viewing*, where he's found this cache of old family videos and his father, who is in the process of now living a new life, having left the boy's mother, is taking these videos and taping over them with home-made pornography that he's making with his mistress. It's as though the only way he can actually sustain a level of sexual excitement is in knowing that his exploits are being recorded and are being used to erase this previous life.

It makes it more important because they're recorded, it's on video.

Exactly, and I do think that we do perform in a way when we know that something is being recorded. I mean in this conversation that we're having, I am much more careful in the choice of words, and in the way that I'm expressing myself, than I would be if it wasn't being recorded. When you take that dynamic and you put it within a family, it's bound to create these strange perversions that are bound to then be misused or appropriated and exaggerated by people who have other agendas.

In Felicia's Journey *and elsewhere, your characters are shown to live in the films in a continuum of narrative life; but also with all sorts of elements from their past intruding into the narrative continuum. And this business of layering experience, memory, recollection, is this the most important technique that you bring to films? Is this the most important part of what you're trying to do?*

One of the most profound experiences of my background is as an Armenian, having this piece of history that you know at one level has happened, but which you don't have the visual evidence to exploit. We are living in a century when we demand images, when we demand to be shown the scene that will make something clear and will serve as evidence. When a genocide has occurred and it's been denied, and where there's not a visual reference, there's no iconographic moment that the public can seize on as being representative of what that experience is, it's extraordinarily vulnerable. You are relying then on the witnesses and the stories, and we understand that there's a degree of subjectivity. And that to me is the most uncomfortable aspect of where my upbringing had to redefine and format itself. And I suppose that, when you look at the latest film, *Ararat*, you understand that there is a whole community of people that might have expected that that film was going to be a very literal rendering, a historical document that would prove once and for all that the genocide happened. And yet that's not my experience of it. My experience of this genocide is that history rather is formed by the way that competing versions of an event try and struggle to determine their authority.

But the Armenians are still convinced that they are losing out in this struggle and that the Turkish denial, as they would see it, is stronger than the Armenian assertion of massacre.

That is a profound and very sad situation for any people to be in. And as a dramatist working from that community, I think that this notion of denial is laced through all of the films at some level. *Ararat* in a way is again about how vulnerable that history might be, and how dependent we are on someone to listen to it and appraise it, and to give it a sense of value, because it can be so easily erased.

But you weren't making an overtly political film in that sense?

Absolutely not, but what's fascinating is how the document, the very fact that there is a film called *Ararat*, has now become this political tool.

Let's go back to that scene you described earlier on, which was your experience of going through Customs and having to explain to an Immigration officer what you were doing. And there's a scene in Ararat *where the young man comes back, having filmed in the area of Van, in Turkish Armenia, secretly, having filmed Ararat, and the Canadian Immigration officer wants to know what's going on. And the climax is, what's in those cans of film? Is it film, or is it, because by then everybody thinks it is, heroin? And in the event, the young man is let go and then you see the Immigration officer with the can open and it is filled with heroin. And somebody asks him, 'Why did you do it?' And the officer replies, 'Well, I think, I couldn't believe that he thought that was what he was doing!' I wonder whether it's a metaphor for saying that importing these memories into a country like Canada, if they are too virulent, is as dangerous as heroin?*

Well, I think it's the most provocative point that the Christopher Plummer character – the Immigration officer – makes. Earlier in the inspection when he confronts the boy by saying, 'What are you bringing into this country?' he's not really talking about what's in the can, but the whole notion of the experience, and this legacy of hatred and violence. And can this country, can any country, be the repository of those grievances? And this is the paradox of the multicultural system, that we want people to keep the more folkloric aspects of their culture, we want the dancing and we want the food. We want those things that we can immediately share and have access to, but we don't want those unresolved and dangerous and often quite explosive elements that are also part of the culture.

But it's true, you would break up the home culture, the new culture, if everybody were continuing to fight the battles which they brought with them.

Absolutely.

So how do you resolve that?

I think it's an ongoing issue. I think that you resolve that by conversations between individuals, by the way you negotiate with strangers, by the way you negotiate. And *Ararat* certainly is full of those, and says history is not really being defined by these grand gestures, the film premières, or the large broad strokes, but rather in the way that individuals address these issues, in hallways or in Customs offices, or in places where we can be infused at all times with the humanity of how these events change individuals.

We need to say something about just how you work, and your films have these complex structures. How far do you know before you start shooting what the structures are going to be? Are they scripted in such a detailed way?

What is scripted is the idea that there is a mosaic. The editing of the film is another version of the script, in a way. Because then, the alchemy that you've generated through performance and camera placement and music will alter the shape in ways that you can't anticipate at a script stage. But what the blueprint of the script allows everyone to understand is that it is a fluid process, that there is a dramatic coherence but also to underline that this is only one part of the evolution of the film.

But the things have to fit pretty tightly, although there are certain scenes where either you leave them deliberately vague, or they do steal up on you, such as an incestuous relationship in The Sweet Hereafter?

That's a very good example. When you were to read that moment, I think that the incest is quite evident and clear. But the way it's filmed, and the way it's cast throws some confusion onto that, and that ambiguity is something that then has to be addressed in the editing.

So your sense of the timing as to when to bring the incest theme back, that was something which you only felt in the cutting room.

Absolutely, and if you were to read the shooting script of *The Sweet Hereafter*, the voice-over that Nicole, the incest victim, has was very different than what we see in the final film. What you need to read is very different, often, from what you need to see.

But the question of the composition of scenes, I think the crucial shot in my mind here is in The Sweet Hereafter *when a school bus goes off the road, it's filled with children, it careers off on to a frozen lake, breaks through the ice and then sinks. And you see that from four hundred yards away, from the point of view of the person who witnessed it. There's not a single shot of screaming faces . . .*

Well, of course, because the whole idea there is to show the sense of helplessness that the father watching this can only imagine what's happening in that bus at that moment. To suddenly put the camera there I think would dispel and trivialise what that character's experience is. And that's what I think the great challenge is in directing a film, to find a way of visually representing these moments which address how the characters themselves experience those situations. For instance, in many of the films the emotions are buried and perhaps there is a sense of coldness even. But the music and the lushness of the visual image works against that, so that we as viewers are aware that there is an emotional life beyond what we are seeing. In a film like *Exotica*, where there's something figurative about the aspects of dialogue and the way that the characters present themselves, there is something – these are shattered people, these are people who are just living in shells. But the music would suggest that there is something else welling underneath, waiting to erupt in a way.

And what often wells up, of course, is violence. And the threat of violence, but it's very frightening and it just erupts like a firecracker, as

I guess it does in real life.

I think so. I think so, and I think that those moments are unexpected and they are catastrophic often. They're catastrophic because we have so little control over them.

Does that imminence of violence actually frighten you as a person?

What I'm most frightened of is this notion of how we react and would protect ourselves from that, knowing, of course, that there is no protection, that at any moment our stability and sense of control of our lives can be taken away from us. And that helplessness that the character, Billy Ansel, feels as he sees that bus disappearing; or let's say the helplessness of an entire culture as they see their communities eradicated as certainly happened, or is depicted in *Ararat*, how we can prepare ourselves for that. This is why the character of the adjuster was so fascinating.

This is an earlier film.

This is an earlier film, which is based on the notion of an insurance adjuster who has this obsessive attention to his clients, who is trying to rematerialise the life that they have lost, while his own life is completely shattered. And there are professions and occupations which allow someone to deal with neuroses and fear that would otherwise not be socially acceptable. But that the parameters of the job, be it an insurance adjuster or litigation lawyer or a Customs officer, these are jobs that allow you access into other people's lives in a way that would otherwise be outrageous, and allow you to deal with issues that are unresolved in your own personality by potentially exploiting other people's pain and sense of vulnerability.

I want to end with an installation that you did in London at Burlington House. It was called Steenbeckett, Beckett *being your television version of* Krapp's Last Tape, *the 'Steenbeck' being homage to a machine we all love, which is the machine on which countless films have been made where you can synchronise the film and the sound, and view them and edit them. But of course, they no longer exist, they've been junked. There is Krapp, looking at all his accumulated tapes, and at the age of almost seventy deciding that that's the end, there's nothing else. Were you also, in that installation, looking back at what you've done, looking at your huge accumulation of film and digital and thinking, what is your equivalent of Krapp's monologue, looking back, as it were?*

Well, my equivalent is this idea that I am an artist who is working at a particular juncture where the material aspect and the weight of these archival mediums is evaporating. With it, perhaps, a sense that there is a rare aspect to the accumulation, the very physical weight of experience. This is what the installation was trying to address, actually, that the last shot of that TV version was a twenty-minute take of John Hurt. And I was aware as we were shooting this on 35mm film of the cumbersome nature of the technology that we needed to record this moment. And how in a few years that would be obsolete, as a Steenbeck is.

Isn't that an improvement, isn't that an advance, some would say?

It's an advance, but I would also suggest that there was this moment where the very physical vulnerability of the medium reflected a corporeal aspect of our own experience, which made the decision to record, and how we recorded, and how we preserved, a more considered choice. That we were aware that how we were transcribing our experience was not as spontaneous, now we are in a time where, with the digital process, we are able to record everything . . .

And it doesn't matter.

It doesn't matter.

It appears not to matter.

It appears not to matter. And I think what's so touching about *Krapp's Last Tape* is that very physical process reflects a relationship to his own past which we can identify as being human.

Yes, you said somewhere that it's important that we remember that time, i.e. the memory, occupies space. And I suppose if the digital medium appears to exist out of time, does that also mean that it is less valued because it doesn't occupy space and therefore we understand it less well?

Well, that's very interesting because of course we get into that whole Kantian dilemma between the phenomenal and the nominal. And that we have a sense that our lives and what we experience is really tailored by the instruments and the perceiving mechanisms we have to take that in. But there is a whole other world outside of that which is governed by laws that we can't even begin to imagine. And yet we live under the illusion that the world we see is the world that exists, and that perhaps the old technology was able to correspond to aspects of our own physical selves, in a way that made that definition easier to understand. That we are now in a time where we don't have any comprehension of how these materials work and so we surrender aspects that are profound decisions that we have to make and we assign them without considering what that might mean later on, what the implications of that might be. We divest ourselves of a degree of responsibility.

WILLIAM FORSYTHE

The body teaches you a tremendous amount about the world

There's general agreement that William Forsythe – Bill Forsythe – is one of the world's leading choreographers. For the last twenty years he has led his company, Ballett Frankfurt, to a very special position in the league tables of contemporary dance. The company has a signature style – Forsythe's own choreography. He's extraordinarily fertile and inventive, turning out at least two or three works a year. Almost every other dance company in the world wants to work with him, or to perform his pieces. Why? Because, say his supporters, he's taking dance into the twenty-first century by deconstructing classical ballet. Now there's a word – deconstructing. No review or article about Forsythe is complete without it. But just what does it mean? His detractors – and there are some – accuse him of modish, politically correct, postmodernism, expressed in glossy, pumped-up athleticism. A few, from the very high classical tradition, say that deconstructing the great tradition can only be the work of the anti-Christ. In that case, if the devil has the best tunes, he also seems to have the best dance steps. Last year there was public outcry when the Frankfurt City Council announced that they could no longer support Ballett Frankfurt at existing levels. So in 2004, after a historic tenure in Frankfurt, creatively comparable with that of his idol, George Balanchine of the New York City Ballet, Forsythe moved on. For the moment, though, he's extremely active backstage here at one of his main performance venues in Frankfurt. As a young man of just fifty-three, Forsythe will not be short of offers.

So let's deal with Balanchine first. You weren't taught by him but by one of his dancers. What's the nature of Balanchine's appeal to you?

I like the mechanics of dancing. I like how it feels and I like how you think about it. And I was taught by someone who danced in his first company in America, and someone he also trusted as a teacher of his style. And, what it was, at least as I remember it and experienced it, was a kind of euphoria that comes through identification with a kind of universal mathematic, which is what ballet is. It's an extraordinary testament to how we intuit, let's say, the universal laws of physics that are everywhere. There's no space without it.

Expressed through the joints of the human body?

We're designed because the world is such. We didn't develop as a species without physics; we grew up, or grew into, this world with physics acting on our bodies the whole time. So the Balanchine style or technique, whatever you call it, was taught to me as a very complex series of torsions, you know, which are based upon something called épaulement, which is the relationship between the head, the hand and the foot, and the very prescribed turnings and counter-turnings and counter-twistings. So what happens, if you engage in this, and reduce your focus to this one action, if you prioritise your consciousness towards creating these forms that are inherent in ballet, you actually arrive at a kind of euphoric state. And I was taught this as a kind of euphoric meditation.

I think you also said that you admired and loved his tremendous mechanical simplicity. Now is that consistent with what you've just said about the euphoric state that it induced?

Well, there's two different things. There's the style of dancing from Balanchine and there's his choreography. At one point you have to separate the two because he does have a school, and the school teaches this style of very rigorous épaulement. The choreography itself was dependent upon this school, that the dancers all had access to this technical ability. And the choreography is spectacularly musical – I mean, that is the whole point of the choreography, it is there for music and as an interpretation. Whether this is the only way to make ballets now, interpreting music, certainly begs questioning.

Mm. But there was no doubt that he was the key influence that you had. When did you first begin to understand that you wanted to move beyond Balanchine?

I think I wanted to first move through Balanchine; and that was important that I first tried to imitate, and the first works I did were very clearly imitations. I wanted to be able to understand what this was, this making of a ballet like that. So at one point you say, OK, you can imitate the surface of this thing. But he made his ballets for very personal reasons, and I needed to also make ballets for personal reasons.

So what were the personal reasons which drove you to move through Balanchine to beyond Balanchine?

I grew up in a different culture. I grew up in American culture of the fifties and sixties, and my musical influences were drastically different. He did not grow up with rock'n'roll and I did. And right around that time was the emergence of rock'n'roll and I lived it, and quite unconsciously I became a really, really good dancer, a regular old dancer – someone who turned on the radio and danced round the kitchen or went out and danced at parties. I won my first friends in school because I could dance well.

But you knew that dancing alone, good as you were, wasn't going to satisfy you, even though you felt euphoric.

Dancing teaches you a lot. I think the body is incredibly instructive and contains a wealth of information, also information that supplies philosophy with ideas also. I think by dancing I was able to understand a lot of things. I was able to intuit things about mathematics and philosophy and discovered afterwards that what I had thought about seemed to be true. And the body – how can I say this? – the body teaches you a tremendous amount about the world. I would say that the body in many cases becomes an ear, the body itself is an organ for listening.

But how do you get into the sort of state of mind that you can start to learn from your body?

Practice. Practice.

What sort of practice?

Every conceivable kind of physical practice you can imagine. I did ballet for many, many, many years. I danced since I was three.

Why did you start dancing?

You don't start dancing, you dance. I mean *either* you're a dancer or you're not. I'm one of the people who has always danced. I can still dance and I use it as a kind of communion, you know. You use it to get in touch with things, even if it's just moving your hands. I sometimes just arrange my fingers; it's a way of thinking. I mean, the body is a thinking tool.

If the rest of us did that it would be a neurotic twitch, but when you do it, it's something different.

Because I'm conscious of what I'm doing, I'm doing it to look at what the body's possibilities are. If I'm looking at my hand right now, I'm saying 'OK, how does the body configure itself, what is the mathematics here, what are the tensions, what are the properties of the present, when you're with your body?' You say, 'What am I paying attention to right now?'

Can you ever be still?

That's a good question. Difficult. Usually when I'm sleeping. It keeps you thin apparently!

You said that you were brought up in this very different American cultural scene from Balanchine. Given what we all think about the vitality and the creativity of American dance, why didn't you stay there?

What do you really mean by 'stay there'?

Well, you came to Germany.

Well, do you have to be there in order to be yourself, you know? Be where is really the question. So I pretty much took myself with me when I moved across the ocean. And I don't think that I myself have been tremendously influenced by foreign culture, except that theatre culture is organised differently than in America. So I adapted myself to the organisation. But I myself as a person I don't think would be that much different had I lived in America.

So you think you are recognisably, creatively the same person as you would have been if you'd stayed in New York? It sounds unlikely.

The question is would it have turned out differently? Sure, why not, because it's a different system and one is certainly adaptive. And I feel that I probably would have adapted to the situation there and there's no use saying, 'Well, you know, what if and had you . . .?' Rather, I am here and I've been here and this is what's emerged.

Just let me clear up one thing. You talk most of the time about ballet, and making ballets. Universally, people who do the sort of work you do call themselves dance, or dance theatre. Is there something deliberately almost retro in attaching yourself to the word 'ballet'?

Well, ballet's never been retro because it's in my body, so I live with it, it's very contemporary. You can't erase it. If you learn a language, for example, if you've learned English as your mother tongue, it's very difficult to erase something like that. And ballet was my mother tongue in dance, so you can't erase it from your consciousness.

But you never felt that you had to signal that you were doing something contemporary and avant garde by saying 'let's push ballet to one side and let's call it dance'?

Well, this is ballet now. It's one way of thinking about it. It's certainly not all of ballet, it's just a little part of it. Ballet is a normative methodology, so in its purest form it's a normative methodology. And we all learn this normative methodology. Everyone agrees that passé is passé, arabesque is arabesque, and we all try with our own means, our bodies, to say 'OK, this is my arabesque'; and then we have this wonderful ideal that sort of exists, it's a prescription but there is no arabesque, for example, it's everyone's arabesque. So you carry it around with you and if you are going through changes as a person in this civilisation that we're in, then I guess it changes according to what influences or effects you've experienced.

Let's get on to this question of deconstruction, which is rightly or wrongly attached to you, hung round your neck. First of all, do you mind the fact that it's the first thing everybody says: 'Oh Forsythe has deconstructed classical ballet'?

Well, I feel that the word is used rather carelessly. I'm not sure if they mean literary deconstruction, architectural deconstruction. But if I would refer to someone like Paul de Man, who's a literary theorist, and refer to his deconstruction, I would describe it as a non-absolutist environment, which has mathematical implications, which would be a bit like Cantor's Theorem; it is impossible to have the set of all sets. And so a non-absolutist environment would say that it also has to include some absolutes. So it means rather a kind of new political territory which means that one respects rules but also one rejects rules, too, of any nature.

That's the essence of what we're talking about?

To some degree. I think there is an error on the part of many people who use the word 'deconstruction'; they phonetically confuse it with 'destruction'. They hear the negative in it and they use it that way, and I would rather they say something more direct about what they feel I'm doing with ballet. But I don't understand why people see themselves, who don't practise dance, as the guardians of a tradition. You know, what tradition? Which part? There's many lines to this tradition, there's many ways of practising it. In any case I'm only interested in a kind of internal refractive aspect of it, and the analysis of categorical representation. But this is me, and I'm just one of many people practising ballet, so I think to call it 'deconstruction' is a little bit cavalier.

Even your supporters say, one of the dance critics said very simply, 'Forsythe has broken every rule in the classical dance book.' Would you accept that?

Well, I'd like to know first what they mean by rules, and which rules. The rules are not stated anywhere, there's no place where rules are stated. It doesn't have legal status, you know. There is really no legal function to ballet. And to use this word is very interesting. I use it myself.

'Deconstructing'?

Yes. I say it, and I would say, rather, let's change that word to 'prescription'. So if we say arabesque involves a line emanating from the hip, at the least forty-five degrees from the floor, defined by the foot, its relationship to the hip, and going up there to a hundred and eighty degrees at least, for a penchée. Then within that mathematical prescription there is perhaps room for saying 'what if'?

But you're still working within the mathematical prescription of the arabesque, as anybody will recognise it?

Ballet is a geometric, inscriptive art form. We're inscribing geometry. And let's just start there – it's a really basic approach, it's very simple, it's not overtly political but it does have philosophical backgrounds. If you look at the eighteenth century and the emphasis on neo-Platonism as a foundation for abstraction, then you go, 'Why do we believe this is valuable, good, etc. etc.?' So one begins to examine it and say, 'What if one does this to that? Do the results change? Do they change philosophically?' and then perhaps the politics of making it do change.

You use the word 'prescription' – the prescription, I suppose, also comes in the idea of people who say, 'This is what the arabesque is and you shall not change from that' – that's the negative prescription, isn't it, the restrictive prescription?

People never think of prescription as a sort of linguistic form that has no space in it. It's a bit like this pen, that I can't do anything with, this pen on the table here, it's solid and it's fixed. But this is language, this is a linguistic prescription, and language is malleable and suggests change already. And because I like to think algorithmically, I like to think of these prescriptions as little language machines that produce these things called arabesques or pirouettes. One says, 'Well, why not look at it as a sort of research project and what happens if the prescription is altered by one word, two words, and if we replace this with that, what emerges?' And so basically it's curiosity.

Another quote from the writer I mentioned, who said, 'The classical eye has been replaced by an aesthetic of perfect disorder, where every joint is shot through with energy and drama, traditionally modest movements have been terrifyingly magnified so that an arabesque might seem to wrench the dancer's joints apart.' Is that a fair description of some of the things that you've done?

I think that writer enjoys hyperbole, yeah, and revels in it!

Do you think you're not doing anything as extreme?

Our goals are so much different, our goals are really very workmanlike. We're looking at these things, we're saying, 'Is it possible with this velocity to accomplish that?' And rather than say we're working teleologically and want an absolute outcome – this is not physics, classical physics, this is more like quantum physics – in saying there is a probability that you will fall over, and there's a possibility that this thing will transform into something else, we're just basically pushing the system to say OK, at a certain level what are the probabilities? Will this thing become something we don't know? Can ballet actually produce something we know, produce something we don't know? Now that's an interesting thing.

And how far down that line do you think that you've got?

I'm getting there. I'm getting on down the line!

But at the same time you're always, I think, drawing on ballet's academic heritage, and that seems to be a sort of very strong sense inside you. Am I right?

Academic? Yes, it's most recognisable in its academic form. One always starts from that point insofar as that the definition is pretty clear, it's accepted universally. I think that having investigated that to a large degree we've moved on a little bit at the moment, seeing the body as geometrically inscriptive but looking at other properties like folding, collapsing, or other kinds of effects from physics.

At the time that you were going down this road, were you actively dissatisfied with what kind of choreography was on offer?

Throughout my entire career I have seen wonderful works from really great artists, and I have always been inspired by other people.

So you never had to say 'I reject all that, and this is me and my unique road'?

Well, I wasn't paying attention to mainstream ballet, because it really wasn't what I was doing – I don't do classics. I would say it's almost an idiolect, you know like a tiny language spoken by a little tribe – I mean we're only thirty people, so you could compare us perhaps with a tribe in the Amazon. Here we are in Frankfurt, at the end of the world, in deepest darkest Germany, here we are speaking this little ballet-derivative language. And I would say yes, like a little idiolect – something that we understand and now it's been taken out into the world by various people who say, 'We'd like to also investigate what it feels like to speak that way!'

Are you surprised when people say this is a ballet language for the twenty-first century?

Oh, it seems almost appropriate.

But you didn't set out to do it?

No! No, I mean we're just ballet practitioners!

You came to Ballett Frankfurt in 1984, you were just thirty-five, perhaps that's the right age to start running a company. How clear an idea did you have about what you wanted to do?

I had less ideas about the company and more ideas about the space. The Frankfurt Opera stage is perhaps one of the most beautiful theatres in the world. It's fifty by fifty metres. The audience is relatively small. You can see well practically from every seat, and one has the feeling on the stage that one is rather in a landscape – it's so large. And this influenced very much my thinking about space and making things in space.

But what sort of opportunities did that suggest to you? Just that you had space which you needed to work with rather than dropping conventional sets in?

Yeah. Well, things took time. To walk fifty metres takes more time than it does to walk twelve, and so the temporal structures of pieces adapted themselves to that kind of space. And because the space itself is so beautiful, I didn't want to fill it with anything but light. So I left the majority of scenic elements out, and tried to build a repertoire of light, even building lighting instruments myself, designing them myself and having them built, and deploying them to create unique visual situations for this stage.

Did you know at the beginning that your company would have no soloists, no corps de ballet, just a company of equals?

That's interesting. I don't know if I knew it, it just seemed the right way to work right now. I noticed in other companies where I worked that it always created problems.

Who was going to get the solos?

Not just that, it's just that it makes no sense. If you're going to work on ballet, there is no male ballet or female ballet basically. Men at one point don't wear point shoes, but the primary stuff of ballet is ungendered. There are also degrees of expertise – someone can do a double saut de basque, another person can only do one. Someone can do triple tours, someone can do entrechats huit but someone else can also do an extraordinary entrechats six, so everyone has their strengths and weaknesses. Very few people can do everything extraordinarily well. But what made sense would be to have a group whose talents were relatively equal, so I have only soloists, I don't have a group. And this brings a much different atmosphere into the work. Everyone's equally responsible.

Did you know that you'd have to find over a period of time a different set of dancers who could work in the sort of way that you wanted?

Yes, but that's a slow evolution. That took about eight years.

And in that time you were evolving your method? And you worked through it with them?

Yes, I also worked on their bodies – in other words I always made the work for who I had in front of me – you don't make a work for some non-existent person, you have to look at the person in front of you and see what they're doing. And I also change ballets constantly. The cast changes and something does not look good on that person – I change it. Or if they're having trouble co-ordinatively with it, I change it. There's no point in making people suffer, for what?

Now your relationship with the company has evolved. From the early eighties the credits for your ballets say 'Choreography by William Forsythe, created on X and Y and Z'. Now, its . . .

Created with. Created with.

Well, it's 'created on' that I saw, in the complete list of your works. And then, of course, it changes to 'created with'! What is that telling us about your relationship with your dancers? It suggests a very physical approach of working with their bodies.

Well, I am fifty-three now and I still dance, right? I dance in rehearsals, I go in every night and dance work on my own. My attitude is always the following. If I'm going to dance with you, then you should probably choreograph with me! So we both dance, the dancers and I, we all dance together and we all choreograph together. Because if you leave it over to the other person to just do the dance and the other person to do the choreography, I believe there's a gap forms in your experience. And this experiential gap is, I find, dangerous, and detrimental to the kind of work at least that I want to do.

It becomes active passive?

Yeah, exactly. And it evolves to the point that the dancers are credited for choreography and they're also paid for it.

But that took time, didn't it? That's the interesting thing, because we move from the credit which states 'created on', to a different credit, 'William Forsythe in collaboration with the ensemble', which was presumably a very different process, and then in 1997, Hypothetical

Stream – *a choreographic work 'from William Forsythe' and then nine named dancers!*

Hypothetical Stream was made originally for Daniel Larrieu and his company in Tours and he wanted a ballet and I said, 'I can't come, I'll fax it to you.' So I took a series of sketches from Tiepolo, and I drew any number of vectors, emanating from these knots of suspended figures that were all flying in the clouds, and all very knotted, very Baroque. And I drew a number of vectors, and said, 'These are knots, and these need to be solved, or unknotted.' And the lines that I drew were hypothetical solutions to these knots.

How the dancers would move to unknot the knots?

Yes, or a tighter knot or a more complicated one. And the figures in the drawings were all numbered, so your number, Joan, is number one and, and John is number two etc. And they received instructions how to construct this ballet. And I've done it in three different places and each one is drastically different, and the people solve it themselves.

Have you ever faxed any other ballet like that?

No, no, it's the only faxed ballet!

But in the end, how can nine or six people, or you and the company, all choreograph together? I mean in the end you're making the choice, aren't you, you are the . . . Somebody has to be the directing mind, because I think you've said the trouble is if there isn't somebody with a directing mind it looks like a can of worms.

Well, I start the idea, I'm the initiator, right? So I say I believe that something could emerge from these conditions, and then I name the conditions, which is basically the algorithm to make the choreography. We then work on these instructions, and these instructions then give it a kind of result, and we discuss it. And from that I have to keep deriving other conditions, like variations on these results, until we arrive at something that is agreeable upon. The reason the dancers do it is because of time limitations to some degree. Also, in order to understand the structure, you have to be in the structure sometimes, dancing it. I've had up to eight dancers examine a structure according to certain instructions, internally, that was *Eidos Telos*, and you get a very,

very unique result. In a work based on Virginia Woolf's *Mrs Dalloway*, there was a wonderful introduction to the book at one point, and it said Mrs Dalloway was having moments of vision. So one of our methodologies had to do with identically remembering another person's variation, or phrase rather, and building a kind of architecture of movement around it. But you had to keep seeing this other person dancing in order to perform it, so it was a way of having a vision.

It seems to me that what you ask of your dancers is absolutely huge. There's a 1995 dance where you ask them to work from over a hundred core sequences, and then to develop those in the course of the performance. How do you begin to reach a stage where people know enough and remember enough to make it coherent?

Repetition. Repetition – over and over and over and over again, until one could move through space, and the shape of the hand – in this case that was *Eidos Telos* – the shape of the hand recalls sequences, so if the hand moves in relationship with, for example, my head, in a certain tension, you know that that recalls a certain sequence. And this has to do with a cloud of memory, a cloud of form – in our case a cloud of memory. It had to do with creating a memory, and a kind of metaphoric memory. And it was immediately after my wife had died so I was really concerned with memory at that point.

Because you've said the body is the memory, and I guess that's only something that a dancer can understand.

Well, the body begins to remember autonomously. You don't have to construct memory any more. For example, you remember how to feed yourself with a fork. You don't even think any more, you pick up the fork and it goes. So for us, if we provide certain conditions, end up in a certain shape, this produces memory, and some of it is constructed in consciousness and other is just habit, actually.

Now, music. In your early years, in your Balanchine phase, a lot of music was classical, or twentieth-century certainly. Then at a particular period, the Dutch composer, Thom Willems, started to work with you more or less all the time. His music is often very hard, very percussive, very industrial, call it what you want. What is the appeal of that sort of music for you as a choreographer?

Well, I'd like to take Thom under my wing right now and say that you have to really hear twenty years of music before you can really say what it is. It goes through every conceivable kind of acoustic dimension, and to say it's industrial or something like that is actually a little bit unfair. Yes, these are comments that have been made. Thom Willems gives you acoustic space to dance; he really gives you space to dance! It makes acoustic environments, and so we've done away with the sets, and we have acoustic environments. He's a classical musician, and I feel that it works for classical-based dancing. And he is amenable to our ideas. He likes to understand what we're doing and try to think up something that might surprise us and challenge us.

So at what stage does he come into the creative process?

He can come in at any stage. He can walk in two days before the première or he can hand me a piece four months before. It varies every time. We've had every conceivable sort of time schedule in working over the last twenty years. Thom Willems, though, is also someone who's constantly evolving. We play music – sometimes it's played live on the laptop during a performance. He sometimes pulls back to the point he's practically inaudible. I would say he's an extraordinary partner. He is always interested in the idea. He always wants to know what are we thinking and I say, 'Nothing, we're just, we're just organising bodies!' No, it's fine with him, but he's always interested in the idea.

How precise is the idea when you start working on a new piece? You said just now that you choreographed a dance using images from Tiepolo which you then drew out on paper. Do you ever do anything remotely like that with your own work, that you sketch it out in sketches beforehand?

Absolutely not. Absolutely not. I pray for what the Buddhists call that 'don't know mind'. I try not to know what the piece will be. I can start with an idea and I'll study for years actually to think about something. But when I go into the studio I want to be able to see what is in front of me, I want to not have another idea. In that sense it's not like ballet, not where I have this thing I'm trying to fill, or pass through the prescription. I try to devise methodologies that are commensurate with the project. The project usually has some form as an idea, but those ideas have to become methodologies, and I have to look at what the results are, I have to look at dancers. And that is the biggest challenge, not seeing what I want to see but seeing what's actually in front of my eyes.

So what are you saying to the dancers on day one?

I usually say, 'I've absolutely no idea what I'm doing, because I've never made this ballet before!'

And they say, 'Give us a clue'?

Right and then, then we go.

So the process of discovery between you and the ensemble is an absolutely critical part of the creative business?

I think our curiosity is very valuable – how curious are people. Also trusting – I have to trust them and they have to trust me. That's very, very important.

And do they ever say to you, 'Bill, we've done this before'?

Yes they have! Very valuable comment! I say, 'Well, do we want to do it again?' And that is, I find, a very helpful comment. And I go, 'Have we really?' and they go, 'Yeah,' and I'm like 'OK; well, here we go.' I'm very grateful to them. They're the ones, the dancers are the ones, who have actually pushed me, constantly, to go further.

What external influences matter to you? You mentioned Tiepolo, you mentioned rock'n'roll music. Who are the other influences from the artistic world all around you that matter?

I would say that I'm very influenced by the here and now, whatever is in front of me – a book, a newspaper, a photo, a film, snow falling outside, you name it, that gets my attention. I'm sort of like a cat, you know. Do you ever see a cat sit around and stare at things? In that sense I sit around and stare at things a lot because I'm easily distracted and fascinated by things. So whatever sparks my curiosity or holds my interest is what's in front of my eyes. If I'm in front of a work of a colleague that is really inspiring, then

I'm inspired by it, whether it be a photo, a painting, a sculpture, an installation. Or it could be, like I said, watching the neighbour's cat.

Why does dance matter at all today?

Well, we all still have bodies, don't we? So I would say that's a very, very good question. Does it matter, and to what degree does it matter? I'm reading Hegel right now, so I'm inclined to question some of the distinctions he makes about art. I think dancing is in a difficult position, only insofar as there is this battle between that which is instructive on one hand, and entertaining or decorative on another – sensuous as he calls it. On the other hand everyone dances; MTV is literally a dance channel – that's the way I see it. I turn on MTV and look for groovy moves, as it were, and to see spectacular dancing. There is a lot of dance culture. It's all around us. Maybe as we get older, we get that we see less and less of it, but it's not to be avoided.

So that will continue even if the classical ballet companies and your company didn't exist?

Of course it would, thank God. I would hope so . . . !

So why do companies such as yours matter? Why does this particular kind of dance, ballet, matter?

I don't know that it does matter. I'm not in a position to assess it. We do it, it has a certain resonance. Right now, I am working on projects that make work that tries to make the audience aware of its own attention. So a recent work we made called *Forehand* tried to function more as a musical piece creating a series of silences, and these silences were designed to make the audience aware of their collective attention. It actually worked. And at the end of the piece, I always had the feeling that the audience applauds very enthusiastically its own attention, which I think because of television is to some degree harder and harder to get – you can't zap your way out of a performance, quite frankly.

Were people embarrassed by the silences, because it had put the spotlight back on them?

Perhaps at some point, but finally it became a collective enterprise. And this collective enterprise apparently was from the response of the audience, very rewarding. We're talking a thousand, four hundred people, you know, actually being glad that they became a little community of attentive people.

What's the next stage of your evolution as a maker of ballets?

The question is, I really don't know if it's ballets I'm making. Perhaps we need another word for what we're doing here at the moment. I think that the word 'ballet' causes a lot of contention. We certainly don't want to upset those who have used ballet as a way to fetishise their own hysteria. So I think that I'd rather move on, than work in the arena of the hysterical fetishists, as it were, and just say that at one point this was a place where we moved from, it was at a point of departure. And I have certainly no intentions of trying to define ballet. Ballet is not to be defined by any individual whatsoever; it is an historical normative methodology, and this is where it will always be.

But curiosity, which you mentioned much earlier, that will always be the defining characteristic of what you do?

That's nice if that would be true. I hope so; I hope we stay curious, certainly. I don't think any one person can exhaust ballet any more than one composer can exhaust music – classical music – for that matter. Bach didn't certainly exhaust classical music, nor did Stravinsky. But I don't want to be in a situation where I am also defined by ballet only; because the thinking uses ballet as a structure, a structure that sort of accelerates thinking, and as a place to start from. And I don't want to say that this is ballet now, as we've said before. I don't know if this is ballet now – perhaps it isn't any more – so I shall be the last one to say what it is, and would be disinclined to say that this is the historical line of this art form. It's just one of many lines.

So what about the line in Frankfurt?

Well, the line in Frankfurt is about to experience a rather strong shift in its direction. I don't know whether the line will be able to continue in the form that it's in – in other words as a company – or whether we will have to simply imagine ourselves otherwise, which is to say that we will probably move into more teaching, and actually documenting ideas. We've had several offers right now, like the CD ROM which we've produced already, to produce more instructive things, and to keep the ideas alive.

But you don't just want to become an archivist of your own past work?

No. No, not an archivist, but these are useful tools, thinking tools, for people working in the field, and they're just tools.

When did you last see a traditional production of Swan Lake*?*

Swan Lake, hm!

Or any of the great classical Russian ballets.

Let me think; it's been a while. Yes, it's been a while!

Did you enjoy it?

Oh yeah. I saw Sylvie Guillem in *Giselle*. I did enjoy it, really. It's Royal Ballet, actually, and they were great, I thought that the company was amazing. They know how to do those ballets well. It was so spectacularly performed, and I really enjoyed it and I'm glad that there are those works to see still.

You don't have to set what you do against that sort of work and that sort of achievement?

Oh, not at all. I want to see that work really beautifully performed, I don't want to see a crap version of *Swan Lake* or *Giselle*. I love to see an extraordinary, exquisite, pristine version of that. Just say that my work is not against it, it's adjacent, or beside or around. You can't move through the same space – that space is historically occupied by that work. You can't pass through it, you can't affect it, deflect it, you can't do anything with it. It simply exists as a line, and these other lines in history . . . some will last longer and some will last less long.

GILBERT AND GEORGE

We always try to make an art that is confrontational

Gilbert and George are a hundred and nineteen, no that's wrong, Gilbert and George is a hundred and nineteen. No, that's definitely wrong. Gilbert is fifty-nine, George is sixty, but the artist Gilbert and George is just thirty-four if you date his existence from 1968 when he did his first sculptures at Frank's Sandwich Bar in the East End of London. Or from 1967, when Gilbert, from the Italian Dolomites, and George, from Devon, met at St Martin's School of

Art. Then perhaps the idea that two men should become their sculpture seemed just one of those post-art-school jokes, but thirty-four years on Gilbert and George are still recognisably the artist who became famous with the *Singing Sculpture* of 1969 when the two men in their trademark suits, their hands and faces in bronzed make-up, coloured with dots, mimed and danced their way through Flanagan and Allen's 'Underneath the Arches'. They moved on to postal sculptures, or postcards, written sculptures, and then in the early 1970s to large photo pieces, initially monochrome, later coloured photo images, their surface divided into black grids of squares and rectangles usually with text forming part of the image. While they are perhaps best known in popular terms for their use of explicit sexual and defecatory imagery, their work has a far broader range to it, death and hope and life and fear from the 1980s. Class war, politics and, in their last London show, *More Horny Pictures*, pictures of young male prostitutes. And they divide the critics; are they 'jokers, storytellers with a cool nearly pathological desire for exhibitionism' – according to one – or should they be read very differently? 'The art of Gilbert and George is a method of making everything mean what it usually does only with grander, more vivid force.' They are resolutely beyond current fashion, they have lived in Spitalfields in East London, a strong centre of Bangladeshi immigrants, for years, well before the trendy art world moved eastwards to Hoxton to join them. For themselves, once they said, 'Our motto is that nothing matters'; but on another occasion, 'The function of art is to bring about new understanding, progress and advancement.'

Two people, one artist, how have you managed it for thirty-four years?

GILBERT Because we never ask that question ourselves.

GEORGE And we never argue. We don't believe in discussing or planning or in ideas. How we are as people when we go to the studio is how the pictures will be. They're never based on ideas from the head.

GILBERT And we had this amazing determination when we started in 1969 that we wanted to be artists. And I was from what they call the Dolomites, I couldn't speak English very well, and George was from Devon, and he showed me London and we wanted to be artists together, and it was an amazing vision for us. And we never lost that vision, we still have that every single day. Nothing has changed in that way, the ambition that we want to be artists.

GEORGE And we do believe that being war babies was an enormous thing for us, because I remember as a child that everything was broken, families were broken, people were injured, many people were dead. Houses were filled with furniture which was damaged. And you knew one thing and one thing only, that things would get better. And our generation really believed in that, that you had to get up and sort everything out and go forward and do it.

GILBERT And maybe because when we start in 1967–68, we tried to do something different. And we always believe in accidents, we never believe in what they call searching, we always believe in a dream or something that we fell into it. And so one day we decided that we should become a sculpture that feels the pain, not only the surface, that we were able to speak, we were able to express ourself. And that was totally different than the other sculptors because they only had a surface.

You must have known one another for a certain amount of time before you came together; how long was that period and when did each of you begin to realise that what you wanted to do was to work together absolutely?

GEORGE We weren't conscious of that, we never believed that we decided on it or thought it out or discussed that. We feel more that it was something that came over us, like a cloud that came over us, as though somebody else did it to us.

Did your colleagues think that you were serious?

GEORGE At St Martin's we were taken very seriously, almost

as a threat, really, because the style of art that was current then was formalistic art. It was to do with colour, shape, form, weight, and you discussed art in those terms, you never discussed feeling, meanings, sex, race, religion, money, none of those things came into the discussion about art. It was just another language, the language of sculpture. And we thought that was wrong, because if you took those sculptures out of the building of St Martin's School of Art into the street they wouldn't address the issues that were inside of all the people on the street, they wouldn't even identify them as art.

And those issues you saw as what?

GEORGE We felt that everyone was very, very complex. If we speak to young people in our neighbourhood they talk about employment, sex, race, religion, all these things are enormously important, and drugs, there's an enormous problem now with young people in the East End of London.

GILBERT Yes, we do believe that in 1969, through the idea of making a more emotional art we managed to finish off St Martin's School of Art for thirty years.

Because they couldn't resolve the tension between the formalism of the teaching and the emotion that was bubbling up inside you?

GILBERT Not only us, a lot of other artists, and we do believe that after the St Martin's sculpture department fell apart for many, many, many years and moved over to another kind of school.

Were there any other students who you got on with, or did you feel yourselves very isolated? You say you were taken seriously but you were also seen as a threat?

GEORGE We were part of a very elite group of students on the top floor of the school, it was an unofficial course. County Hall, which controlled all these art schools, didn't even know that course existed.

County Hall, that was the local authority.

GEORGE Exactly. And Frank Martin, who ran that course, ran it as a sort of personal hobby and it was very, very overstaffed with tutors, and people could come from anywhere in the world and just join the course without filling in forms or showing their work or anything. And we did feel very, very special about it.

GILBERT Superior.

GEORGE We never even visited the painting department, for instance, we didn't even know where it was. Long after we left St Martin's, people said, 'What sort of painting was going on at St Martin's when you were there?' and we said, 'No idea, never even went there.'

GILBERT I mean there were a group of artists like Richard Long, Hamish Fulton, Barry Flanagan, Bruce McLean, many, many like that. And we did feel superior, we felt we were able to understand a new vision for art and it did change – art did change.

GEORGE And we felt very much that the work that was going on at St Martin's by the tutors would never become interesting or more interesting for people. You could have shows of it all over the world, it would never grow, it could never become something. It was limited by its formality.

It's very interesting what you say about emotion, because there are three very different artists whom I've met in the last six weeks – John Adams the composer, Bill Viola the video artist, and now you – all of whom are saying, 'The important thing about art is not the form and the structure, it is emotion and what I am doing is to release emotion.'

GEORGE And meaning, yes. That was extraordinary for us because when we left St Martin's there were four or five art galleries in the world, modern ones. There was one in Amsterdam, one in Düsseldorf, one in London, one in New York, one in Italy, one in Belgium, where we could exhibit our works; there wasn't a great choice of galleries as you have now. And all of those galleries specialised in minimal abstract art and concept. So everything had to be either on a sheet of paper or it had to be wood or coal or lead, and it had to be true to materials. And the bad things in art then were emotion, colour, sentiment, feeling, sexuality, all those were taboo.

GILBERT And we felt we were always on the outside in those galleries, we felt we were never in the centre, but the centre was a blank canvas, or a circle or line, that was the centre, and we were what they called, the 'randy outside'. And I remember so well Konrad Fischer, this quite famous art dealer in Dusseldorf, he used to say, 'Oh I love you,' and we'd go out and drink the whole night away, 'But you are something different.' We were something different. But the art world changed. We are in the centre now.

GEORGE We stayed still and the art world moved in a way that we became more central.

They've been desperately trying to co-opt you, haven't they? Over the thirty-four years people have been trying to include you in and say you're part of this school or part of that school.

GEORGE Of many, many movements, yes, movements long forgotten. But you can imagine in those galleries at that time that any art that addressed the vast general public was regarded as an embarrassment almost, it had to be just for the elite international few. And we always remember when we had out first show in Düsseldorf and we had an extremely successful opening and private view and lots of drinks and things, a big night of partying. And then we went into the gallery in the morning and the lady was just finishing cleaning away the bottles and corks and things. And the director of the gallery was sitting there looking very, very grumpy and depressed. And we said, 'Hangover?' No, no, no, he didn't have a hangover. We said, 'What's the matter?' And he said, 'Oh, the cleaning lady, she likes your exhibition.' It's a very, very seventies story.

Yes, that's a giveaway. Now you have lived in Fournier Street in Spitalfields, the Bangladeshi immigrant area. George moved there first, it's been your home ever since. What did you like about it?

GEORGE At the time we moved in, of course, it wasn't the Bangladeshi street, it was the Jewish quarter. All the shops, our newsagent, the tobacconist, the restaurants, the cafés, were all Jewish. And then it became Somali for a while, for a year and a half a lot of Somali people moved in with beautiful filed teeth. And then it became Maltese, very briefly. Directly opposite our house now on Fournier Street there was a Maltese café where we had beautiful food I remember, extraordinary.

But what did you like about this?

GILBERT Well, George moved there in 1964 because it was very cheap and we were able to have half-studio and half-living. And it was quite unusual that we were able to do that, because it was like a ghetto district and very romantic in some funny way. The first time I went to the East End of London and I thought it was just extraordinary; it felt to me like moving into a book, into a nineteenth-century book, all these yellow lights, all these old-fashioned houses, eighteenth-century houses, it was a magic, like magic.

And now?

GILBERT We still love it. We don't want to know exactly what is going on because we know that we cannot change anything, so we love it. There are a lot of people who say 'Oh my God, all these trendy people are moving in,' but I don't care about that. Living is living.

GEORGE It's very interesting. For fifteen years all the journalists used to say, 'Now that you're successful artists, why don't you move to a nicer part of London?' And for the last fifteen years they've said, 'Oh, it's become so trendy. Isn't it time you moved on?' So they always wanted us to leave. We always felt that it was dangerous, it was rough, it was romantic, and London was, at that time, much more dangerous than it is now in many ways, we feel that. But we felt that we were at the centre of the universe. We had the most marvellous nightlife in those days. All the European and American people who came to London felt that London and Britain were falling to pieces, that it was all very wretched and collapsing into anarchy. And we saw that, but at the same time we thought it was the most actual place in the world, it was more modern than anywhere else.

Now, from that environment, or from that time, the Singing Sculpture *evolved. How did it evolve?*

GILBERT It evolved because we were absolutely alone with nothing to do, and we wanted to be artists, but we'd just left St Martin's School of Art and nobody would touch us in a million years.

GEORGE We went to every single gallery in London, even the

ones we'd never heard of, just to be able to say that we'd been to every gallery. We just got the list; so even galleries near Sloane Street or galleries that didn't even show modern art, we went to. We presented an idea of our intentions for the future as artists, and said, 'We'd like to offer an exhibition,' and they all said, 'No!' And we felt enormously proud. We thought we really were doing something amazing; doing the right thing: everybody said no!

What were you offering them; were you offering them the Singing Sculpture*?*

GILBERT Oh yes, even that. We were offering them full of different ideas.

GEORGE We went to the Tate and we said we would like to present a living sculpture called *A Christmas Piece*, where we'd already organised with the RSPCA to borrow animals and we would recreate the birth of Jesus in the entrance to the Tate. And we would stand there as two living figures. It didn't occur to us that maybe wasn't very right, we would be Mary and Joseph in a way, and there wouldn't have been a baby but there would be the animals. And of course again they turned it down. But then we had two enormous pieces of luck, I must say, because there was an exhibition travelling around the world called *When Attitude Becomes Form*, and every city it arrived in, the local curator was invited to add artists to that exhibition. And it was coming to the ICA in London and we were so excited we were going to be in this group show. And then, much to our amazement, the selector, who we knew, didn't select us and we were horrified and we felt completely miserable about it. And we felt the only thing we could do was to be a living sculpture at the opening. So we went to the opening and stood there with these multicoloured bronze heads and hands . . .

GILBERT In the middle of the room . . .

GEORGE In the middle of the exhibition, completely still for the whole evening, and it stole the show entirely.

Did it take a lot of guts?

GEORGE Did it take a lot of guts? No, I think we just felt it was the only possibility and we had to seize that moment, if not it would be lost. And then, during that evening, a young man came up to us and said, 'I am Konrad Fischer, you do something with me in Düsseldorf, uh?' And that was the most famous art dealer in the world at that time. Every artist would cut their legs off to join that gallery, and he was asking us to do it.

GILBERT But we were trying to go towards the music world as well, the pop world.

Hence the Singing Sculpture?

GILBERT Yes. And we went to the Marquee and we did one evening there and we did full of other stuff. We were not sure if we were going towards music or art.

And it could have gone either way?

GILBERT Yes, it could have gone either way.

And then the Red Sculpture, *that was a bit further on, that was 1976; your hands and faces painted red, and a very elaborate ninety-minute choreographic movement imitating marionettes?*

GEORGE Very severe, a very severe work that one, very emotional!

GILBERT It was very interesting, like the *Singing Sculpture*, all the sculptures now, we were doing this eight hours non-stop. We went on the table and did it for eight hours and everybody told us, 'How could you do that, how can you do that without, what they call, having lunch or having tea or going to the toilet?' But they didn't realise that they were staying there in front of us for eight hours, many of them; even more emotional, they were crying in front of it, they felt all their life was coming down in front of them. There were many people that were totally emotionally crying. But that's what the idea was, to make a living art that was not only on the surface, that it was speaking, that was the idea.

But the Red Sculpture, *what sort of evolution from the* Singing Sculpture *was that?*

GEORGE It's much more internal and much more complex in terms of content. The *Singing Sculpture* was like a waterfall that you watched and watched and watched!

GILBERT And that one had more like bloody life in dusty corners, no? They were all symbols that we had, repeated phrases like 'bloody life' and 'dusty corners', again and again. It was an hour and a half long, the whole piece, and all these slogans that we try to make them think about life.

GEORGE But you have that same effect strangely; like now we just came back from Lisbon and you just see these rooms full of young people completely eating the pictures off the wall, just talking together in huge groups.

What do you think they see in them? Do you talk to them at an exhibition like that?

GEORGE Sometimes when we have an opening we have a little contact with the vast general public and then we leave, of course, and come back to the studio.

But what do you think they said that they see in them?

GILBERT They see freedom, I really believe that. It's very funny because two to three days ago, a girl knocked on our door and she was from Lisbon but she's studying here and she wanted to come and work for us. Because she saw the show and she was so in love with all this expression, but it is expression that frees them, because they want to run away from their father, the city, they want to liberate them, and in our work they see a certain liberation. Sexual liberation, full of other liberations.

Well, I suppose Paula Rego's work about abortion in Portugal, that is very issue-based and that is very focused. But the sense of liberating her people from political and legislative oppression . . . clearly she gets a tremendous response when she isn't banned.

GEORGE Of course, I mean we realise that because we had an exhibition in Athens which preceded the one in Portugal. Both of those museums were very interesting, they didn't discuss the issue of any picture not being in the show. You had total freedom – that you cannot have in London, Paris and New York – in Athens and in Lisbon. And that is because for those people to say 'maybe we shouldn't have this picture', or 'it's a little excessive' or something, would be like going back to the old days of the regime, yes. So they're bending over backwards to be more modern than anywhere else. It's quite refreshing.

Are you saying that there are works in London, where your Hayward

Show was a big one, works which either the curators excluded or you yourselves excluded because you thought that they would not be acceptable to the London audience?

GEORGE We had enormous trouble in the Serpentine, there was a group show in the Serpentine and we wanted to put one or two of the *Naked Shit* pictures in, and there was an enormous row, they absolutely refused to show one of them. And we've shown that picture in many, many countries.

GILBERT But five months later we showed them all at South London Gallery, but the South London Gallery is a gallery that was totally unfamous, but it became totally famous with that show.

But you are going to show all your works with all the 'objectionable four-letter words' in them at the Serpentine in a few months' time.

GEORGE That's very exciting. In June of this year, 2002, we will be showing for the first time ever the whole *Twenty-Six Dirty Words* pictures. They were never shown together. We created them, we showed some in Holland, some in Germany and some in New York, and in June they will be together for the first time, and that's quite exciting, I must say. They're twenty-five years old, it's Her Majesty's Golden Jubilee, it's the *Dirty Words* Silver Jubilee.

But do you really think that people need to be liberated from our fears about four-letter words?

GEORGE We do! We do!

You think you need to feel liberated or the audience do?

GILBERT Oh yes.

GEORGE We don't think that we're free and we're helping the audience, we feel that together with the viewer we're doing it, we're walking down life's road hand in hand with the viewer. We don't know exactly what we do when we make a picture, it's only when it's finished and it starts to be exhibited that we begin to feel what we were actually trying to say in that picture. We're not that conscious.

GILBERT We're not so conscious. Even when we do this kind of show, we are not doing them totally deliberate because I think we are like schizophrenic; we don't know exactly what's going on, that we are pro and against it the whole time. And even like the *Dirty Words*; if you look back, they create this extraordinary feeling of the anarchy that was going on in England and this aggression that was inside a lot of people. And we didn't write those words on the walls, we don't swear! And so we were able to create this subconscious landscape that is very, very, very powerful and is of that time.

Where do you pick up your references? You imply – after all, you live in the world like the rest of us – that you are absorbing what's going on in the world. Where do you get your raw material from?

GEORGE We don't feel that way, that we're showing life or reflecting life in that way. We like to think that we're forming our tomorrows, that we're making pictures that don't exist in reality, that maybe tomorrow will be a little bit more like our pictures than it would otherwise.

GILBERT And we feel we're getting them all around us. We always say, our subjects you can get a hundred metres away from our house; and even like all these religious feelings that we feel that we have to liberate ourselves. Personally, I've felt I always had to liberate myself from being a Catholic man. Because up and down Brick Lane you see this amazing confrontation between East and West, the Muslims and the Christians, on every lamp-post, stickers day and night, it's extraordinary, this battle of religions, of religious feelings. For us it's very exciting.

GEORGE Sometimes you have the call to prayer at the same time as bell practice at the other end of the street, that's extraordinary.

But that's wonderful . . .

GEORGE Beautiful. We love that, we love that.

That's not antithetical, it is about prayer, isn't it?

GEORGE And we think that's a very world thing, that we can see stickers on the way to breakfast on the lamp-posts which say, 'Jews and Christians, why don't you just give it up! Do not die in ignorance, give it up, don't be silly!' We think that's extraordinary, it's amazing that nobody actually bothers with those stickers.

Until September 11 there were thousands of stickers all the way along Brick Lane. They were all removed overnight after that.

GILBERT And sexual frustration.

GEORGE Which is also on the street, all the time.

GILBERT I think that's an amazing subject.

All the cards for prostitutes in telephone boxes?

GILBERT No, no, no, hidden sexuality.

How does that show itself?

GILBERT Hidden sexuality like what do you call, if somebody feels he is gay or he is that and that, they're all writing it on the wall, because he's terrified that if mother knows it or father knows it, or the vicar is sending him to the dungeon . . . all that stuff.

GEORGE Especially with written text. What makes a person write these things on the wall is extraordinary, all the incestuous ones around us because it's a Muslim community, sex your mum, sex my dad, sex your sister, extraordinary. There's very few people who actually go out and write sexual things on the wall, but it must be an amazing driving force. Or people write on the back of a white van in the dust, 'This van is nearly as dirty as my wife last night! She, da, da, da, da, da.' It's extraordinary the power inside a person to make them do that.

Yes, 'If you think this van is dirty, you should spend a night with the driver!'

GEORGE Very good, that's a good one, that's a good one.

Oh, that's real, that's for free! Let's roll back to the philosophy which underlines this. 'Art for all' is the flag that you have flown under, but you show in galleries, but most people don't go to galleries. Most of the ways in which you can show your art are not available to all. So how do you square the desire to do art for all with the available places where you could express it?

GEORGE Well, first of all we must say that more people go to more exhibitions now than ever before in the whole history of mankind, it's quite extraordinary the world over. Modern art has never been more famous than now. In the 1970s we always used to say that you could walk from our house in Fournier Street to Marble Arch and ask every person you passed to name a living artist and they wouldn't be able to! They would be able to name a living killer, a living politician, a living musician, a living sports person, but not a living artist. And that has changed, everybody in London knows the name of two, three, four living artists, it's quite an improvement.

GILBERT We always try to make an art that is confrontational, that is visually confrontational; it had to be visual, that everybody is able to read it. I think that's what we would call 'art for all', that it's not elitist. You will read a letter, you read it you understand; if like it or not, that is up to them. That's how we always did that, we always try to promote our art, we used to leaflet in Liverpool Street station in 1969, we used to give away cigarettes to make them come. And we were always very concentrated on making cheap publications that people could read and even to make an appearance always, all the news we were doing, all the interviews, you are able to create an atmosphere that they don't have to be in the gallery, they just have to hear the words, and that's how we did it!

GEORGE And we still have to do that when we have exhibitions – in Athens recently or in Lisbon now – we still have to persuade the directors of the museums and the press department to do it in our way, in a more democratic way. We feel we have a more general understanding of how the public can come to see an exhibition who normally wouldn't. In Lisbon, we had the front pages of the two national papers in Portugal, that's extraordinary. The Euro was pushed to one side and the Taliban the other side, and a huge image of ourselves saying, 'Come to see this exhibition.'

GILBERT And there has to be a certain provocation, you have to be questioning what is there as art, then you are able even to stimulate the viewer. You have to question what is in front of you, all the time.

Is one of the things that you're saying that you don't go in for obscure symbols? By and large you use the human being in an absolutely recognisable form, not distorted, not in any way transformed; vegetable life, even the countryside from time to time, the cityscape. So from that point of view every single image that you use, sexual organs, anything like that, is completely readable, familiar, and available to everybody?

GEORGE And then we can be more complex by that use, then it becomes more elaborate. We never liked the idea of the artist using a language which excludes ninety-nine per cent of the world's population, we don't think it's necessary; that it's only white people in London, Paris and New York in certain boroughs who would even understand the work, we think that's so elitist and cruel to the vast general public.

How did you come to the idea of a form in which your photo pieces and your fixed wall pieces exist – you've been working on them for over twenty years now, I think? What made you think that this use of an overtly, very rigid fixed grid was going to be something which would let you develop and then become very free with your forms later?

GEORGE I think the language changed, the visual language changed as we went along. Unlike children or artists or amateur artists, we didn't start off with the canvas and the box of colours; we came from sculpture, so we had to find a way of making the art work. We didn't have a form ready-made from college.

GILBERT Because we tried out at the beginning to do drawings; and everybody loved those drawing so much we thought, 'Oh my God, there must be something wrong with that now, because they only like our aesthetics of the hand!' And we think, 'Why should the hand be important in art, the vision has to be important!' So that's why we changed very, very slowly into a new way of making art through the lens. But at the beginning thirty years ago we didn't know how to create a big image out of negatives, nobody did that before.

Did you in fact enjoy using charcoal, and the drawing?

GILBERT No!

Because those country pieces are beautiful, they are lyrical. But I can quite see that you'd regard them as being well within a very orthodox aesthetic.

GEORGE Yes, even those were based on the negative image because we took a photograph and then copied the photograph with the charcoal.

GILBERT And not only that, we made them old; we made them specially old so that it looked like maybe we found them in a fourteenth-century house. And: 'Oh my God, G and G are already there.' And that's how we did them.

GEORGE We wanted to be established.

GILBERT Again we tried to make them so that we didn't do them, they existed. But then we started to create this new idea with photo pieces, and we pushed them together and we'd scatter them further, all round the wall to create a bigger piece. And then we are trying to push them together and make them into a shape, into a square or rectangle. And then we realised that the grid was very good in making compositions, because you are restricted, and that's very good; you are not totally free, and we believe that's very good that you are not totally free. So we were able to make amazing compositions and we always say our art is campaigning art, we are not trying to make a beautiful picture; we are trying to provoke, campaigning, have ideas and that's it.

But of course there's been a big evolution from your earliest grid pictures, where, on the whole, one square or rectangle has one image in it and it is arranged in a very ordered way. And then you suddenly discovered that you could spread the image across different boxes. It's a big step, isn't it?

GEORGE I think there are two developments. One is the visual language, that we were able to be more complex technically, and as we grew up, as we felt different, thought different, behaved different, we went through many different emotions and feelings ourselves.

How complicated are they to make? Each one of your wall pieces, photo images, they are one single piece?

GEORGE They never start off as one single piece, they're all done subject by subject. So each subject is another negative and that's superimposed into the picture. And it's very, very laborious.

GILBERT All the subjects are taken against black, and every subject has a negative, and we are shooting on top of the same paper many, many different images. So we have to cover some parts, all done in the dark room. It's extraordinarily laborious. And then we colour it by hand, that's why we only make one each.

You must have technical assistants?

GEORGE We have a few assistants at the last stage of making the pictures when we colour them, in order that we can both do colouring. So it speeds up the job a little, so they carry them around and help with the donkey work of it. But when we are making the pictures in the studio then we're totally alone.

What did you have to learn to become good at what is, I suppose, a fairly sophisticated technology?

GEORGE Well, we just trained ourselves as we went along, just experimented.

GILBERT Driven to making more and more powerful images. But now we want to change maybe, because we realise that they were done with enlargers, and now we are trying to arrange them with scanners. The scanners are just now good enough, they didn't used to be as good as an enlarger, but now maybe they are going to be as good as enlargers, so we would be able to scan them and do them on the computer, the cutting in and that.

GEORGE We wouldn't even need to have a photographic process any more, you could actually take the image digitally, or we can take it even photographically and scan that image as well. And we could have a printout machine so you wouldn't have to do all this dipping into the chemicals.

GILBERT And all the colours we can combine...

GEORGE Colours we wouldn't have to do by hand.

GILBERT We could combine black and white and full colour totally, it could be a revolution for us.

But there's no room in the processes you now have for second thoughts, you can't go back and say, I don't like that.

GEORGE No, absolutely not. Once the original drawing is done you are fixed for ever, you cannot control it because the paper is blank until the picture is finished. We can't dip the picture until all the subjects are in.

So if you get something wrong, back to square one.

GEORGE We'd be absolutely wrecked, yes. But we've never got anything wrong so far.

GILBERT It's all based on numbers on the back. We always have 1, 2, 3, 4, 5, 6, 7, 8, 9, 10.

Did I hear you rightly, that you hardly ever have to throw a work away because you've got something wrong?

GEORGE We never did that, never that, never one.

No second thoughts?

GEORGE No, never, not one. We say that how we are that day made us do that picture and we have to respect that. If you have another thought, that's another picture; it would be another one.

GILBERT What we are, that's what we are and that's it, we accept it totally. We never change our mind about that.

What's your working day?

GEORGE When we're actually creating the pictures, it's a very, very heavy day. We get up at six, the cafés near us open at six, have a quick breakfast and we start and we work normally around the clock or a little bit more, but never less.

GILBERT But it depends what we are doing. If we are taking images, we have to be creative, so we have to be loose, we have to dream more. And it cannot be rigid, no, because we have to feel the world. And then even when we do the design, we have to be totally free, we always jump in and out of the studio, back into the street, walk up and down, come back in again, do another drawing, run out again. That's how we do it, we always say we are doing it like being in a black bag. We don't want to know – that's our motto always – don't know, we're just feeling it. But then once the designs are done, the initial design, then we never change, and after that it's only making it, and making it we are doing it many, many hours, we do eight hours, nine hours a day.

GEORGE But that's just work, really.

Do you only work on one photo, be it your wall piece, at a time or do you have a number on the go at the same time?

GEORGE We will work on the whole exhibition, and when one picture is finished they will all be finished. So we do the first thing to each of those pictures, the second thing to all of those pictures, third thing, and then in one magic day they are all finished at the same time.

How large is your darkroom, your studio?

GEORGE Oh, we have an enormous studio, we have three studios, in fact. We have a studio behind our house, a studio behind the house next door and a studio behind the house next door to the one next door.

So it's not that you think of one wall piece at a time, you are thinking of an entire show?

GEORGE Absolutely, yes. And we never work on the whole picture, we only work on a panel at a time, yes, each panel is separate.

Can you see yourselves changing from the form of expression of the grid-like boxes?

GILBERT Through these new idea with scanners and computers I think we could go much further. But we like our expression, we like the imagery, we like what you call visual language. We want to keep to that, very much so.

GEORGE We like the rectangular classical picture on the wall, we think that's a very, very democratic, normal, fantastic thing, and within that we can be very complex and very anarchic or aggressive. But we like the respectable form. We don't like for ourselves to have an eccentric form that will alienate a lot of people.

And what happens when you are not working and you are not collecting images. What do you do, what sort of state are you in? Presumably you're constantly receptive to the world around you and what's going on?

GILBERT Oh, we are designing shows, like at the moment. We are designing shows, we're giving interviews, we are designing books, and that's an amazing activity.

And of course you've got a huge archive, haven't you?

GEORGE We were going into the archive this morning with the people from the Serpentine because they're trying to research how the *Dirty Words* pictures were seen at the time they were created and how they're seen now. Because we remember that when we did those pictures, many friends in the art world around us thought that we'd gone completely crazy, that this was a little excessive just to take these very rough words from the streets. And they really didn't like those pictures. But those same people today say that they 'love the *Dirty Words* pictures'. And when you say, 'Hey, hang on, I remember you saying . . .', 'Oh no, no, no, I always loved them.' I'm sure they genuinely believe it.

And do the people who say that they love them, are they the ones who you think might buy them? Or is it a question of 'I love Gilbert and George's Dirty Pictures, *they are so dirty', but in fact they wouldn't dare have them on their own walls?*

GEORGE Well, I think we did sell them quite well when we made them, they were very inexpensive at that time as well, of course.

GILBERT I mean it's more like what they call the *Naked Shit* pictures, that's because they are more expensive, everybody likes them but no collectors actually want them on the walls. It's quite difficult to live with one of those pictures. But we don't do them for that; we always want enough money to do what we want, and nothing else.

In fact, are you rich? You must be!

GILBERT No.

GEORGE Not by normal artistic standards I'm sure, no.

Are there some of your canvases, images, which have never sold?

GILBERT Oh yes, many, many.

Yes, and . . .

GEORGE There are difficult pictures . . .

GILBERT A lot of difficult pictures.

GEORGE If you think it took the Serpentine twenty-five years to show the *Dirty Words* pictures, that's quite extraordinary, a quarter of a century before they could be accepted.

You represent your own selves, your own bodies a great deal in your work, but you've also talked about humiliating yourselves. What do you mean by that and why is it necessary?

GILBERT I think we started that a long time ago in 1969 when we did *Gilbert the Shit and George the Cunt*. It was the first time that we confronted our public and humiliated ourselves. And we realised that there is enormous freedom in that, we are able to free ourselves and nobody is able to attack you after that.

And did you find that humiliating yourselves in that way gave you a subsequent strength?

GILBERT Yes.

GEORGE A strength and I think it gives us an amazing contact with the general public, because the general public knows that many artists are very superior towards the viewer. Even when we were more socially involved with the other artists, they always had a very low opinion of the general public. They thought they did very superior modern art, they had one or two collectors at some galleries, but of course those people out there would take years to be able to understand it. And that's not true, everyone is very complicated and able to understand things. But I think we did an art that the viewer felt they could trust us, that we weren't looking down at the viewer, that it was an experience together.

GILBERT Not only that, then we started to do these drinking pieces. We always used to go out drinking with a lot of other artists, and every other artist used to go back in the studio and do some nice clean canvas, and it was, well, what the hell is that? We thought, might we do the drinking pieces now? We are drunk, we do the drinking piece. And so that became, what you call, an amazing freedom for us.

Was it in a way defensive, though, in the sense that nobody could say anything worse about you that you had not been prepared to say about yourselves?

GEORGE Oh yes, we pre-empted absolutely!

GILBERT We always do that, always did that.

GEORGE But we always said that we don't trust the idea of a happy artist. Nobody would really trust the idea that I was an artist and like life and like art and like everything artistic, and have artistic friends and so on.

But you don't hate life, everything you have said makes that clear?

GEORGE We celebrate life but we like to be able to realise that there's nothing in the world that is not also inside of you or us or anybody. Anything, any horror in the world, we're also capable of.

GILBERT But I do believe that we went through unbelievable difficult pain, and I believe that that's why we are not able to remember anything. We are able to remember very little because it feels like an enormous mad cloud full of dark and crazy stuff. We don't know anything what we did. It feels we are not aware of this mad schizophrenia that went on for forty years now. It's extraordinary. I really believe we were never conscious, we never wanted to be conscious, never looked back. Always, next day maybe it's going to be a better day. That was always our motto, it's always 'next day'!

Now these days, the artist as personality is probably more of a personality, it's easier to be a personality. Do you think that you fall into the trap of personality by having made yourselves the subject of your art?

GEORGE We think that most people think of our pictures in terms of their own life and their own experience. And they think that we're in the picture as the people speaking to them, like every letter they receive will be signed by the person who wrote that letter. I think that's how people see it.

GILBERT I don't think we are personalities.

Oh, come on!

GILBERT No, I don't think so. I think we are, what you call, like some crazy living sculptures, no. They know Gilbert and George as a name, but we became some untouchable in some way.

Isn't that dangerous, to be untouchable, if by untouchable you mean you have such a position that people daren't criticise you?

GILBERT I mean untouchable that we are able to take a bus, every night to a Turkish restaurant and everybody knows us, but we are still able to do whatever we want. There is that barrier that we have been able to create.

GEORGE Nobody would bother you as an artist. And art is still very unfamous compared with other forms, really, compared with people on television or sports people or politicians.

GILBERT Artists are nothing.

Do you have a thing against the critics? You just said that you're criticised more and more. I think somebody once said, 'Traditionally with modern art it's the artist and critics against the public; with you, it's you and the public against the critics!'

GEORGE That's a very good quote, yes. No, we do believe in that.

But do you feel hard done by?

GEORGE We have enormous support from the critics as well, yes, it's very strange.

GILBERT I think they did a very good job in some way. We wouldn't like say that to them, because we created this love-and-hate relationship, and that has been going on for thirty years non-stop. And then that is very good for an artist that you are always under pressure.

So you learn from the criticism, do you?

GILBERT No, we don't learn, we hate them but we wouldn't tell them that.

GEORGE Not at all. And it's also very interesting that young people and young collectors love the art that the critic is against. They feel really in the centre of the advance of life.

GILBERT What did you used to say about Brian Sewell?

Brian Sewell of the Standard*?*

GEORGE Oh yes, we always say that we never met anyone who's said to us, 'I used to love modern art but since reading Sewell, I'm not so sure.' So we know from that that he never converted anyone.

Yes, but of course David Sylvester, regarded rightly as the greatest of the art critics, said – this was of the Naked Shit *pictures – 'Most artists this century have tried to do naked, and have only succeeded in doing nude. Gilbert and George have done naked.'*

GEORGE Yes, that was very perceptive of David, because very few people realised that at first.

GILBERT But he's very good, David Sylvester, because he always used to say to us, 'Art critics are only parasites.' That's what he'd call him.

GEORGE It was very good because we said that 'You're the greatest living writer in the English language,' and he said, 'No, no, I'm just a parasite, just a parasite.' So I said, 'Well, maybe you're the greatest living parasite.'

In recent years you have often talked about the loss of your friends, through death – a lot of them younger than yourselves. How has this concern with death shown in your work?

GILBERT We did many pieces before that, in fact, to do with death – *Death, Hope, Life, Fear*, 1980; *Death, Faith and Bloody Life* and *Dead Heads, Dead Bored*. We did that in 1975 to 1985, but after that, when they started to die, we stopped. We never mentioned that word again, in fact.

Shouldn't you?

GEORGE I think it is very, very clear in our pictures without having to be spelled out as it used to be. We think even the *New Horny Pictures* we did are like huge Lutyens cemeteries on the Somme or something, all of those boys advertising in the magazines. Some are almost certainly dead already, as the magazines were taken from four or five years ago. One day all of them will be dead and then it will be like a huge memorial to those people. They will never be immortalised by anybody else except in those sixteen pictures.

GILBERT And it's very good, it is like tombstones. They describe themselves, their age, and a little story of what they did, it's extraordinary.

GEORGE That was the moment when we were able to make those pictures, the *New Horny Pictures*, it was the moment we were looking at a previous catalogue of ours and found ourselves staring at a picture called *Dead Head* with an amazing multi-coloured cemetery. And we thought, 'Why are we looking, why are we looking?' We looked and we looked and we looked, for hours. Then suddenly we realised that those advertisements which we were collecting, the sexual advertisements, and hadn't been able to use in our pictures, were the same as tombstones. The age of the person, how many years they spent on earth, their name and a sentence about their life. And in that moment we realised there was a moral dimension to the sexual advertisement and we were able to use them in pictures.

Will the art of Gilbert and George die when the first one of you dies?

GEORGE No, I think if we fell under a bus today the pictures will live on, I'm sure of that.

But will the artist Gilbert and George die when the first one of you dies?

GEORGE We always cross the road together. So maybe we have to be careful!

HEINER GOEBBELS

I love to disappoint expectations, in a creative way

Fortunately you can't fit Heiner Goebbels into a neat artistic category. He's not a man to be glibly pigeon-holed. He's certainly a composer; undoubtedly a man of the theatre. He's unquestionably a leader in the creation of that elusive concept, music theatre – or, as one writer put it, a work by Goebbels is 'a beast slithering between the three conventions of opera, theatre and concert'. Over a period of almost thirty years his work has ranged from sound plays for radio, to so-called 'radical' chamber music, to the big set pieces in the concert hall, theatre and opera house for which he has become famous. Some, like *Black on White*, or *Hashirigaki*, take place in the theatre, though musicians make up the performers. Others, like *Surrogate Cities*, are concert pieces, though they do have a visual element. His latest work, *Landscape with Distant Relatives*, is labelled as Goebbels' 'version' of an opera. Typically even such a cautious categorisation left some of the audience confused.

I think I need to give a very compressed idea of what a piece by him is like. Take *Hashirigaki*, the most recent work seen in Britain, at Edinburgh and the Barbican. The title is the Japanese word for 'running, writing fluently, outlining'. The performers are three women – a Canadian musician, a Swedish dancer (very tall) and an actress – and a Japanese musician, and they all play, sing, move, dance and speak. Ah, yes, the words. Gertrude Stein's *The Making of Americans*; the lyrics from Beach Boys' songs. But the music ranges from the Beach Boys to traditional Japanese music, and it's all performed in fantastic costumes and an ever-changing set of objects, lighting, real images, and playful objects. To the very square question 'What does it all mean?' Goebbels tends to answer 'That's up to you' – which some regard as an evasion. The fact is that most critics and most audiences go with the flow, and take from Goebbels' pieces a deep, instinctual sense of purpose and connection. As I said, he defies categorisation, and he intends to keep it that way.

So what are you deep down? A composer, a director? Will the real Heiner Goebbels stand up?

I think I like to switch. I am easily bored, and I change my working field every seven years. And that's why I have now several professions. A very distinctive quality which I highly estimate for my work is to be able to have a distant look. And to be able to have a real distant look, I think you need to look from another profession at what you're doing. So when I'm working as a composer, I sometimes look at it as a director. When I work as a director, I look at it as a composer, which means when I stage a piece I have very much in mind the whole rhythm of the show, the whole link between the scenes, which I think is of special importance. When I work as a composer, I listen to it also as a director in terms of does this interest somebody who is not involved in the material? Because I think in the arts, and maybe not only in arts but in other professions as well, you get very easily too much stuck in your own material, and then you lose the overview. You lose the real relationship between who's attending such a performance and what is he bringing with him by way of attention, and all that.

But you can't be equally balanced between the two, can you? That just doesn't sound likely!

Well, maybe I'm schizophrenic! No, I think I can. In this opera which you just quoted – *Landscape with Distant Relatives* – I really cut a lot of pieces in the last months after the first series of performances, to make it a bit shorter. And especially sections where others said, 'Oh, this is the best musical thing,' or where others said, 'But that's the most beautiful scene.' And I had really equal reasons from both professions to do that. Because I said, 'Yes, it's a beautiful scene but it's too slow, and this makes the whole thing very lazy, and that's why I have to cut this beautiful scene.' So I think I really can switch, yes.

You started life as a composer, working with sound on radio. But doesn't that sound as if composing, because it came first, matters most?

No, I never considered myself so much as a composer in the first time, because before I did radio works, I worked as a composer for theatre, which means I made the music for a lot of very good German theatre directors. And I made music to Shakespeare's *Richard III* and to *Iphigenie* by Goethe, and to Kleist pieces. And to four-hour-long pieces, sometimes I made ten minutes of music, or fifteen minutes. But I was sitting there for two months attending the rehearsals, which means I was bored as a composer very easily. And also I was very disappointed how the music was given away as a chance for developing an image. It was at most used between the scenes or for some atmospheric illustrative things. But at the same time I had a lot of time to learn the skills of a director, because I was sitting next to him and I was not so busy – I couldn't be so busy in the music. So I think this was a very important step for me – already in the early days, 1978 and 1979 – for what I'm doing now.

So the integration of the theatrical experience and the compositional one was there from the very beginning?

From the very beginning, and if I look even earlier I think that for me as a fifteen-, sixteen-, or seventeen-year-old boy, I was very much into classical music, I was very much into pop music, I always played the Beatles and the Beach Boys every day at the piano. But I was not into contemporary music but into contemporary arts. I went to all the exhibitions, I went to the Documenta exhibitions, which I could get in these days, and probably this is also a knowledge which helps me now working with visual elements.

A very broad-based educational experience, because you never learned theatre as such in an academic way?

No. No.

So it was entirely learned by sitting in and watching other directors do things and make mistakes?

Which is probably the best way to do it!

But thinking of your composition – I can't think who your music links up with. You've never been associated with serialism, or any of the more academic forms of music writing. You've never dabbled with Darmstadt. I don't know what your musical origins are.

It's even worse – I've never been in Darmstadt, even if it's twenty kilometres from here; I mean never at these studies. Of course, I was in Darmstadt to go to a concert or whatever, but I never was at these Ferienkurse, you're right. There's one composer who I feel closely linked to, and this is Hans Eisler, because probably he might be responsible that I became a professional musician. Because I studied sociology, I was very into politics, and

I was connected also to some political movements here in the early seventies with Joschka Fischer – now Germany's Foreign Minister – and Daniel Cohn-Bendit and this 'sponti' scene as we say. And I made some music in the evening for fun, but I never thought that this could be connected in a way which balances both elements out.

That is politics and art?

Yes. And then I read a book from Hans Eisler where he discusses a lot of things, like mathematics, politics, history, arts of course, philosophy, and I loved his music as well, his songs definitely. And after reading this book I had the feeling this is really possible for one person to be connected like every measure. And this is a unique quality of Eisler I would say. It's not that there's a composer who has a political message on top; it's something which is really somehow connected in his body. And you hear it, you hear it in his temperament, you hear it in his melancholy, when he doesn't exclude such feelings in his exile songs – after words from Brecht. And you hear it in the always forward-moving rhythm which steadily pulls his music. So I had already a very good relationship to his musical qualities. But I had also the feeling that reading these famous talks with Bunge in this book, that this was a very true basis for the combination between music and politics. And I think this might have been the moment, 1974 or 1975, where I decided, OK maybe I can go into music studies and think about the profession as a musician, as a composer.

But you couldn't be less like Eisler, could you? After all, a man who was thrown out of Nazi Germany for Marxism, who was then thrown out of the United States for being a Communist. Now, unless I misjudge you completely, you're not that sort of ideologue. You're not driven by those sort of political beliefs, are you?

No, but I think I'm driven by a great scepticism, especially towards arts and politics, and this is something which I might have in common with Eisler. I mean he was very, very critical, overcritical about moments where this combination was not convincing.

So I suppose it's perfectly possible that you should have as an ideal somebody who embodies art and politics in a particular way, and you just make the combination in a very different way because you are not ideological.

And I think there's another reason why Eisler could be such an important influence. He always insisted on a true relationship. And I never intended to tell something with my music on a subject with which I'm not involved, where I have no experiences. I never said I could do a representative political statement for somebody starving or . . .

A political prisoner, say?

Yes, I never did that. I think this might be important on a political level definitely, but on an artistic level, I don't think it really works. And this is something probably I also learned from Eisler. And I learned another thing, which is that he always said that progress in arts, progress in music, needs to be made with maybe a step back. You can't progress all elements at once. So, for example, when he writes a march, he would change the harmony a little bit, he would make a rhythm break in the middle – which is very unlikely for a march – but of course he would also keep some marching quality in order to make it work.

When you were starting your performance career, you worked in this rather wonderfully named 'So-called Left-wing Radical Wind Orchestra', which doesn't sound as if it was an altogether serious name, was it?

It was a name we were given. Somebody announced us as '*Linksradikales Blasorchester*', and we said OK. We didn't choose this name, so we call it 'So-called Left Radical Brass Band'.

But was it entirely serious? Or did that indicate a certain distancing from really high-ground radicalism?

Yes, and from any fundamentalist position, either musical or political, yes.

At that time, too, you felt that concert-going and the concert experience needed a change?

It was not made for concerts, actually, this band. This was really made for demonstrations, for speeches, for any political moments in Frankfurt, which happened really every two weeks.

But apart from that, in general did you have a view that the music world needed to be shaken up, and it needed to have new elements engendered in it?

This was not my first idea. The first idea was really to bring music into a field which excluded music for a long time, or which excluded culture for a long time. The '68 Movement didn't really accept and respect the necessity for culture. I mean, the only thing you could hear were songs by Joan Baez, or by the Rolling Stones, but that's about it. It took some four or five years, until the beginning of the seventies, until it was possible to play the cello somewhere.

So what you were doing was unfashionable, by saying classical music has a role to play in the political movements – politics doesn't just have to be associated with rock and pop?

And it was also the idea to take this cultural question seriously, to develop the music and opportunity to perform as well as all the other qualities we tried to develop. We tried to develop the way we were living together, how we were making demonstrations. We tried not to exclude anything. I think that was the main element of this movement.

And is that something that you carried forward into your work in the theatre, with your music theatre pieces – the idea of very broad collaboration with a large number of people in different forms?

Exactly. And what I also learned in this 'So-called Left Radical Brass Band' is that there was a collective working method possible in music which I didn't know before. So, for example, there would be a demonstration next week, so I wrote a piece. And then I came back to the orchestra and they said, 'No, it's too difficult, we can't learn it in one week, you have to get rid of that, and our flute player is sick so let's change it!' And we changed it and it worked. And to have this deep experience, that a collective can be even artistically more effective, and on this specific political and social point more important, this was a very good experience.

Now, I'm going to go forward to the time when you started writing really big orchestral pieces, to 1994, when you did the work called Surrogate Cities *for Frankfurt, which we only saw in Britain in 2002. It's a large romantic work, large orchestra, and the typical ingredients of your music – blues singers, a Jewish cantor, vocal improvisation, Baroque, and so on. One critic wrote of it that 'it reinstates the collective power of the symphony orchestra'. Now, if you accept that description, did you find it rather odd that, with your background, you were coming back to something as mainstream as a symphony orchestra in a concert hall?*

No, I think there are two reasons why this description might be right. One is that a lot of contemporary orchestral musicians who dissolve the orchestra into a high number of soloists, they give away this collective power; they give away this ability to affect an audience more directly. And on the other hand, my biography has another important chapter in the sixties. I was living in a small German city with thirty thousand inhabitants. We had, by some accident, a cultural administrator who had very good connections to an agency. So whenever one of the big soloists of the sixties, or the big orchestras, was touring he was able to date, let's say, Munich, Berlin, Frankfurt and my own little town, Landau. So I heard the big soloists like Sviatoslav Richter on his first tour in the West; I heard Karajan with the Berlin Philharmonic; I heard Sergiu Celibidache; I heard Kyril Kondrashin with the Moscow orchestra; Rostropovich on his first Western tour. And I think this influenced me a lot, because I was very much touched by these high soloists and these high-quality orchestras.

And the sheer physical sound of the full orchestra?

Exactly. And I think what an orchestra should be like is to enlarge collective possibilities, and not necessarily to split into a number of individual voices.

I think you've also said, coming back to the question of your relationship with artistes, that you learned an enormous amount from working on Surrogate Cities *with the orchestra, which was the Junge Deutsche Philharmonie – young players – and that they pushed you to do things, or enabled you to take risks, which you would not have been able to do with another set of players. How did that relationship work?*

It was a wonderful experience because it was the first experience for me with a big orchestra. And it was also, as the title suggests – *Surrogate Cities* – a portrait not only of an orchestra but also of a city and the way a city functions. And it was really a great experience that, within the two weeks of our studies with this work, the various orchestra sections were working in different rooms. In one room there were the wind players, in another room the brass players, and in another room the drum section. And I went from room to room, and especially I had my biggest fun when I was in the corridors, and hearing these different sections working, like in a big factory, or like in a city where you have these different professions working in different locations and buildings; and how then everything came together was really very enjoyable. And also it was a very flexible and open communication with the musicians, who could help me a lot.

Did they make suggestions?

They made suggestions, the conductor made suggestions. I am still very open to all that. And they say, 'OK, but if you make it pizzicato instead of arco, I'm sure it will become more forward moving' and things like this. So we changed a lot.

There has to be something that is written down, doesn't there?

Ninety per cent was written, or maybe even more. But I'm sceptical that written material can already really transport your intention. I think I have always to examine that with the considered result. And very often the paper doesn't give you the precise indications.

We're talking about form here. Was writing about the city itself important? This was a commission for the city of Frankfurt, therefore it had to be about cities. But did you feel there was something important to be said about the urban experience of our time?

As I look back for the last thirty years, I have only spent my time in cities. I think that really cities are a way of living together which enables us to deal with confrontations much better than we can in the countryside. Living together in cities, even with such highly controversial ethnical and cultural differences, enables us on a small territory somehow to learn to accept, to respect the other. I think of my children, how they grow up in the school here, with a lot of nationalities. Their experiences and their knowledge are so rich and so bright, that I'm sure this will help them to go into a future. And I think this is something that cities are really good for.

But was Surrogate Cities *about that?*

Part is about that. Part is also about the different layers which you can observe in cities. When you make excavations, then you can really read the ground, and you can see about the history. So maybe my way of working was a little bit like the archaeologist. I try to discover history, for example, where you mentioned the Jewish cantors, a history which is no longer in such a way being performed. I tried to work this out with a living cantor, and we listened a lot to these documentary recordings of the twenties, and he said after he noticed what I was interested in, he said, 'Why don't you use the original recordings, because you will never find in the world a cantor who is able to do it like this any more.' Because in these days, in these twenties and thirties, you didn't have this split between the professions. There was a cantor who was able to sing in the synagogue at the Sabbath, and the next evening he was singing in the Metropolitan Opera. There was no split between the professions. And we have lost this. And so you find this kind of singing in one piece, you find some old Baroque work, you find some sounds which are technical or mechanical, and which really drive us crazy in the city. You find them integrated in an orchestra.

I want to talk about another piece of yours called Black on White, *which is a theatre piece for an orchestra, the Ensemble Moderne. And you get the orchestra to do all sorts of things – not just play the instruments which they're paid to play, so to say, but instruments that they have never played before. They play badminton, they throw tennis balls at thunder sheets, they play a flute to a singing kettle, all sorts of wild and wonderful things. But one of the things that strikes me is that you get artistes to break out of their own particular skill. You see them in a much more whole way, don't you?*

I think it has to do with the fact that I love to disappoint expectations, in a creative way. So when people come to such a performance and it starts as a concert; I mean they are sitting with their back to the audience, OK, but they are still sitting as an orchestra, and they are conducted. And then it explodes, at a certain moment, and they start to play with balls, as you say, and they start to hurt the expectations. Because what I hate is to be able to predict what's coming next in a performance, and that's why probably I switch also between a concert and a theatre piece or a music theatre piece or a performance or an installation. And because I also think that theatre, and especially music theatre, is so much a complex fusion of a lot of elements – light, sound, words, movements. What you usually get when you see a music theatre performance is that all these elements are somehow ordered in a hierarchical way, so they're always there to make an explanation specially deep and clear. And I think I try to do the opposite. I love it if pictures are rather opening up, pictures are widening the horizon of the viewer. And also I like to develop the individual elements of theatre. I like to work with light, not only in a way that it makes the performer seeable. I like to work with light in a way that respects the light bulb as a sculpture, or that is able to develop the force of a light itself as an artistic force. Which means that I have to work with light from the very beginning, from the very first rehearsal I have the light, because otherwise whenever an element comes late into the creative process, it will be less important, it will be only illustrative.

It'll be secondary.

That's why I try to develop all the elements at once, which is difficult. And I have to keep them a bit open for a while until they are settled, until they link to each other. But this is exactly the reason why also the performers are not only playing instruments but they are also singing and dancing and speaking and developing their whole range of possibilities.

Is it chaos at the beginning? Because that means you have your lighting designer, your sound designer your costume designer and all the performers there.

You can call it chaos if you would be an authoritarian director. Then you would say, 'Shut up, it's too noisy'; and, 'You can't cross the stage while I'm directing this Shakespeare here.' What I do is really, you're right, it's absolutely the opposite, but it's never chaos. It's very creative; and you need an open eye, you need not to be disturbed, you need to have a high attention on everything that is happening. For example, the costume designer goes on stage while we do a very delicate scene and she's changing the hats of the performers; and the light designer is turning the light into a back light rather than a front light. And then, if you're really open to this and if you're really curious about all these elements, then you discover so many possibilities. And if you don't consider it as chaotic, it will be a very rich experience for everybody.

And at what stage does this have an effect on the sound? Do you find yourself saying that lighting is so extraordinary that what I hear, and what I need the audience to hear, must be different from what they hear at the moment?

Yes, that's very often like this. I develop, in a creative state of improvisations, pictures, sounds, scenes. And then I go away for myself for let's say three, four, five months, and I compose a piece. And I bring the words into an order, and I bring the costumes into an order, and I bring the development of stage into an order. And I try to reflect all these experiences; for example, to say this light was so strong we don't need any music in this moment, so I would rather put it there. I'm really reacting very strongly to these experiences.

When you get all your artistes and your creative collaborators in the studio together for the first time, what do you know about the piece that you want to do? You're not there with a tabula rasa, are you? You know you're going to do something called Black on White, *don't you?*

Very often, for example, I know some temperature, I know what I don't like. I might not know the text I use. I might not have the music already. But I might be looking for a certain poetic quality. And in the case of *Black on White*, for example, our first rehearsals had nothing to do with the Edgar Allan Poe text, which came up later. We worked with texts about gardens and trees – I don't know why, I can't even explain – and we had no written score with the first rehearsals, because I knew that the Ensemble can play anything I give them. But if I give them any scores now they would be too busy reading, and I could not see if they can do anything else – if they can play badminton at the same time! So I had to get rid of any score and just rehearse without it. And I have a certain feeling, I think, sometimes. In *Hashirigaki*, I knew some pictures which I read; in Kafka, I knew some colours, I knew some orange I wanted to see. I was not sure it would work with Gertrude Stein. I was not sure it would work with the Beach Boys.

And then when you have, as it were, composed it, and you're ninety per cent there, do you go back to the performers and put it together with the final ten per cent of input from them?

And that's very fast, actually. For *Hashirigaki* probably we took up to a few weeks. For my new opera, *Landscape*, we took a little bit more than two weeks. Then everything is clear and we do that very quickly.

I was struck by the front page of the programme for Hashirigaki, *which read very simply: 'Théâtre Vidy-Lausanne;* Hashirigaki *by Heiner Goebbels'. I accept everything you say about your democratic approach, but that is still Heiner Goebbels as* 'auteur', *isn't it? In the end, you are the person who is saying 'this is my work'.*

Yes, I think I can say that because I bring most of the structures in the piece. And I judge the overall temperature, and I inspire everybody to work in this direction, even if I'm not able to be very explicit about it.

When you're just composing and you don't have things like the lighting or the staging to . . . to stimulate you, how do you actually create, when you just have to put music on the page?

That's a good question because I think this might be a reason why you'll always find samples in my work of documentary sounds, of sounds which are usually not in an orchestra, sounds from the outer world. For me, I try to develop a balance between the real live performed instruments and between sounds which are usually not to be found in such an orchestra. And I think this is for me represented in a social experience with the power relationships; so to say, when you have a synthesiser or when you have the rhythm of a sampler, which you have to accept as a conductor or as a musician. Then you have a resistance, you have a partner with whom you have to deal. You can't create your own world just as a string quartet, as an orchestra by yourself. There must be something which is stronger than you. I think this is a relationship which I really deeply need, which I deeply try to balance out, but which I would always love to be present even in a concert hall.

Do you allow other people to stage your works?

Yes. Actually, I would love it if this happens more. It has just happened recently that an opera house in Freiburg, in Germany, they staged *Surrogate Cities* with a dance company, with actors, with singers, with the opera orchestra. It was a very successful production.

The idea that you don't write things down much, and therefore only you can stage them. That's not true?

No, that's not true. The score for *Black on White*, for example, is completely open to adaptations, even with other ensembles, with other instruments, including instruments which were not in the original cast and things like this.

Now there are many different elements in your pieces, different kinds of music, different traditions. You've said some very interesting things about working with disparate cultures; you don't want them to be homogenised, you're not seeking some false synthesis. You always want them to keep their own distinct character.

Maybe it has to do with what I said about the elements in theatre anyway; so when I'm talking about light, I could have been talking about an Indian singer, or an African Griot singer with a cora. I think I want to keep the elements transparent; I want to keep the different quotes or cultures or languages which come into a performance, I want to keep them transparent. I don't want to paternalise or fraternise or cover them over; and I rather keep them pretty much clear. And I might rather put something in opposition to them, but not in the way of making a melting pot.

A few oriental bells and whistles on rock music, that sort of thing?

No. That's not it!

So the Japanese music in Hashirigaki *is absolutely itself, and it is played by a classical Japanese musician. And it just happens to sit side by side with the Beach Boys and with other kinds of music?*

Yes. The open question is why this works. Because you could

easily say yes, it has nothing to do with it, so it doesn't work. I think there must be a possible link at the moment where these two cultures or where these two musics touch each other; there must happen something – not necessarily in the music maybe, in the light or in the costume or in the staging – but there must happen something which makes it at least on the same level usable. So, for example, when you mentioned the Japanese elements in *Hashirigaki*, after a while I discovered that the use of percussion in the Beach Boys' recording is very similar to the use of percussion in Japanese traditional music. That's something that you can really find in both kinds of music, and that's why maybe it works.

But you only discovered that. That wasn't your starting-off point?

No, not at all.

How do you avoid being a mere collagist? Because that seems to be one of the dangers of just putting together this and that. And all the critics say – it's not just me – that that's not how your work comes over. Do you sense this as a danger, that you're just sticking things together?

Yeah, I think it's a danger, it's a great danger. The more possibilities you have, the bigger the danger is. And I think the more preparation and careful investigation – research – you need beforehand. I'm very superstitious in a way; each material, even in a degree which we won't be able to perceive very consciously, has its secret or its truth. And so I'm very careful with the choice of material; with the library of sounds, for example in *Hashirigaki*, then I really try to use only Beach Boys' sounds. And even the cymbal which is sampled and separately performed should be a cymbal which they used in this recording session, because I think if it would be another one it might sound different, it might evoke something else, and we lose the overall cohesion.

You were once quoted as saying that you don't regard yourself as a revolutionary director. Why do you think you said that, and does it really reflect what you do?

I don't remember that I said that but I think there's a lot of very conservative elements in my perspectives on theatre, on the qualities of theatre, also on my perspective of the orchestra, I love the collective sound of it, and maybe that's not very revolutionary at all, maybe that's very conservative. And in theatre I don't believe in representation, I don't believe we can really pretend to be somebody else on stage. But I believe in a lot of emotional stage effects, which I also use in my pieces. But what I really try is to avoid the hierarchy of the elements, how they are used in conventional theatre.

If I said that I thought that you were quite a romantic director, and that some of your pieces, certainly Hashirigaki, *had sentimental moments, would you mind that?*

No, not at all. Especially *Hashirigaki*, it's definitely a melancholy piece, and it makes great use of the melancholy in the Beach Boys' songs and the melancholy in the Gertrude Stein writing, and that's why they both go together so well. And this is also an element which I appreciate very much in Hans Eisler.

Have you ever had a creative block, where you simply didn't know where you were going to go next?

I have always creative blocks, when I have a new task, because I don't want to repeat myself. So I easily accept too fast the commission which is a bit hard of my possibilities, or experience. Like *Surrogate Cities*; the commission was of course way too difficult for me, and I accepted it because I'm curious and I wanted to go on a new field. And of course, then I had a constant creative block for one and a half years before I was able to write something. But I think these blocks can be quite productive. What we should avoid as artists is always doing what comes in our mind first, and for this, these blocks are very important. You have no idea how much time I spend throwing ideas away which come to me first.

There's a sort of censor in your mind saying that's too easy?

Yes, that's . . . yes, exactly.

And for whom in the end do you create? Are you creating for yourself – I know you've got a commission – but are you creating for yourself, for your audience, for society?

I would never say I create for myself and I think I would never create anything if it would be just for myself. I have nothing in my desk which is unperformed. I have no symphonies laying down which have not been performed. I always need the commission, I always need the reason from a theatre, from an orchestra, from some musicians, from some actors.

If there wasn't a commission, would you work at all?

No, I would be maybe a taxi driver! I don't know, I wouldn't work. I really need that. I rarely did anything in my life just from an internal need.

You wouldn't sit down and say, 'I have to write music because I must write music'?

Oh! No, I hate that, I can't do that. I always react. I always react. I'm much better in reacting to something than inventing something. Sometimes it's opposition to what I've done just before. For example, after *Surrogate Cities*, this huge orchestra score for one and a half hours and one hundred musicians, I definitely wanted to do a piece without my own music. So I did a piece with music by Prince, Bach, and Schubert and Beethoven, which was called *The Repetition*. After doing *Black on White*, where eighteen musicians are the performers on stage, I definitely wanted to do a piece only for one actor, who does all the music. So Max Black turned out to come in this position. So it's very often a reaction to what I've done before, or a reaction to the purpose of a commission which inspires me much more than a blank page.

It's a kind of perversity, isn't it?

Yes.

Creative perversity?

Yes, yes.

But there's no sign of that going away?

No, unfortunately not.

ANISH KAPOOR

One doesn't make art for other people

When talking about the work of the sculptor Anish Kapoor, you should beware of the adjectives. They can get very overheated: 'implacable, yet whimsical'; 'hysterically sublime!'; 'tactical and dreamlike'; those are just a few phrases to be going on with. Maybe it's a response to the intense colours he uses – cobalt blues, crimson reds, impenetrable blacks, all applied so that they seem to soak up the light, and soak up the action of the viewer's eye too.

Now it may seem odd to be talking about colour in relation to a sculptor, but you can't talk about Kapoor's work without referring to it. The colours are at the service of the shapes – excavated holes in blocks of stone and rock; highly polished discs or bowls, like domes of heaven, said one critic. Kapoor's objects take on and disrupt the orderly space of galleries. 'Exuberant, irrational, vital forces thrusting through floors or walls' – there go the adjectives again! Critics may have occasional reservations about his work, but they can't shrug it off with a throwaway phrase. It's definitely not that sort of work. Anish Kapoor is rising fifty, and can look back at most of the art world's badges of honour: Venice Biennale, Turner Prize, Documenta, retrospectives in all the right places. More recently he has stormed the bastions of the most prestigious arts institutions, creating the vast installation *Marsyas* – there he filled the Turbine Hall at Tate Modern – and he designed the settings for Glyndebourne's 2003 production of Mozart's *Idomeneo*. His work reveals a simple profundity, says one writer. It's a primal experience, says another. Kapoor himself insists, 'I've nothing to say,' which is where, here in his Camberwell studio, we begin.

Why do you say that you have nothing to say?

One of the currents in the contemporary experience of art is that it points to the experience of the author. That is to say it dwells in the author. It seems to me that there's another route in which the artist looks for content, which is different from meaning. It may be abstract, but at a deeper level symbolic content is necessarily philosophical and often religious. I think I am attempting to dig away at – without wanting to sound too pompous – the great mystery of being. And that, while it has a route through my psychobiography, it isn't based in it.

So at least you are walking away from the romantic idea of the artist – that it is the life of the artist, the view of the artist, the experience of the artist which is absolutely central to the art – and you take the artist with the art bag and baggage.

I am. I think I'm saying that there is another position. Maybe it is my Indian roots that prompt me in that direction. Of course, I also see a connection thereby with the minimal art of the sixties and seventies. The idea that the object in a sense has a language unto itself, and that its primary purpose in the world isn't interpretative, it is there as if sitting within its own world of meaning.

You make the distinction between subject matter – and one can certainly see that your pieces are not about subject matter – and content. Your sculptures are full of content. But just fill out that antithesis.

Putting aside subject matter is saying that a content can arise. It does this seemingly out of formal language considerations – about form, about material, about context. When that subject matter is sufficiently out of the way, something else occurs; maybe it's the role of the artist then, as I see it, to pursue this.

And can that content at a certain stage even migrate into something that is more like subject matter, without being explicitly a subject?

Yes, I think it can. Let's just underline this by saying that artists don't make objects. Artists make mythologies. When one sees a work by Picasso, Let us say, what we look at is the mythological context in which Picasso worked. It's as if one's looking beyond the image, beyond the work as displayed. One is looking at Picasso's mythology, which is about money, fame, and a life lived in truly creative endeavour, or so the story goes.

So how does this distinction between content and subject matter work out in the case of a series like Barnett Newman's The Stations of the Cross*?*

The important thing there is to look at the work. On the face of it you are absolutely right. The moment that you are, as we all had the opportunity recently to be, in front of those works, they seemingly have nothing to do with the Stations of the Cross. They are a series of black-and-white canvases with 'zips' – these areas without colour, without painting, in a field of otherwise painted stuff; nothing to do with the Stations of the Cross other than that he has very carefully made the title part of the content. It's as if the words then act as another form in the process of looking. So therefore one has to ask oneself the question about where this content arises. Is it about whether the content is resident in the viewer, or whether it is resident in the work? Now that's a subtle yet very clear manipulation of the act of looking.

If it weren't in the work, though, you can't always invest what you take to it, can you? There has to be something immanent in the work.

Precisely. There's something immanent in the work but the circle is only completed by the viewer. Now that's a very different position from a work with a subject matter, where the work itself has a complete circle of meaning and counterpoint.

It tells a story, you recognise that story, you tell it back.

But here is an incomplete circle which says 'Come and be involved. And without your involvement as a viewer, there is no story!' I believe that that's a complete kind of reinvention of the idea of art.

And is that what you hope and think people do with your art, because after all now, after twenty-five years or so, people come to an Anish Kapoor and they expect to see eternity, don't they? So they arrive in the gallery and say, 'I'm going to lose myself.' Now is that a helpful thing for you?

Well, as I was trying to say earlier on, artists make mythologies, not objects, so perhaps this is one of those mythologies that's come to reside in and around my work.

Did you set out to make it?

Yes. And I could also say no, in that meaningful mythologies – after all, things don't get to be even remotely mythological until they have some deeper resonance – I believe that one cannot set out to make a work that's spiritual. What does it mean? What is a contemporary iconography for the spiritual? Do we know? Is it some fuzzy space? Is that enough? I believe these things come to be because there are other resonances.

Are you aware that you have changed what you do because people suddenly started saying 'I go to a Kapoor and I see eternity and I lose myself' etc? Has there been any reflex back from viewers' reactions to you?

It must be there to some extent, but one doesn't make art for other people, even though I am very concerned with the viewer. It is in that abstract eye of the beholder that some circle, that I've been trying to talk about, the circle is completed. I make art for myself.

So if there were no commissions at all, what would you do in the morning?

Oh, that's great, I'd love that. I would come to the studio and do my thing. What one does in the studio, in fact, is to pose a series of problems to oneself. You can come in and say, 'Yes, I have this funny notion that I want to make a blob of gooey mass of certain dimensions, that has a certain effect.' And then, having made it, I've got to look for some deeper meaning, for some reason for this thing to be in the world. There's enough stuff in the world anyway!

But you can't invest it with a meaning after you've made it.

Oh, those processes are complex. One can find a way to do precisely that. Naming is one of those ways. Context is another. What happens if I put it next to another object? How does that change its reason for being, its effect on the body? One of the phenomena that I've worked with over many years is darkness. Darkness is a fact that we all know about, an idea about the absence of light. Very simple. What interests me, however, is the sense of the darkness that we carry within us, the darkness that's akin to one of the principal subjects of the sublime – terror. A work will only have deep resonance if the kind of darkness that I can generate, let's say a block of stone with a cavity in can have a darkness, is resident in you already; you know it already. This is not a verbal connection, but a bodily one. That's why sculpture occupies the same space as your body.

Do people ever say that they are frightened, particularly by those bottomless black pits? Of course, they're never pits, they're usually quite shallow, but that's the point. Do people say they're frightened by them?

It has happened. I showed a work at Documenta in Kassel, in Germany, in 1992, a work called *Descent into Limbo*, after Mantegna – *Christ descending into the limbo of the nether world*. You entered a room about six metres cubed. In the floor, a space, in fact a hole, but made in such a way that it was a space full of darkness, and read like a black carpet on the floor. You make a room, close the door of course, there's always a line, people stand outside and wait, which in this case took about forty-five minutes. There were people who went into that room and hugged the walls, were terrified that this kind of omphalos at the centre of the room would suck them in. There was a man, who stood in line for forty-five minutes and went into the room, took his glasses off; he was so furious, he'd done a lot of things in the name of contemporary art but never stood in line to look at a black carpet! So he took his glasses off and threw them. And of course then they disappeared into the void of the work. This is total success in my terms!

But your other colours, your blues, your reds in particular, these are the most intense, sensuous, light-affirming colours as well. And actually, I've never found your blacks that terrifying, they are restful, the eyes just shut out. But your blues and your reds, I mean they couldn't be more about life, could they?

Red is a colour I've felt very strongly about. Maybe red is a very Indian colour, maybe it's one of those things that I grew up with and recognise at some other level. Of course, it is the colour of the interior of our bodies. Red is the centre.

Brancusi's great adventure in form, it seems to me, is a proposition which is modern, which is about upwards, onwards, the rocket, the form that's phallic and forward. Donald Judd's great adventure in form, it seems to me, was to close form, was to enclose form.

Squares, rectangles . . .

Exactly, and to bring colour into space. I think, if I might be so bold as to dare to put myself in that lineage, I'm interested in the idea that form in a sense turns itself inside out, that the inside and the outside are equivalent to each other, that we don't just enclose. The form is continually in a warp and continually turning itself inside out. Now I have a feeling that's a very contemporary idea about form.

I'm interested you mentioned phallic because I get the impression sometimes that when people look at your works, the one thing that they feel they can't quite mention in their English way is that of course they are womb-like. Womb-like is the easy bit. Vaginal and things like that.

Anti-phallic, the opposite of phallic, the opposite of Brancusi. Inward. Downwards.

Downwards!

If one took a platonic model, one might say the back of the cave, away from light, towards darkness.

But you actually penetrate to the back of the cave, and penetrate is the word.

Rather than the front of the cave, which is light and forward and out towards the open world.

But the fact is that your shapes are very apparently simple, even when they are deceptive. What I'm curious to know is that you have this intense and complex theoretical basis; but when it comes to making things, you're doing things with a deceptive simplicity, and that's a very interesting transfer, isn't it?

Yes, the eye is a very quick instrument. The eye gets it immediately – I'm interested in that moment of immediate recognition. An object lives in a space in a particular way, you walk into the space and then you say 'Yes that's it!' or 'That's not for me!' – whichever way it goes.

Yes, or it's just a black carpet!

But it's an immediate translation. The theoretical stuff comes later, it's sort of irrelevant. I'm much more interested in the effect that the body has, or that the body receives from a work.

Let's talk practicalities for a moment. You said that you're a terrible carver – indeed you do very little at all – so what makes you a sculptor? Is it an instinctive three-dimensional urge?

I think I understand something about space. I think the job of a sculptor is spatial as much as it is to do with form. The idea that an artist has to make everything themselves is . . .

It lingers there, doesn't it?

Well, it lingers, it's certainly not true however, it's certainly not necessary, and I doubt that it's ever been true. The problem with stone carving is that it takes months and months and months, and I have a very dedicated, wonderful team of young fellows who do a lot of the preparatory work for me. Roughing out a stone is just damned hard work.

But finishing it off you'll do?

Well, I'll do some of it, where it's necessary. Much of what I make is geometric and has a kind of almost mathematical logic to the form.

Yes. You're getting the proportions right.

The proportions, of course. I have a small stone yard in Battersea where I go every morning, talk through the current projects with the guys. They then do a day's work and I'll see it the following morning. And then, of course, as we come to finishing something I'll spend more and more time there trying to resolve things.

You work both with organic materials and with inorganic materials. Clearly, I would say, the appeal of the organic – the rock and the stone – is in no way greater than what you can get, the subtleties, the effects, with the inorganic. That's not a barrier for you in any way.

No. I do like the idea that artists nowadays work in all sorts of materials. I've just shown you a work I've been making with smoke. To be an artist in any of a huge number of ways, seems to me to be a huge psychological liberation. Picasso worked incredibly hard to liberate himself. You know he was able to fracture the world and make cubism, and then to reconstruct the world and make these very whole organic kind of images, and then very sexual things towards the end of his life. We can now, if we can liberate ourselves enough, open the possibility. The art world is so much more open.

Yes, in the work you've just mentioned, pushing smoke into a room, then extracting it so powerfully that it turns into a column of smoke; the moment I say 'column of smoke' I think, of course, of the biblical references, the column of fire and so on. And I was wondering, 'Why isn't that a work of art?' but only for a second, because I will remember that as much as many other flat paintings on a wall!

Good! Let's think of Moses and the burning bush. One can hardly make a move in the right context without immediately calling up a whole series of mythological references that are already in our cultural pot.

Simply because you choose to have them in your cultural pot, and of course you are Indian and you are part Iraqi and you are part Jewish. Were you formally taught these things, were they formally or casually talked about in the family conversation?

Somewhat. My grandfather was the cantor in a synagogue in Poona – a small town not far from Bombay – but my parents were fastidiously areligious. So while some of this was around, it's much more that I feel that the symbolic world, which I insist is the nub of a problem for an artist like me, is latent in most actions I would wish to make as an artist. And the work is to find that latent content.

But it does sound as if you have a great deal of this in your own cultural and personal bedrock.

I feel it's important, yes. I mean one can hardly be Indian and not know that almost every action, which hand you eat your food with, for example, has some deeper symbolic level of interpretation.

But quite a lot of the time, understandably, you wanted to avoid the Indian tag. I was rather shocked when I came across an article from 1998, not that long ago, which said you're the most successful Indian artist living in the West! Nobody would say that now, so is that why you can talk about the Indian influences much more openly, because you're not pigeon-holed?

In the late seventies, when I first started making work as a professional artist, I was making objects out of colour pigment. They looked more Indian than some of the things I'm doing now. What was interesting or problematic for me then was that they were referred to as exotic. The exotic is a tag that seems akin to the touristic as if one were viewing the work from the outside. My job was to get a view from the inside.

It's a bit like decoration as well, isn't it?

Precisely. You have to get beyond that seemingly decorative façade. The exotic's always been a real problem for me. However, I am Indian, that is part of me and I'm proud of it. Indian life is mythologically rich and powerful.

And incredibly rich in colours. Just because you use bright colours, which Western artists are frightened of using, why should you have the exotic label stuck on you?

Well, things have changed now. The art world has changed, but maybe the way we have learned to look has changed in the last twenty-five years, and the exotic is much more acceptable. There are many artists now, younger artists, who work out of the exotic.

Chris Ofili. Extremely exotic. And who could be more respectable than that at the moment?

Indeed.

What do you think of the idea, though, of cross-culturalism, when it is raised? Does it mean anything to you?

If what we're saying is that we're building a kind of bridge, in Heidegger's sense, between one bank of a certain cultural reality and another bank of a different cultural reality, then maybe there is some moment of crossing, 'Mister In-Between' can be powerful and new. If, on the other hand, rather Madame Butterfly-like – it all comes back to the conversation about the exotic – from which one can extract those bits that are attractive, and have them reside in a resident culture, then it's cheap and trivial.

It's bells and whistles, isn't it?

Yes, precisely. 'Mister In-Between', I think, has opened a whole host of possibilities which are tremendously exciting.

But what you're not saying is, 'I'll take a bit of English because I'm here, I'll take a bit of Indian because I'm there, and I should put in all the cultural references of which I'm a part because that acknowledges them all, doesn't reject any of them and is fantastically politically correct.' That is certainly not you!

Yes, but then one wouldn't be taken seriously as an artist if that's how it went.

There's quite a lot of talk about that sort of multiculturalism in the art world, isn't there?

Yes, and it's extremely trivial, and to be put to one side.

Which we'll happily do! Back to when you come in to work – I think this is important – what do you feel as you're coming in to work?

Either immense determination that on this day I am going to do so and so and so and so, or – which is equally interesting and much more difficult – I don't know what I'm going to do today.

Are you frightened by that?

No. Having said what I've tried to say about uncovering a symbolic world, I've learned over the years it is in that cloud of unknowing that something new can occur, that it is precisely in those moments when I don't know what to do, boredom drives one to try! 'I don't know what to do. I'm going to try so and so today.' And just trying it out. Then maybe there's a host of possibilities, which one might pursue for weeks or months or days, or whatever it is, either getting somewhere or not.

Do the dead ends worry you?

No, I think the dead ends are really interesting. I used to empty the studio out and throw stuff away. I now don't. What I find is that there will be a whole series of dead ends, constantly, that a year or two down the line I'll come back to them and wonder, 'Why didn't I see this before? – it's so obvious!' In a sense reinvesting in little moments of insight. There isn't a project. I'm trying to say one does not set out with the idea that 'I've just had a great idea and now I'm going to go and perform it'. Almost all art that's made like that doesn't go anywhere, even if it appears to at first.

Except when you did your huge PVC and metal figure for the Tate Modern, Marsyas *– that was a project.*

That was a project that came out of a whole lot of other projects. I started out making, two years before, a little model out of cardboard stockings.

Yes, it's over there in the corner of the studio and it's twelve inches by six inches.

Exactly, which proposed the idea of some kind of quasi-architectural space with this membrane stretched across it. Now I didn't realise when I was asked to take on the Turbine Hall that that's what I'd end up doing.

And you already had that in your mind?

Yes, including the model on which it sits, which is a proposal for a visitors' centre for the Salvation Army down on the South Bank.

And the interesting thing about that other model is that while one could recognisably see it as being related to Marsyas, *what you then did was the twists and the turns in the membrane – that's what makes it different.*

What we're saying is that work grows out of other work. That there are very few 'eureka' moments of 'here is a completely new, unforeseen idea'. For me anyway, all ideas grow out of other ideas.

But you also say that you've got to be ready when you come to work to face emptiness. Is that worse than boredom or just a different way of expressing it?

I think it's more resolute than boredom. Boredom is that terrible time after you've had your sandwich at lunchtime when all those endeavours seem fruitless, but vital to live through that seeming, day after day 'oh God, what-am-I-going-to-do-with-myself?' feeling. The fear of the emptiness that it implies, the fear that is 'have I got something else to do, have I done what I have to do, and how can I encourage myself to keep on going?' I'm not an artist who has an agenda that's set by the work. That is to say I haven't made a decision – unlike some very great artists, of course – to make work out of steel, or whatever. I do all sorts of things and hopefully tie them together by some emerging content. So they may be diverse in their form, but not their content.

And everything you say about the continuity, that has a rather reassuring sound to it. But are there moments when there really is the emptiness that you described when nothing seems worth doing and you don't know what you're going to do next anyway?

Well, I haven't had one of those periods for a good long while. The last time that happened to me was rather interesting. It was in the early eighties. I'd just done a show in New York, the first time I'd ever made a show in New York, and at the time all the galleries were in SoHo and every time I'd go out of the apartment I was staying in, I'd meet people on the street and they'd tell me how wonderful I was. I was probably about twenty-five years old. And do you know what, I believed every single word of it! I loved it! You know, as I look back on it, it was a good show but it wasn't the best show I've ever made. It sold within the first three minutes, and I came back believing all that stuff. I came back to the studio, which was empty, there was no one to tell me how wonderful I was, and I spent the next two and a half years making almost nothing. A deep lesson not to believe in one's own mythology, I'm glad it happened so early, I'm thankful it happened so early. Emptiness is what artists have to live with. The difficulty is not to rush to fill the emptiness up.

And how did you get out of it?

By slowly getting back into the studio and making some new things. It took me two and a half years, which is a long time and not a long time. A long time if one has to live it every day, but in the bigger span of things perhaps not. And so what it's taught me is that one must not believe any of those mythologies about oneself as an artist.

And now, if you get a bad review, or somebody says Marsyas *is big and heavy and clunking?*

Which happened!

Which happened. You take that in your stride. But it would be difficult if everybody were saying, 'Kapoor's run out of steam, he's repeating himself!' Can you imagine how you would keep your sense of self-belief and integrity under those circumstances?

Well, one doesn't know those things until they occur. And these things happen. I remember William Feaver writing about my drawing show that I did at the Tate, and saying, 'This is the worst show the Tate's ever done.' Well, that floored me for a little while, and then you kind of get on with it. I sort of think of it as column inches; little does it matter, in a way.

It's said sometimes, 'Oh, Anish Kapoor's very ambitious.' Now that can say more about the person who said it than about the person about whom it is being said, but still, how ambitious are you?

I am very ambitious.

To be what?

To challenge myself. To make art that I've not made before. As I was trying to say earlier, the modern world has a huge range of possibilities, whether one's talking about spaces to show in, or materials to make work with. I'm ambitious to try and occupy as much of that territory as I can allow myself to. What I see this as is me battling against my own limitations. The image that I've conjured here of Picasso liberating himself in order to be able to make a fractured world, or a world whole, is a battle that he fought with himself. At least that's the way I see it. And I think there is something about opening one's heart to the possibilities that one doesn't even truly or readily know are there – emotional possibilities as much as anything else.

What are your limitations as a sculptor?

Oh, they're manifold. I don't know. Do you know, much of the work that I've made over many years now proposes the idea that for every form there is a kind of counterpoint in non-form. One of the things that I see myself working with now is not the non-form, because in a way I feel I've done some of that, but the form. What happens when there's form and no non-form? Where can I go with that? That's a battle I need to investigate.

The phrase you used about Picasso, about integration and disintegration. It strikes me what would be really interesting is what happens when you decide to explore disintegrated forms rather than the amazingly integrated forms, or is that what you've just been edging towards?

It may well be. It's very hard to imagine what that looks like. We live in a fractured world. I've always seen it as my role as an artist to attempt to make wholeness. Do I have the emotional wherewithal to be able to recognise the fractured nature of the world, and take on the death that that implies, rather than the resolved completeness of the death that is implied by my background, which understands death as part of life? There is something else.

Is it almost a rediscovery of how, say, cubism might apply to your work, what happens if you apply those principles?

Quite, that's what's been hanging around in the background here. Yes, I don't know if I'll go there.

You've observed that there are at least three stages of an artist's life – the first ten years they say, 'Oh that's very interesting, haven't seen that before'; in the second stage they say, 'Oh we've seen that before, but it's still quite interesting!' Then you come to stage three. Now presumably you are at stage three where you are having to say, 'What am I going to do next?' Do you feel you're at that stage?

Let's see. Well, I'm certainly not in stage one. It's very hard from my perspective, from within the story, so to speak, to know whether one is in one's mid career; I expect I am in my mid career. And I think I do feel that there is still everything to prove. Being an artist is a very long game. I hope I'll be around making art when I'm eighty, and I think the idea that somehow one has done what one has to do and therefore you can kind of steadily carry on – well, it's not something I recognise. I feel there's everything to do yet.

So you never think 'I wish I'd been an engineer, and how simple life would have been'?

Not at all. I feel this is an immense gift. One does afford oneself the luxury to be able to come into the studio all day, every day, and spend one's life making aesthetic propositions! What a luxury, and one that I will carry on with.

SIMON McBURNEY

The moment you think you've arrived is the moment that you should stop

It used to be called Theatre de Complicite (firmly unaccented); a tightly knit group of performers and artists associated with the idea of physical theatre. In recent years it has undergone an interesting abbreviation, just Complicite will do, its fans not only attracted by the early notion of the body as the principle vehicle of theatrical expression, but also taking on trust that the company offers something innovative, exploratory, unpredictable. Increasingly, too,

Complicite has become associated with one person, the director Simon McBurney, though 'director' is a wholly inadequate word to encapsulate his theatrical skills. Twenty years ago it was very different: a group of four, trained in Paris; mime-based, slick, physical comedy. The evolution over the last two decades has been profound and extraordinary, taking in work such as *Mnemonic*, about the Ice Age man whose body was recovered in an Alpine glacier, to *The Noise of Time*, about Shostakovich's last quartet, to *The Elephant Vanishes*, a dazzling creation about rootlessness and anomie in Tokyo. At the heart of the company's work is Simon McBurney, increasingly seen as one of the most important theatrical creators in Britain.

So what are you, how do you describe yourself?

Normally when people ask me what I do I say I'm an actor, and that's what I always wanted to be and that's the way I approach work even when I'm directing it. I used to perform on the streets with friends a lot and that was perhaps as important a training for me as going to a school, as university, as studying with Jacques Lecoq in Paris. Because to go out on to the street and not know what you're going to do and to start performing, to start improvising, is absolutely terrifying, but also the most exhilarating thing you can do. Because if you can make a piece of theatre begin from nothing, in a place where there is nothing, with people who don't expect to see it and who then perhaps, if you do it well, become riveted and with whom you have this extraordinary brief exchange, which is so intense that it's a little bit like a *coup de foudre* for a moment with a lover, and then it all disappears; if you can do that and if you can survive under those circumstances, no stage in the world will ever hold the same anxiety for you ever again.

But you're other things as well. You clearly have to be very good technically, or you have to understand the technical skills that go into your productions. You're very aware of sound and music, and all these in general are not the sort of things that just an actor would have.

I suppose as an actor you become very sensitive to rhythm, not just rhythm as you look at it from the outside as a director might see it, but within yourself; you become used to the idea of hearing your fellow actors, responding to them in space. When you perform in the theatre, as an actor you have an overall sense of a play as well as the individual scenes that you're working on, and that's what I mean. The other aspect, when I say I'm an actor, is that as an actor you make this imaginative leap into being somebody else; that's to say the muscle of the imagination is as important as any other of the muscles in your body. And so it is something about this instinct in space and time which for me I associate with being an actor rather than a director.

And it's fascinating you use the phrase 'the muscle of the imagination', given that the principal association we have with you is of somebody involved in physical theatre, and also your use of the body, and clearly even with the imagination you have this sense of the physicality of the imagination. It's not something separate from the body.

Yes, you see, when you ask me to describe myself I think that I have to go back in time. I had a teacher in Paris once who said, 'If an actor has forgotten what it's like to play as a child they shouldn't be an actor,' and that is something that I've always retained, the memory of playing as a child and making an imaginary world not just as a way of passing the time. I just remember it as a child being something absolutely essential to my life. I mean I'm talking about playing games, about imagining other people, and it's part of the way that it helps you actually see the world.

Hold the idea of play there for a moment if you will, because I want to find out before that why, after you'd been at Cambridge, where of course lots of people acted, you moved to Paris to study with Jacques Lecoq and Philipe Gaulier, what made you do that? Did you know enough about them to feel that that was the direction you wanted to go in?

No, I knew nothing about them. My father had just died at Cambridge, I had a very passionate love affair that collapsed, and one of the things I felt was that I wanted to run, I wanted to get out of the situation that I was in, get away somehow from my past. And I had heard through different sources, one of whom was the director Ron Eyre, about this school in Paris. I'd heard about one or two people who had been there, but I knew nothing about it. All I knew was that it treated an actor as also a creator, as a writer.

Was there an element of being actively dissatisfied with what you could get from the British theatre as it was then constituted?

I think it was a desire to be able to find my own voice. I think that was the big urge within me. I had a very strange few years. I seemed to be able to make people laugh quite easily, and I was rung up and invited to perform. A man said, 'I'm going to open something here that they have in Los Angeles, I hear you're very funny, I really want you to perform.' I said, 'Well, what is it?' He said, 'It's a comedy club and in Los Angeles it's called the Comedy Store and I'm going to open one here in London.' So I said, 'Right, OK; well, that sounds interesting.' So I went up on the train and in a strip club in Soho upstairs was a tiny little sweaty room. We all got up and performed, various people like Alexei Sayle and all sorts of people that opening night. And I performed something about eating an orange with a fellow actor who was a woman called Sandy Toksvig.

It was quite a first night, that, wasn't it?

It was and Emma Thompson did the sound effects for me, sitting on the side of the stage. And so I was then invited by an unknown radio producer, called Griff Rhys-Jones, if I would work on the radio. I felt, in this world of potential radio shows and leading on to the television, I felt as if I didn't know where I was, I was completely lost.

So you needed to find your roots somehow and that was the attraction of going to Paris to Lecoq . . . ?

Perhaps, yes, it was always this thing of escaping for me, of a kind of rootlessness, not feeling quite at home.

So what did Lecoq . . . ?

Other people felt very at home with the idea of following in a British tradition; I never did.

Ah, so already then you had some sense that you didn't want to be part of a British tradition?

I just knew that I felt uncomfortable and I knew that somehow I needed to find a way of finding out what it was, how I wanted to perform. I knew that there were other forms of performance. I had seen some fantastic theatre in London at the Riverside, when they started to bring in theatre from abroad. London was not a centre for international theatre by any stretch of the imagination, but what I had seen I had found incredibly exciting because it suggested to me that there were other worlds, there was another way of looking at this world. I grew up without a television in a very sort of strange, empty Victorian house, with no central heating, with parents who were kind of misanthropic and took me on holidays to where there were no other people. So we would end up in Iceland in completely the wrong time of year, living in tents which were in fact bought for the South of France! My father was an archaeologist and so we spent a lot of my childhood under canvas, and the moment I was doing something that everybody else was doing, or I was on a path that I was expected to be on, I started to feel uncomfortable. I always remember feeling that I have to find a way of looking at the world. My father was an archaeologist so he dug in the earth to find out the truth about the past; I sometimes feel that I am trying to dig in the world around me. I'm involved in another kind of archaeology to look for another kind of truth, and the moment I find I am separated from that life – every time I have gone out and performed in the cinema, for example, if you do two or three films on the trot, you suddenly have this impression that you're becoming separate or separated from the world around you.

And the people and audiences.

And the people and what life consists of.

I just want to row you back to Lecoq there, because this was clearly such an important experience. Did he give you some sense, or did that training give you some sense of a direction and discipline which could merge some of this welter of emotions?

Well, what he gave me particularly was a rigour continually to return to being involved in life, not losing sight that the root of the life of the theatre is being involved in life itself. When I saw him just before he died he said to me, 'I am nobody; I am only a neutral point through which you must pass. I have no style, I have no technique. People come to me in order to better articulate what they themselves want to do'; and that's principally what he gave all his pupils. Some of his pupils have ended up as writers, some of them have ended up as architects, some of them have ended up as actors. They seem to span many, many different disciplines. You know, people have a very great misunderstanding about what he taught and they think that perhaps it's mime or perhaps it's something to do with physical theatre. It's curiously not to do with any of that. I return to the same phrase: what he taught us more than anything else was the main muscle we exercised was the muscle of the imagination.

Now, twenty years ago you met the three other founding members of the Theatre de Complicite, Annabel Arden, Marcello Magni, Fiona Gordon, just tell me briefly how you met them and how you all knew that you could work together?

Well, I don't think we did. I think what happened was that one of the things that I said to myself leaving university was that if I was going to work in theatre, I promised myself I would never stop working. So I had a desire that whatever I would do, I would not be waiting around for a job.

You'd not be 'resting'.

Certainly not, no. The first desire was to make a piece of work. Annabel I knew from Cambridge and Fiona is Canadian, and Marcello is Italian, and we were all available and we just said, 'Let's make something.'

Did you know what you wanted to make?

No, not exactly. Well, what I wanted to make was what I didn't see in the theatre. I wanted to make something which I wanted to see. It was a hunch without really knowing. I knew that it was about how people were not able to express themselves. What it ended up being was sitting in deckchairs on an imaginary beach for about an hour and a quarter doing absolutely nothing but making people roar with laughter with doing nothing.

How long did that take to develop and to produce?

It took about six or eight weeks to put together, and then we simply got up on stage and started to perform. And through the performance we continued to develop the piece and change it, and it was really through the performance that something began to develop and in a sense that process has remained with me ever since.

So that was a crucial discovery, that you would devise things in rehearsal, of course, but that they would continue to grow during performance?

Inevitably as you're performing you invent, and this was another thing that Jacques insisted upon, that actors should take responsibility for what they do on stage. He encouraged us to imagine that an actor is also in some way a writer, not just an interpreter of work, that you have a fundamentally original and creative input when you work. And so it was a little bit like getting into a boat and rowing out to sea without being entirely sure where were we going but wanting to take advantage of the currents and the winds and feeling somehow that fate would steer us in the right direction. But as I say, we thought we were doing it just for a year, just for a summer perhaps, and for some reason it touched people. There was always a point of view on what we were doing.

Which came from all four of you? How did the point of view evolve?

It came through arguing and reading and stopping, and through a process of discussion, I would say.

Which everybody who joined the company knew was the way they were going to be asked to behave?

Yes, it was chaos, working through chaos, you never quite knew what you were going to do each day, but you knew that you wanted to make something.

One of the other phrases used is that somebody said the whole process of creation involved a rather aggressive environment, aggressive in the sense that so many ideas were generated and thrown away. Now, do you recognise that?

When you make something, if you are a painter or a writer, or a sculptor or a musician, a degree of energy is required to make it. And I'm not sure that it is always aggressive, but when you have a great deal of energy it can appear to be more aggressive than it is. I mean, you can talk about a waterfall being aggressive, but in fact it is just a very powerful forward movement of energy, although I think sometimes my engine house is a kind of anger.

And did you ever use aggression knowingly, in a calculated way, in order to achieve a certain effect in the production, or to get the production to a point where it could begin to work?

Well, I don't remember that; the only thing I ever remember is having a huge amount of energy in order to push this boulder up the hill, to get it up to the top of the hill, to get it to the point where you can release it and it will do its own thing.

Did you feel it was your responsibility to do that pushing because, after all, a lot of the works for over ten years are described as 'Devised by the company, Directed by Simon McBurney'; this is a very interesting division of function. At a certain stage, do you have to say 'I'm the director, I've got to get this show on the road'?

Yes, that's absolutely true. If there is a degree of aggression then it is because a lot of the things that we were making we made through an instinct. I think many directors know what the piece is going to be before they make it. It's very carefully planned out. They know that somebody will come in through this door, they will perform in this way and they will go out that way. Quite often, directors will ask designers where should the actors come in? Just as a painter or a sculptor might not know what it is they are making when they're making it, so I feel very often I don't know what it is eventually that we're going to do. I take the example of something like *The Elephant Vanishes*. We started working and on the first day I had no idea which stories out of this collection we were going to end up with.

You chose three out of a collection of how many?

I don't know . . . twenty. So I didn't know what the piece was going to be, and I think that the quality of not knowing is quite frightening. I think that fear also produces a kind of aggression not only in me but in other people, and other people's fear can perhaps sometimes make your energy seem more aggressive than it is.

Now this is your most recent piece, based on Japanese stories, you were working with Japanese actors . . .

In Japanese and I don't speak Japanese!

They were people who did not know what the Complicite tradition was; how did you get to the point where you chose the three stories, or did they choose the three stories?

The stories chose themselves in the end. I knew that I wanted to do the title story. I knew I was particularly interested in the story about sleep. I didn't know how they would fit together, if they would fit together at all, and there were several other stories which I thought were absolutely marvellous. In the end I had six actors, and to give you an example of a day, I would come in in the morning and we would do some yoga together or we would do some sort of exercise or perhaps we would do none of that, perhaps we would sit and read a couple of the stories, it varied from day to day. But we would do something collectively together in the morning, and then sometimes out of what we were doing, perhaps there would be some music playing, somebody would be doing something and I would observe that they were doing it and I would somehow encourage them to take it further. For example, I remember once somebody was rolling on the carpet and somebody stepped over the top of them. And then I encouraged everybody to roll and everybody stepped over, and suddenly something emerged which I forgot about until weeks later when I was trying to find the ending of the piece, which was about the idea of the sense of loss of direction which is a very powerful sense in the Murakami stories about modern Japan, people not quite knowing where the direction is. And taking the end of *The Elephant Vanishes* and trying to produce an image on stage of people who have lost direction, we ended up with these people rolling over and other people stepping over the top of them.

That began as an exercise and then was retrieved later?

It was retrieved later, so we did what I call filling the reservoir. You give yourself an enormous amount of different information, you infuse yourself with different information, you read all the stories, you listen to music, you have discussions, and we had to talk a lot about being Japanese, but then I talked a lot about being English, about the sense of identity. We set up exercises about that. I asked two people to stand behind one of the actors to be their mother and father, and two people to stand behind them to be their grandparents and great-grandparents, and I said, 'How far back can you go?' We introduced grandparents to grandparents, I mean crazy things, also quite funny. But essentially that was not in order to put that on stage but to do this thing which I call filling the reservoir so that all the actors have an enormous access to a great deal of information. Why do I do that? Well, somehow when you're making a piece of work, you have to create a common language, because there are many people in the room.

Even though there were texts, you need the language which informs the texts?

That's right. How are you going to perform it, because all actors when they come together in a room, they all have very different points of view. What interests me is that you maintain those different points of view but you give people, you create together for each show – and in each show it is different – a common language by which you can approach the material. If it is Shakespeare then you find a different common language to if it is Murakami; but part of the process is developing the tools by which you can then open up the text and create the piece that you're going to create.

You see, one of the other things about Elephant Vanishes *is that it is expressed with this extraordinarily brilliant soundscape and then video images all over the place, which never look as if they are stuck-on bits of expression. So you are not only trying to produce a common language for the actors, you're somehow trying to produce a common language of expression for all the other elements. How do you keep control of this without going mad and how do you synthesise this?*

Well, you do go mad, it's difficult. But the very simple answer to that is that for me the lighting designer and the sound designer and the video designer and even the stage management all have a fantastically important role within the rehearsal room. In conventional theatre what happens is there is a tremendous sense of hierarchy and you find that stage management sit behind what is called a stage management desk and everyone has their right role and nobody veers out of it. This is very much a sort of class system that's become a model that everybody adheres to.

And with you?

In our rehearsal room it's a great deal more chaotic. You're quite likely to find one of the stage managers working with two or three of the actors on a piece that they are devising to show to each other at the end of the day. They'll be filming. They'll perhaps have suggestions about what they can do with a particular object or a particular piece of equipment, so their suggestions or their creativity will be equally included in the process. The only way that you can keep moving forward, finding other ways of expressing things about this increasingly complicated world that we live in, is by listening and observing not only to life around you but to the other people who are in the room. It's not about a sense that you have to be democratic about these things, it's a question of creativity, that the process of making theatre is a collaborative process. I have no interest in paying lip service to it; for me it's absolutely fundamental. Theatre artists are essentially sort of charlatans and thieves, I mean that's the tradition that we come from. So I make no bones about the fact that I steal from here and I take from there, and we all do it, that's perfectly all right, there's nothing new in the world, there's nothing actually new in the way that you do something. But the point is, how do you take something and use it to articulate what is essentially a core of any given theatrical production?

Obviously it's a very high-risk activity and you've written about the fact that in that particular production, The Elephant Vanishes, *you really faced intellectual meltdown; you didn't know what was happening and you thought, maybe I'm on the wrong lines altogether. That was an absolutely ghastly moment. Did you really think that the thing might fail altogether, might not get on to the stage?*

I didn't think it would not get on to the stage. One of the things that I really learned in Paris all those years ago that Jacques showed us very clearly – he took apart the architecture of space, the internal structure of rhythm and the form of plays and the form of theatre, the movement of things, and showed us, as it were, the nuts and bolts in a fan; it was the most marvellous way of how something functions.

Is that a core skill that you'd fall back on, a core instinct?

Well, yes, I think you can take anything and turn it into theatre. We could take this conversation, we could take this pair of spectacles and turn it into a piece of theatre, use it as the basis for a piece of theatre. If you know essentially what it is that makes a piece of theatre function you can always make a piece of theatre. The question is not that for me any more, it's whether this piece of theatre is truly addressing something which is important, whether the meaning is really coming across. And whether it is not just going to get up there – it can always get up there – but whether when it does get up there, whether it will do what you dream it can do.

So how did you break through that awful moment of darkness in Tokyo when you thought you might be on the wrong lines altogether?

I simply came to a dead end with one of the particular stories, which was very, very difficult. It's about a woman who can't sleep for seventeen days and it's nothing to do with insomnia, she literally can't sleep and in fact she feels better and better and better. So it's a very sort of strange premise, yet at the same time it's supposed to be realistic, and it is told through very curious memory process, and it's just very difficult to make that clear. And I had some ideas but they just simply weren't coming together, so what I did at a certain point was I stopped. I said, 'I don't know how to do this bit and I don't know what we should do here, so we're going to split up into different groups and we're going to stop for a whole day. You can take an entire day. I will take an entire day. Somebody else will take an entire day to try and find a solution.' And in a sense it just simply took the pressure off. Because at that point we're getting closer to production, people are standing behind you going 'What is he doing? What's going on? When are we going to know?' The sound people, the lighting, the video, the producers, there's a great army of people waiting to know. They're trying to build the set and you don't know whether you're going to want this element of the set or that. It's a real crisis point. And at that point I said, 'Stop, let's get off the train. It doesn't matter. Let's take a day. It appears that we don't have a day, to hell with it, let's create a day!'

But that was the breakthrough?

And that was a breakthrough, because it's just saying in the end it doesn't matter, nobody's died.

The journey that you've travelled from being one of four running Theatre de Complicite to the fact that now it's just called Complicite and we all know that Complicite and your name sells seats – you're identified with it. Was losing the other three painful?

David Mamet says that a theatre group can never exist beyond a five-year period, and by that he means the same group of people living together, working together, that ideal of the theatre ensemble which people refer to all the time. What I would say is that there have been many moments which have been incredibly painful through the process of working with this company, many moments where you have marriages which then become divorces, but one of the things that we stuck to right from the beginning was that in every single show there would be a different line-up of people. And although we have remained close, it has remained a very mobile group of people with nobody ever taking it for granted that because you did this show you would necessarily do another show. And the company is the same as any group of people that you grow up with and work with. I see it throughout the theatre world, really. We are no exception in that respect.

So there's never been a fight for the possession of the soul of

Complicite? There haven't been people who have said 'We are the real Complicite and Simon has taken it off into directions which really aren't where we thought we were going'?

No, there hasn't been that. At a certain point, we always talked about the idea that we're just going to bring it to a halt. Having worked in an incredibly chaotic way for about seven or eight or nine years, we all said, 'We can't go on like this.' Annabel was starting to be invited to direct opera, other people were invited to do other things elsewhere. I started to work in film. You want to do your own things. Everybody wants to express themselves in their own way. At that point it was suggested that somebody should become artistic director. Everyone turned to me and said, 'Right, well, why don't you be artistic director to begin with and then perhaps somebody else will be artistic director later?' And I said, 'Absolutely no way. I'm very happy as an actor and as a kind of complete maverick wandering around and causing my own chaos in whatever way.' But then I said, 'All right, I'll do it and we'll just see how it goes.' That was when it coincided with Richard Eyre asking me to create a piece on the writings of Bruno Schulz, *The Street of Crocodiles*, and one piece led to another.

So it wasn't that you seized control? This was not an artistic putsch?

No, part of me would have been very happy simply to have been cut loose and left to go in another direction. And I often wonder what might have happened if I had, because it's a double-edged sword to be associated with a particular name or a company. I find it very difficult when people talk about physical theatre, for example. I don't feel I have any relationship with this term at all, because as far as I'm concerned all theatre is physical. As Aristotle says, theatre is an act and an action, and he didn't mean just the writing of it, he meant that at the centre of any piece there is an action, a physical action.

Well, the voice is physical.

And the voice is physical, it's a sort of tautology, really. For me it is perhaps just an indication of the historical state of theatre that suddenly some critic somewhere comes up and starts calling what we did physical theatre; perhaps because we have no money we perform everything, or perhaps because we wish to involve the audience's imagination nobody goes off stage, or perhaps because we suddenly involve a piece of dance in the middle of what seems to be a naturalistic piece, or perhaps simply because the British theatre had fallen into the trap of naturalism.

You're still way ahead of the British theatre now, aren't you? We began with this question of being dissatisfied with various aspects of British theatre and in a way every time you come back with a new production, the gap between you and what the rest of British theatre is doing seems if anything larger.

Oh, goodness, I don't know, really. I only know that I try to express something that I'm feeling passionately about in the way that I think is going to touch people the most. That's the only way I can describe it. There are some amazing people working in British theatre and some amazing things are done. I do think that there is a problem in the way we educate people and the way people see things, and it is something to do with an historical legacy where theatre in the nineteenth century, once you have the arrival of film and television, in order for it to survive it then becomes a middle-class or an upper-middle-class activity, which seems to appeal to a limited group of people. Whereas, of course, theatre, prior to the twentieth century, was something which was for everybody. I don't say that every performance was for everybody, but there was theatre in every walk of life. I take issue with the idea that television has killed theatre. I don't believe that at all. I think one of the things that television has done is it has liberated theatre because it carries the majority of drama. You don't have to worry about drama any more. There's plenty of that on TV. You can do any old thing in the theatre now, and the idea that you've got to kind of stick to a well-made play is absolutely ridiculous. I do think that some of our major theatrical institutions should also programme things which are for me theatre. I don't understand why somebody like Pina Bausch has never been invited to perform on our national stage and it has always remained dance; that isn't the case abroad.

When you look back over the last twenty years, would you ever have guessed that the work that you do would have travelled so far from sitting in deckchairs and making people laugh about the scene of the seaside to this highly complex work with video and almost every single means of expression that was The Elephant Vanishes? *This is an extraordinary journey. How aware have you been of the evolution as you've been through it?*

Quite unaware except that every time I've made a piece of work, I've wanted to get rid of it, obliterate it and do the next thing, because it was never quite what I wanted. I think the moment you think you've arrived is the moment that you should stop.

Do you ever rest?

With difficulty.

Can you do nothing?

I don't think anybody does nothing. Doing nothing is a skill in itself.

Do you have it?

Well, I think I can learn it. I try to understand it more as I get older. And one of the things that I found fascinating about working in Japan and one of the reasons why I like working with actors who are not only British is that you are constantly being made aware of the different ways in which people see the world. And what's fundamentally different for me with Japanese culture is being made aware that we come from a dualistic society, that we divide everything into good and evil, and right and wrong, and the mysterious and the prosaic.

The emotion and the reason; it's very binary, isn't it?

Very binary, whereas in Japanese society everything is seen as part of the same whole. And therefore there is an understanding that meaning and emptiness can be part of the same thing, and that was why the material was very difficult because I realised I was having to see something in a completely new way. And when you ask me have I ever thought of doing nothing, my mind immediately jumps to being in Japan when I started to understand in a very small way what it means to see the world differently. I found an incredible release in the idea that meaning and nothing, meaning and no meaning were all part of the same thing.

Are you ever worried about running out of energy?

No, I'm not worried about running out of energy. Sometimes I feel very tired like everybody but I'm not actually sure what that's to do with but I know that it's not to do with this desire to keep on looking for something. What gives you energy is that the further you go, the more you discover there is to do. It is what I find most wonderful about modern discoveries in physics, which is something that's really interesting me at the moment, is that the more they uncover, the more mystery appears to be there. That is a great source for energy rather than something which makes me feel tired.

RENZO PIANO

Culture is more about curiosity, not about intimidation

When a thousand-foot sliver of glass pierces the sky over London Bridge station, that landmark skyscraper will be by the Italian architect Renzo Piano. When you visit the new Parco de la Musica in Rome, that's his work too. So is the mile-long frontage of the terminal at Japan's Kansai Airport. As are the curving arches of the football stadium in Bari, in southern Italy. Now, don't get me or him wrong – Renzo Piano is not about size. Space, certainly, but not just size, and certainly not for its own sake. You'd see that at once in the work he did helping small communities in Otranto, Matera, or his native Genoa, to modernise their neighbourhoods through informed self-help. He's not a community architect, in the normal sense of the word, but one who does care about communities. Is there anything I've forgotten? Ah, yes, the Pompidou Centre at the Beaubourg in Paris, which he designed with Richard Rogers, and which put them both, and hi-tech architecture, on the map a quarter of a century ago. A signature building, an icon undoubtedly, as defining of modern Paris as the Eiffel Tower. Yet for years Piano was almost shackled by the Beaubourg 'hi-tech' tag. Still, his office here, very nearby, suggests that he can't quite get away from it, or the area. But as one critic put it, Renzo Piano was more confined by the association with the Pompidou Centre than freed by it.

All that is behind you now, but it's an important place to start with, because Rogers and Piano was to all intents a one-building practice. How did the two of you get together?

Well, that was in 1968 or 1969. Richard was one of the few persons I knew in London speaking Italian fluently, and then we became such friends and almost like brothers in some way, and we still are. So we started about that time in London. But we won the competition in 1971, we called it at that time the 'Centre Beaubourg', the Beaubourg Centre, and then we started to move to Paris, and then we started to work together in that period.

And was there ever any disagreement between you that this should be a hi-tech building of the most hi-tech kind?

No, not really, no. We never disagreed because we were both bad boys, we were genuinely bad boys, in a different way, but we have been so complementary all the time. It was a kind of innocent way to make provocation against the institutional building and institutional culture of building. We were convinced, and I think we were right to be convinced, that culture is more about curiosity, not about intimidation. And the typical buildings in that period, the beginning of the seventies, were very intimidating, those kind of monumental stone, marble buildings. So we were genuinely interested in making that provocation, to make a factory, to make a refinery, to make whatever. Everybody was saying, 'This is more like a factory than like a museum,' and we were very pleased about that.

Were you surprised when you won the competition?

Of course, very, very surprised. And we got that competition among 681 entries. Can you believe that? We made the competition because we are very pleased to be working with Ove Arup and partners and other collaborators. We are very happy to do that. It was like enjoying life, you know; it was really like making sort of provocation. Normally we were working in the evening, because in the day we were very busy doing our work, making money, surviving at that time. And then we won that, and we were very surprised, we can't believe it.

It's been called, as you know, a 'hi-tech spoof'.

No. I think that this is because of all those pipes, but really it's not hi-tech triumphalistic building. It is more about a parody of hi-tech; it's more about introducing that sort of familiarity of the machine instead of the intimidation of the stone and marble and arches. It was really about welcoming people. And it was also about flexibility, don't forget. I mean a few years ago big changes were made. After twenty-five years of life, after hundred and fifty million visitors, some changes were made, and those changes were possible only because the building was really like a machine, like a tool, completely flexible.

So that reflected what you had designed it to be: a building which was capable of being renewed?

Exactly. You know when we designed that building, we really didn't know very much what culture was about; but frankly we were very happy about not knowing very much because it was more fresh. And we thought that a building for culture has got to be adaptable, ready to change with the times, and that was absolutely true. Today a library is completely different from a library twenty-five years ago, and that's the reason why the building has been changed very easily, in a completely flexible way. I even think that in twenty-five years' time they will probably change again, but the building will be like a tool – ready to accept any change.

And there was no example that you were working from; people told you that they needed an arts institution, or rather an arts building which wasn't an institution?

The brief was quite interesting because the brief was already talking about mixing different disciplines, like music, visual art, design, reading and books and information. So the brief was in some way revolutionary because it was already introducing that concept that there is no borderline between artistic disciplines. So that was good. What we made, actually, was to push this to the extreme, making five floors – each like a football field – one above the other, pushing all the fixed elements of the building outside – like stairs, like escalator, like lift, like pipes – so that the floors were really like a completely flexible space, spanning fifty metres, so completely open semantically but also physically open to change. And this is, in fact, what has been happening.

You approached this with the greatest seriousness, and it's interesting reading what architectural critics say about the building. One of them said, 'It was an act of loutish bravado.' But from what you've said, this was a very serious thing. You weren't making gestures, were you?

No, no, it was not gesture making. It was a correct provocation. The proof is that since then, the presence of museums in social life changed dramatically. You must admit that museums were not what they are today. Today they are like new cathedrals, and they have a great success. Probably the beginning of the seventies was the era when all this changed. So it was not just a joke, of course; it was the right moment to change.

Let's go back even further to your origins. Your family were all builders, you admired your father hugely. Do you feel that the sheer practicality of his approach to making buildings is something which is a key part of your character and approach?

It is. I think it's in my DNA, it's also under my skin. I always loved to spend time with my father on his site. But you know it's not just about practicality and the craftsmanship, it's also about dreams. When you are a young boy, six, seven, ten years old, and you go on-site every day and you enjoy that, you understand that building is a little miracle. One day you see sand on the floor, and next morning you see something standing up – strong and tall. And this is a miracle, this idea that you start from something rough, without any shape, and you give a shape. When I went to see my father a long time ago and I told him I wanted to be an architect, he watched me and said, 'Whyever, son, why? You can be a builder, why you just want to be an architect.' A builder is like a god!

It's good.

Because you do things, you think about things and you do things you know. So in his personal view of things, a son of a builder should be just a better builder, that's all. That was evolution for him. I'm joking because he was very happy of course. But being the son of a builder doesn't mean that you imitate just the craftsmanship of the pleasure to do physical things. It's more about the Utopia of making things, starting from informal, rough material and then making things.

You've often said that architects are too pompous, they talk too much about art, and that you prefer to be very practical; although, as you say, the architect is also god but a very practical god rather than an artistic god.

Architecture, funnily enough, is probably the most materialistic discipline you can think about, because it's really about physicality, it's about material. It's about fighting against gravity. And believe me, gravity is a very stubborn thing, it's a very obstinate thing. So it's very much materialistic; but at the same time it's very idealistic, it's probably one of the most idealistic disciplines you can think about, because it's about people, it's about enjoyment, it's about Utopia, it's about changing the world. And you do change the world in some way.

For better or for worse.

You try, yes, you try, and this is what probably everybody

dreams about, but as an architect you do. Because you do a job and you interfere with the way people live and stay, so you have a greater responsibility.

But you also have to solve problems; and you've always emphasised that you're providing a service to solve problems. So there's the practicality as well as the idealism that you've just been describing.

You cannot be just a practical man. It's not enough, unfortunately. Architecture is not just about making good buildings, it's also about telling stories in some way. You can tell stories by making interviews, you can tell stories by writing or by painting or by playing music, but you also tell stories by making buildings, because buildings talk. They sometimes sing as well, in the plans, but sometimes they are like that. So it is both practical, but it is also extremely light and ethereal.

In quite a lot of the writing about you, people say, 'The thing about Piano is that he avoids theory, he avoids intellectualisation; indeed, he's almost anti-intellectual.' But what you're saying is not anti-intellectual. Was there not one particular period in your life where you deliberately fostered an image of excessive practicality?

Yes, of course, because you change. I enjoyed, in a quite snob way, to be a son of a builder, especially in an environment where sometimes architects have played a bit too much the artistic role. But, of course, I totally agree: architecture is art – but I don't think you should say that too much – but it is art. Architecture is many, many things. Architecture is a science, is technology, is geography, is topography, is anthropology, is sociology, is art, is history. You know all this comes together. Architecture is a kind of bouillabaisse, incredible bouillabaisse! And, by the way, architecture is also a very polluted art in the sense that it's polluted by life, and by the complexity of things.

And compromise.

Ah, compromise! But in some way, this compromised art becomes more real and more true than other art.

Because you have to deal with the compromises; you can't walk away and say, 'I won't make a compromise!'

Exactly. So the secret is that you don't really do compromise, but you are confronted by life all the time. So in some way it's stupid to say that architecture is not art, because it's not true; but at the same time it's even more stupid to talk too much about architecture being art, because then you get gestures. You know, the academic is exactly when you refuse to feed architecture by reality, by real life, and by people's needs. It's not about being moralistic, it's just about truth.

Was it difficult to get away from the Beaubourg and from the expectation that, because you've done that building, that was the style of architecture you would do?

Yes. As an architect you do something and everybody thinks that this is your style. So if they love what you've done, they want to do again the same thing. This is the beginning of the end of course, because then you are trapped in a sort of stylish cage; maybe sometimes a golden cage, but it's still a cage. And this is terrible because one of the beautiful things about architecture is that it depends entirely from where you are, when, and doing what. Architecture is really the mirror of the moment, and of the people you are working with in architecture, and so essentially the client and the community you are working with. That's the reason why. Architecture is a bit like making a movie. You know it's about different things. And every time you start from the scratch – it's not true because, of course, you have your own coherence and your own system of doing things. But you have to stay away from the notion of a style, in the sense of a rubber stamp. That's terrible, because you'll get trapped in a very formalistic thing. This also happened with the great artists. At the end of their life, they were obliged to repeat themselves because that was what people wanted and that's what they'd paid for.

You mentioned movies. Miloš Forman, and I think maybe Bernardo Bertolucci as well, said, 'My cameraman is a better cameraman than I am, the actors can act in a way that I can't, the sound man can do the sound, the editor can do the edit, the composer writes the music. What am I? The director.' He said that in the end 'I'm the person who brings it all together.'

I like that, yes. I think you have to bring together things. You need to work with talent, because teamwork is about aiming talent at people around you, and you have to get it all coming to one end, you know, otherwise everything disperses. But in some ways, you have to work on the detail, and you have to work on the global thing. By the way, there are very similar things about music, for example, and architecture. They look so far away from one another – one is the most physical among the arts, and the other is the most light, the most immaterial – but they are quite the same, in the sense that music and architecture depend a lot from discipline, order, sometimes even geometrical order, and then you play with that order. And sometimes you become disobedient to that order, then you break the order, but you need the order.

What music do you like?

I like music, all music but, of course, I love modern music. I've been working with Luciano Berio a long time, with Luigi Nono, with Pierre Boulez, a long time ago, together with Richard Rogers. Since then we are very familiar, we meet all the time, and I love working with musicians. I love also music belonging to a different sphere. I love all music on one condition: that it's music and not rubbish. But music is great. And in some way music is also depending from geometry, and from precision, and from mathematics.

You mentioned community a while ago, and I want to take you back to that because in the comparatively early years, after Beaubourg, you were working with small and rather poor communities, some of them down in the south, in Puglia and Otranto and Matera. You had a mobile lab, helping the people there to understand how they could renew their neighbourhoods by learning the necessary skills. How important for you was working with the community in that way?

Well, it was a very important period. It is still now. Still now. I became eventually goodwill ambassador of UNESCO for the city, for urban renewal, so since a long time now I have a job for UNESCO. And right now, for example, we are working in Sarajevo, and we are making a scheme there for a cultural centre, for an educational centre. So I became familiar with the idea of working with community.

So the community is the client in this case?

The community is the client, yes. You know the art of listening is one of the most difficult arts you can think about, the art of listening to people, understanding people. And the architect must listen, and must understand. You become more sensitive when you work with a community, because then you have to listen to the little sound, the little noise – you need to make interpretation of things. And this is a very good gimmick about understanding. I love the idea of not designing the building but designing the tools that may be used by people to make a building. Any historical centre is always like that, you cannot demolish that, you have to change. You have to go through a kind of homeopathic process more than surgery. Cities, especially old cities, are a bit like human bodies, they are very vulnerable. They need to change by using their internal resource and their internal energy more than by just making surgery. So all this is extremely subtle, and I love working in that kind of atmosphere.

Now you're from Genoa – a Genovese – and sometimes regarded by Italians as not quite Italian, a bit European. Is this an important part of your character, that you are more European than you are Italian?

It's difficult to say. I'm very Genoese; for example, I love sailing, I love boats, I love the sea. My office in Genoa is right in front of the sea. I think the water for me is the best background possible you can have, it's a kind of a natural Internet in which you swim. And water is ocean, the water of the ocean is the interlinking matter of the entire world. For me, Liguria, the sea, the water, are a kind of a constant reference. I also love Italy for many, many reasons. It's quite true that I left Italy when I was a twenty-five-year-old. I started to travel, then I went to London. We came together with Richard and from there I moved to Paris, and I'm a French resident in Paris since now almost thirty years.

So you are quite non-Italian. You're European now.

But I still go back to Italy all the time, you know, and for me then it's true I'm European, because I don't see any difference. I feel only empires, like in Genoa, like in London, like everywhere, in Berlin. Yes, I'm European, that's for sure.

Are you an outsider? Because you've been described as being deliberately outside the church of architecture.

That's a bit part of the snob side, you know. Yes, of course, and I enjoy that, especially because in Italy you have to be outside of the Church if you want to be saved! When I was a young architect, you know, the real trap was academy; so I escaped academy. I got to be above all those defences, and now I don't need any defence, so I don't care. But when you are younger, when you are thirty years old, when you start to do things all around the world like that, you need to build up your defence. But it's quite true. I have a good friend, a writer, that's said many times, 'I came so many times very close to the temple, but I always stop at the door; I never was able to get inside the temple!' Because it's true. As an architect, as a writer, as an artist, you are always inadequate to what you're doing. You never feel like really getting to the temple. You should be like that. And this is the real point: you know how many times you feel so close to beauty, and then you try to grab it, but the arms are too short! You feel the inadequacy of what you're trying to do. The mind goes much faster than your arms, and this is true.

There's another building we need to talk about, because it marks the difference from the Beaubourg, and that is the Menil Collection in Houston, Texas, which is a long, low, wood-clad building, absolutely fitting in with the grey wood-clad houses round about. What does that say about your approach to architecture? Was fitting in with that environment – a very domestic environment anyway, but making something monumental in a domestic environment – was that an important part of what you thought architecture is about?

Yes, yes, a very important part. And especially, I have to say, in that scheme the client was an essential part.

Because they're making demands of you?

Well, a good client is very demanding. A good client is never a client that says yes; no, this is not the good client. The good client is somebody that has a strong dream, and has a strong desire, and is able to tell you this, and is able to understand quality. Dominique De Menil, the lady that was my client on the Menil

Collection, was an extremely intelligent lady – strong lady. She wanted that sense of serenity, that sense of abstraction. We learned a lot about natural lighting, about the sense of beauty of the light, of the day that goes away, the cloud coming, the sense of vibrant quality of natural lighting versus artificial lighting. You know all the sort of suspended atmosphere of that building comes, of course, from us as architects, but comes also from the client. That was our dream.

And by the time you got to the Kansai International Airport in Japan, from 1988 onwards – a building characterised by very advanced computer techniques, because you could only design it by understanding how people flowed and how air flowed – from this came the idea of the organism. Now that sounds as if it is a new idea in your work, the building as a living organism, and almost looking like one as well.

Yes, it's true. When you work with such an extreme situation, like a seismic area in the middle of the sea, and in the man-made land, then engineering, architecture, comes together. I mean that building got to be light to be seismically correct.

Everybody says that it looks like a dinosaur skeleton, but the point is that it's not because you thought that was an amusing shape. That was how the logic of the flow of air and the movement of passengers dictated the shape.

Absolutely, that's what I wanted to say. As an architect you work on mathematics, you work on geometry, you work on inspiration, and fantasy, and imagination. But in the end the shape of that building is not like a dinosaur because we wanted to copy nature; we were just making in a much more humble way, the same job nature is doing – we were just building something very flexible and very light.

Do you get a satisfaction from the fact that when you produce a building like that which works, that the shapes do relate very closely to the deep shapes and structures of nature?

Yes, it is a kind of surprise in some way. It's surprising. But it's never something you think about before. Actually, you have to stay away from it. I mean a dinosaur is a dinosaur, and an airport is an airport! You have to be careful about not mixing up.

Metaphors are very dangerous sometimes, so you never do it that way. You don't build Beaubourg by saying 'Now I make a ship in the middle of the city'! Then everybody says it looks like a ship, or like a spaceship. That's not where you start from.

When you have a commission, how do you start thinking about a building?

That's a good point. First, I never start a job without spending days, maybe sometimes weeks, wandering around. I don't remember one single job, even when they are so far away, that I started to work on without trying to understand the place, and to listen. Place talks, you just have to shut up and listen. And you know one thing you can be very wrong about in architecture is the scale of a building. Scale. As an artist, when you make a sculpture you are working on the real size, but as an architect you have to think about what the building will look like when it will be built in the right scale. If you are standing in the middle of Manhattan – for example, we are working now on the *New York Times* headquarters in Times Square – you have to stand there and you have to think about this tower right there, and you have to project like in an imaginary movie. You have to project that there. Otherwise you may be wrong in scale.

But this preliminary activity, sketching, absorbing, takes a long time. I think one of the words you use is 'assimilating'. What are you assimilating?

You try to understand everything from the place. The greatest compliment I can hope to get in a building is when people say 'It's like this building has been there since ever', like a presence that is natural, you know. This is very important. And this is not something you can make by not understanding the place.

Have you ever had a blinding flash, where the first sketch of a building turns out to be very close to what the building finally is?

It happens quite often. Not because you have a sort of attitude of the genius; it's not like that, because architecture is a passion game, you need really to build things. But sometimes among the sketch you do, there are things that are seminal, and they remain the scheme. When we started working on the *New York Times*, one of the first flashes was about the building being atmospheric, a building that takes the colour of the city. You know very well, one of the most beautiful things about Manhattan is that it changes colour, the city changes. After a shower, everything is bluish, and in a sunny evening everything becomes red, and this capacity of a city to take the colour of the weather is a fantastic thing. So one of the first sketches was really to use a ceramic material that can capture that changing quality of the weather and the colour; and that was one of the first sketches that actually remained, through the schematic design, through the detailed design, and then eventually the working drawings.

You've mentioned your collaborators. Is it a sort of dialectic process; to what extent are they solving problems, or are they offering you solutions?

Of course, it's not at all like the master coming back, and putting on the table the great idea. Architecture is really like a circular process, it's a very crafted process. We craft in the office many, many models. We do. And, of course, we work on computers. But it's like a circular process. You go from detail to general, from general to detail, and you go from silent personal work to teamwork. I actually very much like the teamwork because this is the most beautiful thing, the teamwork. After a while you don't even understand who did what, who got the idea. And this is great, when you don't even wonder who got the idea! It doesn't matter; it's the team. In a good team, you have to establish a very simple rule – everybody is the best – and then you just fight, and you discuss, and you tell the truth to everybody. And if everybody brings ideas, of course, like an orchestra you need the director somewhere, you need to bring all the forces to the same final aim. But it's not at all like the director making the creative work and the other ones making the practical work – this is not true at all.

Have you ever realised in the middle of a building that you are going down a blind alley and that you are pursuing a solution which is not going to be a solution?

Of course. Then you change direction, and you stop and you

come back and you start again. I mean absolutely, this is absolutely true, and you have to have that capacity not to fall in love. You know, this is a very important discussion about intelligence. Intelligence may be light or heavy. If you have a heavy intelligence, then you don't have the capacity to stop and to come back; but if you have a light intelligence, that means that you are permeable to critics, you understand people. It's not because you are ready to compromise, it's because you just understand argument. And then the light intelligence has the capacity to stop and to come back.

And I want you to complete the sentence – you said 'You must not fall in love.' I suppose you were going to say 'You must not fall in love with a particular solution'?

Exactly, you have to be passionate, that's for sure. Architecture is about passion. Passion, it's about passionate world. But you have to have enough lucidity in the passion to understand when something is wrong, so you cannot fall in love with a specific solution – then you never come back. You need the lucidity from time to time to look and to say, 'No, that's wrong! That's wrong, you have to come back.'

You also said that just at the time when you think you've got the right solution, that is the time when you need to pause and think very hard whether it is the right solution.

Of course you do that. You also understand, John, that architecture is about practical things, like going on site, building. And, you know, this is what is difficult for architects. If you write a piece that I'm not happy about, then you rewrite. If you write a piece of music and you are not happy, well, you recompose. But if you are not happy about architecture when it's finished – it's finished. You have no way to go back.

Surgeons bury their mistakes and architects cover them with ivy!

Exactly. So you should better be careful not to make any mistake. But you have to stay away from the perfectionists, because perfection is not possible. There is a moment when you have to come down to building, to construction. So there is a moment when you have to stop, unfortunately, and even by suffering you have to do it. This is one of the tragedies of architecture – there is a moment of no return, and there you have to go ahead.

Were you very disappointed not to get the commission for Ground Zero, Twin Towers in New York?

No, we are doing so many works in New York, you know. And also, honestly, I think Ground Zero is an impossible job, and so I never thought we should even try. The only thing I can say about Ground Zero is that it is a place of such tragedy that I said that the architect for that job should be today a young boy, five years old, still feeding at the school of innocence – because you need time. In a place of such tragedy you should not rush to do anything, you fall easily into the rhetoric and into the symbolism. And in such a kind of tragedy, you have to accept that you may show energy not necessarily by building there, exactly there.

Have you ever made a building that perfectly satisfied you?

John, I think the day I will make a building that perfectly satisfies me I will stop working. I will stop doing new things, because it must be such beautiful impression, and feeling that you have to stop. So, no, I don't think, I never did that.

But do you have a building of your own which you are particularly fond of, which you think solved certain problems?

Well, of course. The truth is that you love all those buildings, you love all because they are all children, and you love them. I'm normally trapped in the building, you know. Here in Paris I work and I live very close to Beaubourg, and in some way I'm a little Quasimodo of Beaubourg! I almost live in Beaubourg, you know, and every time Richard comes to Paris we go to Beaubourg, we go there to have lunch. Tomorrow is a Saturday, I will go there with my family.

And do you notice things that annoy you?

Yes, sure, and I keep making notes, and then I send my friends there little notes – 'That corner is not clean' – so you never lose touch with the project. You stay in love with all those little, big, small children around the world. The truth is that you especially love and give love to the ones that are young – very young, or they are still growing – but otherwise it's very difficult to say which one is your preferred.

And what do you do when you get architect's block, when you're looking at a problem and you think, I don't know how to get out of this?

Yes, normally when you have a blockage, you change the scale, you know. And funnily enough, I have good friends in musicians or writers – Mario Vargas Llosa is a good friend, and Luciano Berio was talking about the same thing – you change the scale, you go on a different scale. For example, you leave for a while that problem there and you start to talk and to work and to detail something there, or there. And then sometimes by a little miracle, you come back, and suddenly you know. But also, in some way a creative process is a very funny one. Sometimes when you are blocked you have to accept to suffer, you just have to watch in the dark. And you watch in the dark for a kind of observation, and then after a while, like when you're entering in the dark room, you start to see more, because the eyes get adapted. So you start to see. So sometimes you have to accept the state of anxiety, and then sometimes something happens.

And do you get upset by it, when it happens?

Yes, but more than upset, it's a kind of suffering. You suffer because you don't feel that everything goes well. But the only thing you should never do is to make a compromise and to find short circuits. You have to accept. And then normally what you do, you change the topic, you change a scale, you change angle, on the same job, and then you come back.

MICHAL ROVNER

I'm very specific in my work, which appears to be very non-specific

It's the people that mesmerise you, continuous lines of people, trudging endlessly, hopelessly perhaps, through a bleak, bare landscape. The four walls of a gallery room are covered with this image of humanity walking to . . . what? Well, this is only one of the abiding images created by the artist Michal Rovner. Her mainly video installations at the Israeli Pavilion were widely hailed as one of the highlights of the 2003 Venice Biennale, and they included a series of oval forms like scientists' Petri dishes, in which human figures grouped and regrouped as if themselves the subject of scientific experimentation. Michal Rovner is Israeli by birth, but works in New York. Her constant journeying across the Atlantic, gathering her material in Europe and Israel but creating it in New York, gives her a bi-cultural dimension that she regards as essential to her creativity. She makes her effects through multiple processing of the basic images – for example, starting with the Polaroid frame of an event or place on location, reshooting that frame in the laboratory, processing that reshot frame, often adding colours. At the end, Rovner has created an image several degrees removed from the actual reality she started with, yet retaining a haunting familiarity with it. She quotes Giacometti approvingly: 'Has the artist erased enough data?' And she doesn't only study people. The way birds swarm and turn in flocks, swimmers floating in the Dead Sea, or an unflinching study of an isolated tin house in the desert – all these have come under Michal Rovner's intense, laser-like scrutiny.

You're not a photographer by training, you began life as a dancer.

I began life as a baby, actually. At some point, yes, I was a dancer, for a few years.

Was that important to you?

It was very important to me. I witnessed my ambition for the first time.

And you were surprised by it?

I was. I was willing to do a lot for it, as a huge effort that I was willing to take. I had that purpose that I believed in, because I was never a good student in school or that kind of external evaluation or recognition; at that point it never was important for me. But in terms of the ambition, it was more an inner stage that I placed myself.

But dancing itself wasn't sufficiently interesting to keep you involved?

Maybe I would have probably kept dancing for longer, except I had to go to the army, because I am an Israeli.

Still, if you'd been really interested in dancing, you would have gone back to it after the army, wouldn't you?

Probably. But it's always some kind of a thread, and when you cut it, sometimes in a new unit of time, you lose something of that process. So I began a new process.

Then, in 1977, when you were just twenty-eight, you started photographing your own farmhouse very intensively, almost making it look like a human being, like a face. What drove you to do that?

It started after a period of nearly two years, where I completely lost interest in taking pictures. And that object, item, you know it was for me so reduced and so dense at the same time, it contained so much for me, that I didn't even want to verbalise exactly what it was. But I just knew it. And later on, the actual house that I did go back to take pictures of again and again was another one, which was on the road somewhere in the desert.

This is a deserted Bedouin house?

I don't know how deserted it was but definitely it did not look like it was in any interaction with any person. And from the angle that I saw it from the first time, it had no doors, no windows, and it did look very much like an archetypal house, almost like the idea of a house that you would find in a dictionary, the most basic form of it. And at the same time it had a great enigma because there were no doors, no windows, so it looked very sealed.

And it was in the middle of absolutely nothing?

Nothing, yeah, nothing. For me it's a very satisfying landscape; if I would be given that landscape, I would say that my plate is full rather than empty. But somebody else could call it nothing.

And you studied both these houses. In the case of your own house, of course, it had light coming out of windows, light coming out of doors, it looks like an animated face. In the case of the Bedouin house it has none of these things, just floats mysteriously in this extraordinary blank, or, as you say, inhabited landscape. What did you learn from this intensive process of looking at these two houses?

I don't think I tried to learn anything about that house first of all; and there is something important here to say. When you're bringing in subject matter, the subject matter is never the item for me, talking about birds or people or a house. It is more that kind of action of going back to something and re-examining it. It is that intense look at something, it is that kind of monogamy, if you would say, in selecting something to be occupied with for a very long time. To me that is the way I work. I understood from that point that this is the way I would be working. And also I find it a very important journey, no matter what the subject matter is.

Is that a kind of obsessive look? It has to be. If you are photographing, as you were, that Bedouin house over the period of two years, it's certainly single-minded. The question is, is it obsessive as well? And even if it's obsessive does that matter?

I don't think it's obsessive because it's my will, it's not some kind of force that is dominating you. It is a very intense mode of operation. It is doing something unstoppably, that you don't feel you should be reasonable and stop with this house, and move to another house or move to another person. And that question of being reasonable about something and how much time is enough to be dealing with something until it's enough, and when do you know that you've reached that point? And Bedouins would come riding on horses, they would look at me and they would say '*majnuna*', which means in Arabic 'the crazy, crazy'! They said I was a crazy woman. That was so interesting for me that there was no way where I could relay my viewpoint over it, my reality to them. We had such different realities in the same place.

In fact, did you ever try to have a conversation with them to explain what you were doing? Did it really not matter that you couldn't communicate what you were doing?

I tried even just for my own safety. I came with a camera, I did look like a strange detective, and I said to them, 'You know, I keep taking pictures, I keep looking at this house because did you notice, when you come here, that every time it looks different?' And they said, 'What do you mean?' And I said, 'Look at the shadow now and if you come in the afternoon it won't be here, and then it would get flat. And then suddenly it would blend with the sky. But in the morning it will come out again. And it's completely sealed!' And they said, 'No, there is a door on the other side,' and I said, 'Yes, but I'm not looking at the other side! That other side doesn't exist for me because I have selected it out!'

And did the Bedouin understand that the house looked different at different times of day and in different seasons of the year, or was this not part of their terms of reference?

No, it was not in their vocabulary at all, you know, my, my action. I think they just got used to me.

Now your own farm is also in a fairly bare part of the country – I think it's called the valley of Ayalon.

I wished it would be more bare.

You want it even more bare.

I wished it would be more.

So what does the desert, what does the bareness do to and for you?

I always find that there is a lot of unnecessary details going on, everywhere. You know I am looking always to a situation where I can either start with nothing or concentrate on something better. It could be noise-wise, it could be visually-wise, where I'm really trying to get to something very basic without too much stuff around.

You strip away what you start with to something far more basic and fundamental?

Yes, but it could be doing that with a lot of items sometimes. I use a lot of variables to do that.

Just before we get there, say something about this crucial time in your life when you came to New York. You were buying books for the photographic organisation you founded, and you fell in love with the place, not in the way that most people do but in a much deeper way than that. What was it about New York that grabbed you?

That it was different than Israel. And don't think I don't like Israel either! But it was a very intense place. I like intense things. It was the opposite of the desert for me. I realise that it's a place that does like ambition and does like people's dreams; it is a place that people stand out rather than wanting them to blend in with the group.

And was that what you felt existed in Israel?

It was a very amplified place, it had a lot of energy. But I wouldn't say that I fell in love with New York. I came to New York because one day I was sitting on my back stairs in the farmhouse looking at the field, and I had an image of myself in New York doing very large objects on very large buildings. And together with the film *Taxi Driver* which I adored at that point, and a marriage that was falling apart, is why I came to New York!

But of course, you never left Israel, did you? You have this twin-centre life; you specifically said that you had to leave Israel to become an artist, but you go there to collect a lot of the material for your work.

I remember that point in time where I felt I should make a decision, and I said I am living here for so many years, I am actually having my centre of my life in New York. And then I sort of looked back at Israel with some kind of sentiments, some kind of longing, and there after a few minutes of going downhill emotion-wise, I said to myself, 'Wait a minute, why do I have to make this decision like this? Why do I have to decide this or that? I do have both places. I might have other places in my life.' At that point I decided that I will keep more places to my map, instead of excluding one over the other.

Yes, because you shoot your videos sometimes in Romania and sometimes in Russia. But one question occurs to me: I'm not aware that you have ever done any work, whether of your photoprints or videos, in and about American subjects. Is that right?

I don't think my work is about Israeli subjects either, and in fact there is a very good example of my work hanging over here in New York at the Chase Manhattan Bank. The footage, I filmed people, anonymous people from the window of my loft in New York as they were walking, crossing the street. And then I filmed people who I brought especially to the landscape, in the desert in Israel in the summertime. So there was that act of creating a thread of those two realities that were very, very different.

But overwhelmingly you either find images, or you place the images in Israel, Romania, Russia.

But I did a lot of work in New York also when I filmed the

television news, at the time of the war in the Gulf, and to me that kind of televised image is very much a part of the landscape of being here.

That's a comment on living in the United States.

I think so, the televised image is something that you live with, that is very much your inner space, your landscape.

I'd like you to say something about how you made that series, which was during Gulf War One. You were here, your family were in Israel, in considerable danger, of course. And then you started photographing the images of the war on the television screen. Briefly describe what the process was, from photographing the images to the finished result.

You know, I'm using different processes, whatever comes to hand, and it's never systematic, and it's not really about that either. The one thing why people would talk about the fact that I rephotograph something, there is a strategy of removing something away from its identity, its locality, or specificness. And that kind of desire to record and erase at the same time, that I would say is a consistent manner. But in terms of the war in the Gulf, in terms of the process, what was interesting for me is that in the same moment where I was watching how a building or a place would be bombed, at the same moment I would take a Polaroid of it. It was on television then, falling apart, deteriorating; I was watching it as it fell apart, as it became from some kind of a structure to a pile of dust. And at the same time, in my Polaroid, it became from a white surface with no image, to something which contained an image. So that was to me interesting process-wise.

What seems to be interesting is the degree of distance that you achieve from the original image to the image which you then present to the viewing world – there are sometimes four processes, maybe five or six – and this as a position adopted by an artist towards reality seems to me to be terribly interesting.

You're right.

So this process: anybody can do it, but what the process represents is terribly important.

You're right, and I think the key word that you use is that aspect of distance, that desire to look at something from a distance rather, without being cold about it or without being careless or without necessarily feeling that it cannot get to you or you c[illegible] disclaim responsibility for it. But seeing it from a distance, ju[illegible] maybe, get a better view of it.

Well, I think that's absolutely right, because you have one pa[illegible] print of a soldier holding up his hands and surrendering. You don't kn[illegible] what nation the soldier is, you don't really know where it is, but that image of the hands held high in surrender is the universal experience of everybody who has surrendered in a war. So you're right, it absolutely is not a cold image, and I suppose that's the interesting thing about your work. By taking things out of it, as it were taking the specificity out of it, you make it universal. Just as an Israeli citizen, have people ever said that your view, your detached view, is rather shocking, almost unpatriotic?

No, I never had that. A few times some artists said that the work is not political enough, and you know then comes the question, what is political? And I think if you're communicating something to people, it is impossible actually to cut off the set of associations that one would have at this time. And even if you present something, for instance, a Richard Serra work, a sculpture, that kind of tilted curve, where if you stand next to it, you could talk about some kind of metaphysical experience. But someone else could talk about what force it has as a political statement; there always is that possible aspect. Just my work is, maybe, not as verbal as some people would like it to be.

Well, it's certainly not neutral, and it seems to me that it's not reaching for a conventional idea. Some people might produce anti-war images, and the message would be 'all war is dreadful'. You're certainly not doing that. I think you are showing, by being universal, how painful the experience of war is.

I think I'm not presenting some kind of conclusion to the people I'm showing my work to. I'm rather inviting them to come in and experience something, which hopefully would present some questions to them, questions about their own viewpoint or their own stand. Even the names that I had for my installation at Venice was, by itself, a question. You know *Against Order* question mark; *Against this Order* question mark. It's something that has to do with humanity that is displayed there, and the whole question of when is order less humanistic than you would like it to be? Or when this order threatens humanity or to what degree you would like to participate in that? I'm not an illustrator!

Are you a different person when you're in Israel? Are you a different artist when you're in Israel from when you are working in New York?

I think I recognise myself as the same person, going from place to place. I appear different, you know, outside. I translate myself when I come to America, language-wise and, you know, sometimes I would behave differently. But inside me the experience is not very different, except I do relate to things in Israel different than to things in America.

What is your routine, when you are on your farm in Israel?

My work routine there or here or everywhere is that I work all the time. My work routine is that I work almost all the time; it means every day, it means seven days a week, even if there is a holiday or whatever.

What time do you get up, though?

Six o'clock in the morning.

Whether you're in Israel or in New York?

About, yes.

Which do you prefer? Do you feel happier when you wake up at six o'clock in the desert?

I definitely like to wake up in the field, of course, than to wake up on the seventh floor of a building. I never like to be high anyway. I always like to be close to the ground, to the earth, I always like to touch the earth. I like to smell it. I like to see people creating something that is very real, has a very real dimension, when I wake up in the morning.

So what are the compensations in New York when you don't have any of those satisfactions?

You know the first class that I had in the Academy of Art in Israel, the professor walked in, Professor Ormer who is now the Director of Television. He walked in with a very severe face, he stood by the podium and said, 'The biggest fear of an artist is to be misinterpreted, and that the work will be shown in the wrong context.' There was a long pause, and he said it in English, in Jerusalem. And I had no idea that there was anything like fear connected with art at this point. And he was quoting Mark Rothko. And later on I understood how important it is really for an artist to be shown in the right context, to have your work being taken seriously, to have your work being looked at with respect. That this was why I needed New York, to find a house, a place, for my work, which I believed in already then. I believed that I have something to say that I would like it to be kept in a serious environment.

And this is also where your early ambition has shown itself, when it comes to getting recognition for yourself as an artist.

I think we all want to get recognition for what we do. I think it's a healthy desire, because we are always communicating, you're always in dialogue with other people. And I definitely am not that person that would be happy to know that I'm dying and somebody will discover my work under my bed and one day they will say, 'Oh, this was dismissed!' You know, I don't want to be dismissed. I would like to interact while I'm here, and to use all that potential to say more in a larger way and to use all I can have, and all I can use, to make it better.

There are two big works which I want to say something about. One is called Time Left *where apparent generations of silhouetted matchstick people shuffle off round and round in an endless circuit on the walls of the room. Some people say this is about the holocaust, or just a dance of death, or the journey through life. I'm certainly not going to ask you what your interpretation is. But I would be interested to know where the idea for something like this came from.*

It's very hard to detect where the idea came from. This idea just showed up, you know, but I was looking to the direction of something like that. I went to Russia. I said I'd like to hire fifty people in the age of fifty; I would like them to come tomorrow morning to that hill, and I'll be there at this time. And while I was on the way, I started to think what I'm going to do with all these fifty people!

You didn't know beforehand?

Not for sure. I had sketches, I had ideas, not so clearly, but I knew that I would know what to do with it once I have it.

When you say sketches, do you mean sketches that you had drawn out, a storyboard?

Yes, I had a little notebook, the size of a hand, and I started to draw some ideas that I would like to collect. And I knew once the reality that was going to appear there. While, you know, in the course of the work there will be more and more ideas coming. But already on the way in the car, I was thinking about something that has to do with the group dynamic. And what is the key element that you would describe as the group, the group act that would differentiate between the individual from a group, and it would be probably the gesture of giving hands to each other.

Because they hold one another these people, don't they?

They did hold hands, all of them. And then it all came one after the other, very fast, the whole idea developed as I would like it to be; lines and lines and lines of people just walking endlessly. And then I said, 'I would like to create a wallpaper like that.' And then I would like it to be like a wallpaper, like a tapestry you know, but then I wanted it also to move. And then I said, 'I would actually like it to move endlessly.' And you know, from that point on, it was just to make it happen.

Did you know all that before you started shooting, or did you discover that when you were shooting?

No, I knew that on the way to the shooting. I decided it. But the one decision that came up later on, after I was shooting, was that I would go to another place and do the same thing, and then go to another place and do the same thing, with another group of people.

So that in the finished product you would not be able to tell the difference between one location and another?

Yes, and maybe it's all from one location. It really doesn't matter. For me at that point in time – and I don't think that I need that any more now – there was something about collecting different materials from different places and putting it into a similar situation, that you would not be able to track down. And the common denominator would take over what separates these from those.

So the work in the laboratory afterwards was, in the case of Time Left, *realising your vision of the piece?*

The work was in an editing room and while projecting it, the one other very important stage was that I've decided to transfer it to a scale of a text. They could have stayed large, they could have had faces, there could have been more persona there, in each one of the images, each one of the figures. Already they had a lot of weight, you know, because of their age and what they went through in life. But I wanted to reduce it to a scale of a text, I wanted it to appear like a text.

Yes, each figure was only a matter of a few inches high.

Yes, and that's in some kind of a subtext. The text is a subtext of my work, has been for a while. You know also with that work *Data*, there is that item of scripts, screening scripts.

Humanity and writing, the human body and the written form, thinking and expression – it's as fundamental as that?

And the fact that there is that kind of text that repeats and repeats itself. You know there is a movement going on but there is a great deal of sense of repetition also.

Are you in danger of giving the impression that you are dehumanising these people?

I was asked that; it's definitely a viewpoint that one could choose, or could have, you know. Whatever you think the work is, you know: be my guest! I think that when you talk about dehumanisation and humanisation, there is a tremendously great concern going on for details, for information. People are so much busy, and I would use that word 'obsessed' with information and data, to the degree that they lose the human connection to something, if you talk about that. And they stay with all that kind of listing and listing, and all that filing system going on of the specificness.

That's a central paradox of your work: that the more you take away from the specific nature of the object, the more you make us aware that they're not just uniform stick people, they are individuals.

I suppose so. Something like this, the less you see the more you see, if you wish to say.

Yes. But you clearly get a huge satisfaction from this. We've talked about distancing, we've talked about objectivity, we've talked about stripping away detail, and this is clearly and absolutely a central part of your view of life.

It is that you get to see something else. You never give up something as long as your eyes are open, and you are looking; your visibility is not going to be taken away from you, and you just see something else. You just get to see another layer of it. It's just shifting from one layer to another layer.

Are you an optimist or a pessimist as a person?

You know I'm not there, I'm neither/nor. I'm very interested to be alive, and I'm very curious about it, and I'm very glad that I'm able to create and to communicate something, and hope that it would make a good effect, would make something good. But I don't have that built-in conclusion that things are going to go wrong or they are going to go right. I think that it's probably both. But I think that things are very fragile, life is very fragile. In a way, to be optimistic or pessimistic is to take a stand of believing in something without making sure that it would be OK.

You're prepared to take the risk that it will be one or the other?

No, I rather not be optimistic and sit with my leg up and not do anything about something, or be pessimistic and say 'It's going to all go to hell anyway.' I have to say, in my work I would say, 'Be aware, it's fragile, think about it, let's look at it again.'

Are you lonely as an artist?

You mean as an artist or as a person?

Well, as a person who is an artist.

I'm alone. I don't know if I'm lonely. I am single, you know, I'm a single person, I'm a single person.

Yes, but that doesn't define whether a person is lonely or not, either way.

I don't feel lonely. I feel alone but how do you know that when you say you are sad or I'm sad, we talk about the same thing? After all, we cannot even go and look inside. It's a little bit like if I would have a matchbox and I would tell you I have a bug inside, and you'll say you have a bug, and how do we know that? And there is that question of reality, what do you see and what do I see? And that is something that to me is always very fascinating and I've been aware of it from very early on: that I might experience something else entirely than someone who stands next to me.

That would be a definition of isolation or loneliness. I mean it's neither good nor bad. And we're not supposed to be lonely in this sociable world.

But I do feel aloneness; aloneness, I feel a lot of the time.

Is that a good or a bad thing for your work?

It is very necessary, it's completely necessary. I create a situation of that even. You know I could have immersed myself with a lot of people all the time. In fact, I'm doing a very major effort to keep myself isolated, so that I can be fully in those spaces from which I'm coming up with this work. I don't need to experience it fully, I don't want to dilute it with somebody else's experience or reality, but sometimes I need that reality or experience. For vacation, I went to a monastery of silent nuns, rather than to go to the Bahamas, to be on the beach with a lot of people! You see that's the choice I would make.

In your last exhibition, at the Venice Biennale, there's another very interesting work of these scientific Petri dishes, and you're looking down on them and you see figures and groups of figures forming and re-forming. Clearly putting human beings in scientific dishes invites the idea that humanity is being experimented with, or humanity's experimenting with itself. Now, clearly some sense about humanity and experimentation must have driven this.

I think it has to do for me with an intense look at something, like a scientist would look at something. It is an intense look to maybe examine it or to be able to read something, by looking at it again and again, read something about its mode of operation, you would say. Reality for me always has been material that I'm using and inspired by. There's a great concern going on with Petri dishes, with culture dishes. There is biotechnology, there is biological weapons, all these new diseases – SARS and AIDS – and people are constantly even examining their own body structure by going to all these various doctors to see what's going on, germs and so on. But that act of putting something in those familiar dishes in which one would examine something, and offer a look from above, from high above, from a distance, at humanity, or group dynamic, that is really what the work is about. Of course it has those other links, references and many, many possible associations, but it is another coherent event staged with my work, except it's just a very concentrated space that I created which is very small and dense, but all the elements are there. You know, there is the movement but there is no narrative, there is no development, there is no advancement. And those various situations which offer what would look like some kind of a pattern that you could also read, like some kind of a text that you might want to decipher or not.

You said once, 'The ambiguity of my work is not a lack of opinion.' Does that give us an idea of the tension between the rationality of your basic understanding but then the distance that you place between your rationality and the final work that you present to the audience?

It is ambiguous to the degree that it is not giving specific details or conclusion or direction of how one should read it. But it is at the same time a text you could say that is placing itself, not all over the place, in such confined paradigms; and there's quite a stretch that I would ask someone to do with their viewpoint. All I'm offering is another look at something, another viewpoint at something. But that thing is not just anything; it is very, very carefully chosen, it is very, very worked out, there is a very great degree of care and time and labour put into a very specific degree of density – the scale of it, the size of it, the luminosity of it, the pacing of it. I'm very specific in my work, which appears to be very non-specific.

And you want us, the viewers, to read it, because you use the word 'text' a lot, and to view it in such a way that the importance of the detail comes out.

But those questions that you ask would not come through when you're talking about abstract art. You would not ask, you would not necessarily come up so much with that reference about tension, the tension between the starting point of my work, which is reality. There was a point in time, in reality, that on a certain day and time, very specific people were taken to a specific place and were giving some kind of orders; and I've used a certain camera with a certain film, and there was a name to the cameraman even. There was a name to the kind of water I was drinking. I was wearing very specific clothes, because I'm a very specific, actually, person always. You know, I did want not to have any eggs in my sandwich at the day, like always I would never eat eggs! And I wanted the bread to be dark and not white, and many, many details going on. I did not want to have larger Petri dishes and the very generic ones. I did not want to have two lamps in the room, I did not want to have regular light, I wanted to have very generic floors and light and so on. But why is the work not specific enough? Because it doesn't give you all those details about the reality, about the names of the people. Why do you need all of that, actually?

Oh, I'm not saying that it's not specific enough, I'm trying to tease out the nature of the process.

It is just as specific as it needs to be, because in fact there is something underneath it all, in the core of all of it, that does not need so many details, and does not need all these specifics. And that is actually much simpler than it appears to be. Not to say that it doesn't ask you a question either, but it's simpler.

BILL VIOLA

You just did not make works of art for Christian saints. I mean this was very uncool

At first glance the image look motionless. It's on a high-definition plasma screen, of course, but the stillness of the face or the group or the surface of the water is visually familiar. Then, as you look, the image moves fractionally, very, very slowly, hypnotically. And the faces break into the deepest of emotions, the groups create a kind of balletic interplay between the individuals. The water is disrupted by bodies plunging in or triumphantly emerging. You continue looking as each incremental movement creates its own point of drama, not as an isolated moment, but as a continuum of experience.

Is that a slowed-down film or a moving image? Neither, it's a video piece by the American artist, Bill Viola. There's no one quite like him. One critic has called him the Rembrandt of video art, another has credited him with reinventing the language of art no less. Others, though, have queried whether Viola, a Californian devoted to Buddhism, Sufism, and Christian Mysticism, offers more than what has been called 'vacant exaltation' and 'fast food spirituality'.

Viola has reached this position at the age of only fifty-one. He has more than a hundred works behind him. The first work that really brought him wide acclaim in Britain was the *Nantes Triptych* of 1992 – three large side-by-side screens, showing a woman in labour, a man submerged in water and the face of the artist's mother as she lay dying. The shock of his parent's death wrenched Viola's work on to a new level of intensity and personal awareness, and that piece is in Tate Modern. In 1996 he created a single work for Durham Cathedral, where a naked human form appears from the depths of the water, breaks surface, draws in breath and then sinks back. Typically for England, more fuss was made about the nakedness of the body than about the spiritual significance of the image.

By now, Viola was well into the exploration of themes of spiritual and universal experience. In 2001, his show at the D'Offay Gallery, in London's West End, revealed works of extraordinary emotional range, from the quietism of *Catherine's Room* to the visual and aural intensity of *Five Angels for the Millennium*. There, five bodies erupt from the depths of the water. Ah, water – a running obsessive theme, explained apparently by the artist's so-near death from drowning as a young boy. In Berlin in 2002, Viola revealed his most ambitious work yet, *Going Forth by Day*, a projected image cycle in five side-by-side parts, each lasting thirty-five minutes and running simultaneously. The five parts deal with:

Fire Birth, suggesting the beginning and the end of the world; the *Path*, an endless journey through life; the *Deluge* when a physical cataclysm overcomes the order of everyday life; the *Voyage*, a parable of death and rebirth; and *First Light*, with a moment of pure ecstatic renewal at its climax. It's Viola's most ambitious work, both as an artist and as a film director.

But let's go back to the beginning. There was no art in your home, so where did the impulse for the visual come from?

Well, I would have to say, I was born with it. The family story that was told to me was, I was sitting with my mother one day when I was just about three years old and she was trying to draw things on a piece of paper for me. And I apparently wrenched the pencil away from her and drew an almost perfect speedboat, with the bow cresting up above the waves, and everybody was astonished and my mother kept this picture. When I got to kindergarten the teacher was already singling out my paintings and drawings to put up in front of the class and on the walls, and pretty much was always an artist in that way in terms of the visual.

And you did drawings ten feet long as a child, didn't you?

I invented this planet that was inhabited by humans and, of course, aliens, I forget the name – oh, yes, it was called 'Klamph'. And I started drawing the landscape of it, in a kind of a horizontal almost oriental scroll-like way, and I kept adding more and more sheets of paper with sticky tape, until I was out at about ten feet. Then I had the great idea, if I do say so myself, to end the landscape on the final sheet and make it identical with the beginning of the landscape on the first sheet and I wrapped them around and put the last piece of tape together.

And that's what you're doing today?

Exactly, except it's really expensive tape!

When did you discover that you had this condition called 'dysgraphia', where I think the brain wants to write words as pictures?

Actually, I only really discovered or deduced that I had that by the fact that our eldest son has been diagnosed with that. I've just seen so many similarities between us and how he's been growing up, that when we were told about this, which I hadn't any idea about, I just saw myself because I remember struggling with trying to put together concepts logically and trying to form ideas in time in a way that was sequential. Even to the extent that when I would go to the movies as an adult with my wife, and being in America most of these films aren't terribly complex, I would have to lean over and go, 'What's going on?' Because I just figured later I'd always watched movies like that. I was being completely carried away by the imagery, you know, and I wasn't focused on what the characters where saying, and I wasn't really able to follow the plot too well.

But as far as you're concerned, there's another aspect of the way your mind works that you've talked of: a lot of your images are based on sound or generated by sound. How does that work?

Well, if you really consider a blind person, part of the training that one goes through when one becomes blind, rather than being congenitally blind, is how to read the world through sound, the remaining active sense. And therefore the cane, which I always thought as a kid was simply something you moved it out in front of you, so that you didn't bump into anything; it is actually a sound-producing device, tap, tap, tap, that creates the awareness of space through echo, and we all know submarines and marine creatures such as dolphins and whales have used this sort of echo location. So, for example, right now in the digital age, I can stand here with these microphones and this digital recorder. I can clap my hands and we can record that, and I would be able to put that sound into a computer, do some acoustic analysis and be able to put together a rough image of the room, simply by the delay at which the various echoes, the wave fronts, came back from the various surfaces in the room. So sound is really space, it's a sense that exists all around us. You hear things behind you that you can't see. And in my mind when I work I really have felt the limitation of the camera and therefore have always recorded simultaneous sound and picture, which you can do with video as opposed to film, it's a part of the same machine, as a way to get this larger field of experience into the recording itself.

But your use of sound is usually very subtle, it's very often the merest background, or just a suggestion. But I suppose that's what you're saying, that the mere suggestion of sound to you produces the intensity of image?

Yes, as long as the sound is not music or dialogue, which it most commonly is in films, basically because they arise from literature. I mean whether they're the actual depiction of a novel or written by some screenplay writer as a new original screenplay, they're still derived from written language. So I've really not been that interested, as you know, in the two major components of films, dialogue – therefore plot – and music. And as long as those more self-conscious elements aren't put in as a way to move the action forward, then what you get is this more passive reception of sound, whereby two microphones in a stereo configuration at right angles to each other can produce a very three-dimensional impression of the sound field, of the cars going on the street, the raindrops hitting the pavement. And they can appear to be at different distances from you and you can really feel immersed in a three-dimensional space, which is what's going on in the gallery. Even though, having said that, there have been, you know, numerous examples of where I actually constructed a soundtrack around an image, using most often some sound that was actually recorded with the image. I see video as an 'image-slash-sound' medium.

One other early experience of a very, very different kind was your near-drowning. Did you nearly drown?

Well, I've kind of replayed that a number of times in my mind. Talking to a trauma physician once in Phoenix Arizona, we were sitting there over dinner, a small group, museum people take you out and there's a couple of other kind of art collector types around; and this guy's kind of looking at me, I felt there was a kind of connection and finally by the time dessert came he leaned over and said, 'Have you had a near-death experience?' And I was just shocked, I thought 'What is this guy trying to come on to me, what's going on here?' And then he proceeded to tell me about people in the emergency room that have basically clinically died and come back and he's seen that a lot and he knows these patients throughout life because some of them he keeps track of. And he knew. And I never really thought about it in those terms. But what happened was, as I found later, it had all the classic elements of that. I was jumping off a raft with my cousin, my uncle was on the raft, and I had one of those inner tubes, those inflatable inner tubes and I'd literally just forgotten to hold on. I jumped in, plunged under and within an instant I was in this completely magical, extraordinary world, of colour, blues and greens. I saw plants sort of wafting in the currents, there were fish, and I was so fascinated and captivated and felt so comfortable. And the feeling I had – I mean as a ten-year-old your emotions are really a major part of your consciousness, so the memories were mostly 'feeling' memories – and I remember this big hand coming up, grabbing me under my stomach and yanking me up; and it was so rude, it was an interruption and terrible feeling, it was disappointing. And then I broke the surface and then I remember spitting, then I started crying and then I became a ten-year-old boy who was terrified. But the feeling is I glimpsed this world that was one of the most beautiful things I've ever seen.

And what was the sound of it?

You know what, gee, that's interesting, I don't seem to really remember the sound of it.

That is peculiar, isn't it, that the most important physical experience that you've had . . .

. . . Didn't really have a sound. And speaking about sound, Peter Sellars, the opera director who is a dear friend of mine, was here and he knew that I was working on this piece and he on his own accord just came to Berlin to be here when it was shown. And, of course, being Peter Sellars he didn't come for the big power dinner after the opening, he came four days early when we were still aligning projectors and doing technical adjustments. And he had this book with him that he was reading, *The Luminous Mind* by Kalu Rinpoche, who is one of the great Tibetan spiritual masters who passed away in 1989. And he read me this passage, I was getting goose bumps, it was a passage of a discussion of the transition through the various levels of the 'Bardo' states, as the deceased is moving on to the next life and the next rebirth. And in this text, the last stage one passes through, pure consciousness, almost dissolving again into the universe to be reconstituted again, that last state is defined by sound and it's the sound of the roaring waterfall. The description of it is that one is at the bottom of a huge waterfall or buried under a mountain and there's this deep roaring sound. Peter was reading this to me standing in my piece, *Going Forth by Day*, at the section where the deluge had just come down (we didn't have the sound on at the beginning), with this huge amount of water pouring out, washing these people away. Right next to it on the right is the *Voyage*, a small house with the deathbed scene going on, with the man, the son and the father and the daughter-in-law, you know. I'd never read this book. I might have heard that sound then, when I nearly drowned, I don't really remember.

So that was your experience. I suppose as a result of that the way in which you've used water, and the very powerful images of bodies in water, whether in The Messenger *in Durham Cathedral, or in* Five Angels *for the Millennium in London in 2001, where there are bodies coming out of the water and then sometimes going back, and in the very first image in* Going Forth, *where it represents both rebirth and death, the question is whether you'd been recreating this experience of near-death drowning in your work in an extraordinarily productive way?*

Yeah, I guess so, that's something I've really been very reticent to pursue. I'm really happy to keep that very intense experience in my life at a very young age, which I consider to be a blessing, obviously, since I'm still around to tell the tale, that's one thing. But nonetheless, just to be able to be given that knowledge, because for all human beings who we are, what we are, knowledge of death is the supreme knowledge, that's why culture exists. That's why all of these great works of art exist. It's those of our kind who have come to the edge of that precipice.

But are you saying, if I hear you right, you deliberately keep this slightly at a distance because you want it to be there as a reservoir of creativity?

I don't want to over-analyse it. You know, I think that's one of the worst things that artists can do and I think that's one of the most critical pitfalls, danger zones in the practice of contemporary art today, in an age where theory has really taken over. The theorists are really driving the research now, which if you look at physics the same thing happens. It's like the experimental physicists versus the theoretical physicists and their relationships oscillate over time. Well, in art practice, we happen to be in a period where the theorists are driving things very strongly, and in a way that is almost antithetical to what works of art are. I mean the presence of theory in an artwork or an artwork as a demonstration of kind of theory to me seems really ass-backwards. You know, I love that quote from Proust where he says, 'A work of art that contains a theory is like an article of clothing on which the price tag has been left!' So I just wanted to keep that separate. But I would certainly agree with you, and I know it's true, but in this piece, *The First Light*, the fifth image of *Going Forth*, it's kind of the end and the beginning of the cycle in a way, but there's a moment in that piece, the rescue scene around the water and the desert. There are four people who are left on the edge of this body of water of unknown dimensions in the desert at the breaking of dawn. You see the whole thirty-five minutes is taken up with this sunrise, which we created with computer-controlled lighting in real time. You see the light coming and gradually they're getting more and more tired after having been up on a rescue operation; there's a woman who stands among them and she is waiting for her son, who will not be coming back; there's an ambulance that's there at the beginning and it leaves without its flashers or sirens on – there's no one left to rescue. And then these people, one by one, get very tired and they fall asleep. And so it's just four sleeping people around this pool of water, in fact becoming the image of the very thing that they were involved with throughout the previous night; that is, they become like dead bodies around the water. And while they sleep, a disturbance appears on the water and this young man's face appears and then his shoulders and chest and body, and he effortlessly glides up out of the water dripping wet and floats up into the sky. When he reaches the sky, the drips coming off his clothing and body falling into this water become rain and a big rainstorm, one of those desert rainstorms that comes in from nowhere, and wakes up the sleeping people who totally missed the event. And then they quickly gather their things and one by one they move off as the sun is rising. Now, the thing that really made me somewhat nervous and that was one of the aspects of working on this piece, is I was very concerned in professional terms as an artist where for the first time in my life, this image of the man rising up was done with wires like in *Crouching Tiger, Hidden Dragon*.

I looked for them but I couldn't see them.

Yeah, well, we erase them digitally. But I realised that I had never in all my work done something that had this degree of fantasy. I did a piece called *Five Angels of the Millennium*, which you mentioned, and those angels are in the weightless void of an underwater pool. And anybody that looks at those images knows that these are actual in a practical sense; literally there's a bunch of guys and they jumped in the water at different times and the camera was orientated in different ways, but it's completely natural. I mean, it doesn't defy any laws of physics that we know. And the same with *The Messenger* in Durham. But this was the first time that I'd used this kind of technique, this technical trick, and I was very concerned about it.

Too artificial?

Yeah. I mean, I think what my impulse was, when the people were sleeping, the four actors that were lying there, we had them stay in position, what I thought I should do would be to have the guy waiting above, and then he would literally just drop into the water, make a big splash and submerge. I would run the whole thing in reverse, which would be again, quote unquote, 'natural'.

Why didn't you do that?

I don't know.

Are you still uncomfortable with it?

No. I've seen it here in Berlin and we did three versions of the digital wire removal and there were some problems we had with the high definition, it was a little unsmooth, it was jumpy and it just didn't look right. Then once we clarified those technical issues, and it was really literally gliding out and the wires were removed perfectly instead of a little bit dubiously, then all of a sudden the whole thing locked in and now I'm very pleased with it.

The imagery, as you spoke about it, the idea of people being asleep when this extraordinary event happens, it recalls the Ascension, the Resurrection? You have strong streaks of Christian Mysticism in you but you don't, I think, ever address the Crucifixion, the Resurrection as such. Now are there elements of that in that particular panel? But do you choose not to go quite that far in expressing and interpreting the Christian experience?

Well, that's a good question. I would say that certainly visually that panel is based on, or was inspired by, I guess is a better word, because I don't sort of believe in this restaging, appropriation kind of approach to things where you reproduce something. There's a painting by an artist who I dearly love, called the Master of the Osservanza, he's a Sienese artist from the fifteenth century. We don't know his name, he did a lot of work in the church of the Osservanza and so that's why he's called that. There's a beautiful, very famous resurrection scene that he did of the soldiers just waking up, bathed in this kind of mystical light that comes from nowhere as Christ is rising up out of the tomb. In this case the lid on the tomb is not ajar, it's closed – even more mysterious – and that early dawn light is breaking, which as a student in university when we were looking at a lot of that imagery, I was so turned off to it that I figured it was sunset, you know. And, of course, obviously it's dawn. There are flowers coming out of the ground, there's fruit on the trees, it's the actual re-appropriation of the pagan fertility rites, which so many Christian rituals and feast days are, and this one being the vernal equinox. That was sort of the visual inspiration and it gave me a lot to work with, thinking about how to sort of stage this thing.

The content was my own, about the flood and the woman losing her child. And so I would have to say that I'd answer your question 'yes and no'. I am very conscious that I am using not only just visual compositional elements that have been apparent and used in Christian art, but also the actual meaning of some of these very important events for Christians. And the way I look at it is that the resurrection happens every spring. And we live through the resurrection every spring, human beings are constantly being reborn; that the resurrection in its more expanded sense and not focused on the very important Church holiday of Easter per se, and the whole story of Jesus Christ per se, is a much larger universal image for mankind. It is the hope of renewal, it is watching nature every winter die and every spring be reborn.

But you're not blotting out the particularity of the Crucifixion, you're just using the experience in a more universal way?

Yeah, I'm really interested in the root structures of experience. Because if you go way, way back, these things are so tied to who we are as human beings; they're almost, at this point, I would have to say, built into the operating system. Whether the Christians acknowledge that there is such a thing as the transmigration of souls, as Pythagoras taught, that there is such a thing as your soul literally goes out of your body and eventually appears in another body. Whether or not you subscribe to what Christians say, there still is this imagery and this iconography and these beliefs in rebirth. And the most powerful thing about the Christian message and the Christian faith for me, what they gave to the world, which other religions have a real hard time with, is they brought the gods, the sacred beings, the divine beings, right down to earth.

Into human form . . .

Right into human form to the point that they give birth like us, and they suffer pain like us, they bleed like us, and they die like us. That was so powerful, that image of the Son of God actually dying a mortal death. And then, of course, you realise the image of the Madonna and Child, a totally benign beautiful image that's given comfort to millions of people around the world, is basically a mother and child. I mean we've all experienced that, we all know what that means, we all know the comfort that's in that image. We all know, unfortunately, there is a large group of people who also know what it means to lose a son. One of the parents' most absolutely worst horrific nightmares you can ever imagine, is to outlive your children. Here's this faith that takes this very universal human element and brings it into the context of sacred.

The irony, if it's irony, is that at art school you hated art history. And then you discovered the Sienese masters. Also, if you'd said at the time to your colleagues and your contemporaries, 'What I'm really interested in is reinterpreting Christian iconography', they would have said, 'You cannot be serious! Christianity; please!' So you're wonderfully traditional and old-fashioned. But did you actually have to start to be brave to do this, or did you just say, 'To hell with it, this is what I'm interested in and this is what I am going to do'?

I think probably the latter. I guess versions of that have happened to me all along, that I have always sort of just gone for it. And the turning point for me in terms of your question was in 1983 when I just got back from Japan, where I really encountered traditional culture, full on, for the first time, and was deeply moved and impressed by it. And someone had mentioned to me I should read St John of the Cross's poetry, and I was in a bookshop, and there was this little thin paperback, *Poems of St John of the Cross*, and I picked it up and I read the introduction, about this man's life and I was just so touched, and I was shaken because it was so much like the experiences that I had had and so deep in a human way for all of us. And I was working on this piece about inside and outside and I had this plan to build this room within a room and very quickly, I mean it was like a flash, it was like the whole piece was there in front of me and I didn't know what to call it. And so just one day, the little voice in my head says, 'Well, just call it what it is.' So I titled it *Room for St John of the Cross*. And in 1983, and probably even now, you just did not make works of art for Christian saints, I mean this was very uncool.

People said that, did they?

Oh yeah, it was written about in the critics; oh yeah, definitely. And then a lot of people who saw it appreciated the work.

Second only to the experience of your own near-drowning, the sight of your mother dying is certainly one of the most important, if not the most important, images in your art. As she was dying, did you hesitate for a moment, saying 'I can't put a video camera on my mother's face,' and yet you did? How did you go through that particular transaction with yourself, or wasn't there one?

It was a necessity for me in a way. I mean, you just feel so helpless. Here's your own mother in this state. She basically woke up one night, in the middle of the night and she had a brain haemorrhage. She woke up with a headache and an hour later she was unconscious and my father called me from Florida and I got on the very next plane. And then you arrive and there she is with tubes and wires and little beeping sounds and little oscilloscopes going on. And it was a cruel irony: the technological world that I've devoted my life to is now not only keeping my mother alive but keeping her from me, because I'm not the expert, you know. All families feel that when they go into hospitals these days. It's like you are a complete lay person and these experts know what they're doing and so you can't really administer to your own parent and so you end up holding hands a lot, whispering in their ear and stroking their head and stuff, which we all did. You know, there's a way that you were kind of separate from her. So I guess the helplessness of the whole situation over a period of time, and it was three months from the time that she had her haemorrhage to when she passed away, and she was in a complete coma, you couldn't talk to her. And video for me by that time, 1990, had become my own lifeline to the world. I just felt that I had to do something, I was going nuts. And I asked my dad if I could: 'Would you mind if I . . .?'

What did he say?

He said: 'No, no; that's OK', luckily. He was pretty sensitive. And for me there was an image in front of me for the first time in my life that I could not understand, I could not accept, I could not grasp. It was like the forbidden image, the worst image that you could possibly imagine and I just had to not run away from that image or close my eyes to that image, but go right through that image. So I took out the camera and I made actually very few video recordings: a couple of days when she was about three weeks before the end; and then a very short little session a week before the end. And then the last image which is at the very end of *Nantes Triptych*, where you're in close-up on the face and you don't see the light in the eyes any more. It was taken late in the afternoon of the day she passed away, she passed away at six o'clock the next morning.

Now when you did this, you've explained why you did it, but did you think it was going to become part of a work of art?

Oh no, absolutely not.

This was a purely personal reaction: 'This is me, I use the video and I have to try and interpret this event with my chosen instrument of expression.'

This is, 'I'm drowning and if I don't hold on to some line I'm going to go under.' So that was absolute necessity and I just went back home after that horrific event after the funeral and just took those tapes, it was like the little box of ashes, I just put them in a little place on my shelf.

So how many years later did you say, 'That's going to be part of a video'?

Well, that was actually very soon. What happened was, at the end of 1987 I got a grant from German Television to make a film video. What I proposed was to do a recording of the desert in various states and that I would go out to the desert for six months, instead of the usual two weeks or three weeks which I had been doing for years. I really wanted to see what would happen if you got beyond that taking, taking, taking that you always feel with cameras. I said, 'What would happen if I lived in the image and how would I change over the course of time, in the process of spending six months out there?' What happened was, I met this massive writer's block half of the way in and I just could not pick up a camera. It seemed ludicrous. I was in the most incredible spiritually awe-inspiring landscape, one of the best on the planet, the American South-West. And there I was with this little tiny tube, with a little hole in it, that every time I put it up to my eye, it was almost painful, it was cutting out all the good stuff, it was ridiculous. And then from that point on I went into this downward spiral of starting and stopping. And I just was going down these blind alleys for a year and a half and then finally the whole thing dried up. And for the first time in my life the whole creative force that had carried me so far, starting with the kindergarten teacher who put up little Billy's drawing and nobody else's, all of a sudden I didn't have anything left. It was truly frightening and I was just completely depressed and immobilised. And that's when the phone call came from my dad: 'Mom's sick, get on the plane.' And I flew there and I had a hundred and eighty-five tapes at that point, twenty minutes long, each of raw material, sitting on my shelf from the desert. And I finally got back home after the funeral, and waiting for me is this letter: 'We are going to request that you send back the money, unless we have a rough cut on the producer's desk in six weeks.' And I was like, 'Oh man, you know, we have to give back the money,' and we didn't really have the money but, 'we will have to give it back somehow.' I just couldn't handle it. So finally my wife Kira said, 'No, we have to do something.' And the last place I wanted to go was the editing room and I forced myself to go in there and I pulled out all this desert footage. And then like a ton of bricks it hit me, what I was really working on. I went to the shelf, pulled those other images off, put them in the machine and sat with one hand up to my face, cracking a little slit in my fingers looking at this image that I didn't ever want to see again . . .

Of your mother dying?

Yes. And then forcing myself to log it, gradually make peace with it. And then all the desert stuff just came right into that and I made this piece called *The Passing*.

So, you filmed your mother; you have appeared yourself occasionally; most of your pieces otherwise, the great majority, are done with actors, even when they are actors who are expressing very, very painful intense emotions. Have you ever been attracted by the idea of doing portraits of real people?

Do you mean actors aren't real people?

They're not expressing their own emotions, they create the emotions you tell them to express.

Wait a second. The first project I did with professional actors was in 1995 called *The Greeting*, with the three women, based on the early sixteenth-century Pontormo painting. And I was very uncomfortable in the whole situation and when the commission came through from the National Gallery in London to do a piece based on the work in the collection, I realised I wanted to do this quintet, these five people undergoing intense emotional stress because I was a scholar in residence at the Getty Research Institute in 1998 and the theme of that year was representing the passions. We looked at the passions in different artworks in art history and philosophy. And what happened was, it really took me to another level and actually gave me a way to get into, to understand, the Old Master paintings that I'd been interested in for many years before. I knew I wanted to do something with actors and that's really when I kind of started.

And I first called up the woman who's in *The Greeting*, Susanna Peters, and I said, 'Susanna, you've got to come and I want to do some one-on-one stuff with you.' And I really wanted her to take me through the ropes of how to direct someone in a very intimate way, close-up in your face, like getting someone to cry. So we spent a couple of days together and I was very nervous about it and very uncomfortable, to the point when she really started crying. I just grabbed some tissues and got up immediately and walked up in front of the camera and gave her a tissue. She said, 'What are you doing?' with the tears running down her face. She was really great, very gentle, very understanding and she showed me what it was like and I was so deeply impressed. I know what you're saying, it's not her emotion, but I'm sorry, she was really crying. She had to go somewhere in herself that was real to express this emotion. That was very powerful.

I can understand that and it does come over very powerfully. But I'm still curious that you wouldn't want to do this, or try this with individuals. Or if you took someone famous, what a challenge that would be, a challenge of portraiture.

Annie Leibowitz recently did a huge photo shoot in the White House with President Bush and his team. And they're very interesting. But can you imagine a circumstance where they said, 'Come and do one of your slow-mo portraits of the President, of Rumsfeld, of Cheney.' Wouldn't that be fascinating?

Yeah, because you know what would be fascinating about it? Time is truth, is the revealer, that's where the mystery lies. And you give it enough time, anything, and you will see some semblance of the inner reality of something. When you live with someone for a whole day, or a week, or when someone sits and you sit with them not for a ten-minute coffee or even an hour coffee heart-to-heart, but if you sit with them for two to three hours and you don't feel obliged to talk, you get an incredibly real portrait of what that person is. And we're doing this for the radio and I think it's appropriate to mention here that I've always been fascinated with listening to the radio and hearing those voices, Robert Siegel, Neal Conant all these people on American Public Radio. And I have images in my mind, very vivid clear images of what these people look like. And every once in a while in the newspaper one of them will appear in the context of an article and I will go, 'That's not what he's supposed to look like. No, that's totally wrong!' And of course, I was wrong, because that is the real Neal Conant or Robert Siegel and that's really what they look like. But I've come to seriously believe that the image that I have had of those people I couldn't see is the real image, is the feeling-being image of a person. The way people with mental disabilities or autism sometimes are said to see through people, the famous story of the people in the mental institution when Reagan came on to give this speech without the sound, they all broke out into hysterical laughter. They said, 'Why are you laughing?' The patients said, 'He's lying,' and yet they could hardly speak. I really believe that that thought-being image is with us all the time, and even if you're talking to someone in front of their face, what's going on in your inner psyche is this being-image residing in there, it's not a visual image. I mean the term persona in English comes from ancient Greek and persona doesn't mean person, it means the kind of inner essence of the person, and if you look at the words persona, per 'through', sonar 'sound', it means from ancient Greek 'to hear through'. To hear through what? 'To hear through the mask.' Because when they did the dramas, they were all wearing masks, because we are all wearing masks.

We give ourselves away with our voices.

And when you hear through the mask, you're going beyond the mask inside. And so that's what's really important to remember about visual images in the age of visual images. They can be masks and shields, and they can cover up the reality.

And time can help you to see through that.

But time will eventually wear that down.

You work a lot with technicians – the production list for Going Forth by Day *is almost a production list for a Hollywood movie – you couldn't do it without them. But what is the relationship between what you want to do and the frustration of having to work through other people? Or is this something that you have had to learn, that you can only realise your vision through other people?*

Yes, precisely. I was not born to be a director, not only was I very shy as a young boy, but also I was always very private in my drawings. Different artworks that I made at various points of my life are always the way for me to engage the world without having to be in it, without having to meet it head on. And here in this later period in my life, where I've come to the limits of my technical knowledge and expertise and the kind of ideas I'm trying to grasp right now are bigger than me and bigger than everyone around me, that I can't literally do it myself, I've had to rely on these experts or specialists to help with certain things.

But you're not driven by the latest technological invention; what you want to know is what is going to be able to realise the idea that you have?

Oh yeah, the idea has to precede technology. I mean, that's what we are: we are beings who have incredible, extraordinary, technological apparatus to keep us alive, keep us functioning and moving us forward. The human brain is probably one of the most complex single objects on the face of the earth. But that is driven not by some technician from MIT trying to make the latest, coolest computer, that's driven by some larger thing in the same way as a thorn on a branch of a bush. Does that thorn know about an animal that's going to come up and try to eat the flowers? How could it possibly know that? But it's there.

So we're being driven forward in increasing layers of complexity and density, by something else. That, of course, is, in a fundamental way, the nature of religion, in any kind of spiritual discipline: to try to touch the untouchable.

Is this the role for art in the twenty-first century? Do you think art has a more important role in the twenty-first century than it was sometimes thought to have in the materialist twentieth?

Yes, I do, very strongly. I think art has a more important role to play in this century than it has had to play in a very, very long time, in terms of history, and the reason for that is, in the age of globalisation, which is an age of fear, it's an age of uncertainty for many of us, it's an age that is characterised by the free flow of information and not only the free flow of information but the uncontrolled flow of information, not in the sense of political regimes, but in the sense of, you can't stop the water, it's like leaking everywhere and it's just flowing out of everything, everything is getting wet. That's really what globalisation is about, and it's not coincidental that the primary fear of individuals in the global age is loss of identity. I mean we talk about identity theft, we talk about loss of language, loss of culture, loss of currency, we're talking about loss of all of the unique things that make you unique in the age where everything's being connected. And so the real fundamental basis of our species as the inheritors of the planet at this point in history, the two forces that have most made you who you are, in the most intimate way in a broader societal way, are technology and revelation.

Those two forces are converging in the twenty-first century in ways we couldn't imagine. And in the age where all these cultures are getting thrust into each other, have no sense of understanding what is the world of someone living in a small village in an Islamic country, compared to ourselves here in the West, where all of these cultures, conditions, traditions, races, societies are literally being put in direct contact with each other, the only possible way to connect with other people is through what was always considered to be the fundamental aspects of the human condition. That is, we are all born, we come from some kind of family situation, we feel love for family members, for friends and we have emotions, we have the human passions of an inner life, of feelings, and we will die. And those universal themes of human existence are no longer just artistic aspects, to use in an artistic way or just something that you have in your private life, separate from the world you live in. This is our society with its rules and everything, those in the twenty-first century are the only possible language.

So they're essentials for survival.

That's the only way to talk to each other. So art has this real, vital place and a vital role to play in this global world.

Do you feel you have any idea of the sort of creative journey ahead of you, because after all at fifty-one you are young?

This is true. Well, there was a TV series when I was young called *The Little Rascals* and it was made in the thirties by Hal Roach. And it was about this band of little kids that had all of these misadventures. And there was one moment when they got on hand-made carts to go speeding down the hill, of course the steering wheel broke halfway down and they went spinning out of control. And at one point the back end of this wagon thing carried around right next to the front end, right in front of the driver. And little Stymie, the little black kid in the group, was shocked, his eyes were real wide and he looked right at Spanky, the little kid behind the steering wheel driving the little cart. And Stymie said, 'Where are you going?' And Spanky said, 'I don't know where we're going, but we're on our way!' So that's where I'm going. Don't ask me where, but we're on our way!

RACHEL WHITEREAD

I don't think I dehumanise; no, not at all

If you haven't seen a sculpture by Rachel Whiteread yourself, the chances are you'll have read about one. The full-size cast of the inside of a house in the East End of London, which no sooner won a prize than the Council pulled it down; the inverted plinth that stood on the vacant plinth in Trafalgar Square; the cast of the inside of a library that constitutes the Holocaust Memorial in Vienna. But it would be wrong to think of Rachel Whiteread as principally a sculptor of the monumental. Many of her most evocative pieces are private, domestic – the underside of a bed, a mattress or a chair, the spaces behind a row of books. Some of these pieces are quite small, and using materials such as plaster, resin, rubber, cement, she explores the spaces we don't think about, the spaces we take for granted, and then jolts us by making them material. Whiteread herself is an intensely private person, avoiding the lifestyle excesses of some of her celebrated contemporaries, and now after years of achievement and recognition, and over forty, the question may be: where does she go now?

But before we explore that let's talk about how you work and some of the sources from which you work. Downstairs in your studio there are a lot of sketches. How important is sketching for you?

Drawing and painting is something I've always done. I studied painting as an undergraduate and I think it's always been very much part of my everyday practice. And also more recently, over the past five years or so, a lot of the works I've made have been very large, and in order to work them out, it's not like I can play with a bucket of plaster to make it happen, and to really think through them and work them out I make a lot of drawings. They're not technical drawings, and people are always asking me, do I use computers, do I use CAD systems? I can just about send an e-mail on the computer, I'm a bit of a Luddite. But I do draw in my own technical way and I use my own perspective and it's just something that I really enjoy doing. It helps me dream a piece and make a piece happen.

Because I was struck by some of the drawings, the watercolours stuck on the walls downstairs. They are minutely worked out with a large number of reference lines, so they're not just impressionistic sketches, are they?

Yeah, I mean some of the drawings you're talking about, they look actually very technical but they're not. They'd be following the line of the edge of something and just drawing something vertically from there, and it becomes the pleasure of drawing as much as the necessity of making something. So a lot of the drawings, they're like small paintings in their own right. So it's a difficult process to describe but it's really more a sort of process, an enjoyment of materials and colour and line.

And you've also said that 'London is my sketchbook'. Now what exactly does that mean?

I think I said that an awful long time ago, but I would say it still is. When I first moved back to London after having lived in Brighton for three years as a student, I'd grown up in leafy Muswell Hill and I moved back to Hackney and that was about fifteen years ago now. And Hackney was a real and still is a very interesting world soup of a place, and there may be lots of things changing about it now but in those times it was a very, very sort of gritty place, and I just enjoyed that part of it. And I would go around with my camera and take photographs and go into junk shops and look at things and go around backstreets and really just exploring it. And all of the studios I had were really in the kind of furthest, darkest depths and it was always an interesting journey going to the studio, what you might find en route. I think this area of London is very much like SoHo in New York was twenty years ago, when a group of artists moved there and then it changed and now it's fashion and not even galleries any more.

You mentioned photography. The photographs of yours that I've seen are very ordered, a lot of straight lines, quite monumental, Roman amphitheatres, the Corinth Canal and things like that. How does that fit in with your work?

The photographs that I take are generally to do with spaces. The photographic part of my work is something to do with trying to find a sense of what people have done to the land, whether it's through building structures, or making great big holes in the ground, or whatever it is that they've done, whether it's a reservoir, or a pyramid. I think it's just the way in which we've affected our world, physically affected it, and I think it's very much a part of the practice that I do in the studio, whether it's casting the inside of a hot-water bottle or looking at a pyramid, I think it's the same sort of thing in effect. Because it's really just about how we have, as a human race, affected the surface of the earth in one way or another.

You mentioned architectural space, but the works that you do, which are inside of a room, inside of a house, staircases, those are not your comment on architecture as such, are they?

No, not at all, actually. I think that the first architectural piece that I made was *Ghost*, which was the cast of the inside of a small room in a Victorian house, and that was really to do with kind of childhood memories and maybe leaving home and doing all those sorts of things. A lot of that earlier work was very much connected to my own history, but I think that changed through *House* which was obviously a sort of political statement as well. And then some of the more recent architectural pieces, a lot of which were cast in this building that we're now sitting in, it was more the notion of how buildings are anonymous, the way in which apartments are often made. These two apartment pieces that were cast in this building were cast physically from the actual apartments that were here, small rooms, a bit like council flats, a bit like this kind of international forgotten architecture. It's just spaces, no one really considers them. It's just got windows and got a door and there's nothing beautiful about them, they're just there. They're purely functional spaces. Actually, when I was casting these pieces the thing that I was most interested in was the space between the walls, so they were cast in such a way that the walls didn't exist any more, so the walls were all slots, and that came from having made *House* ten years ago. There were many things that frustrated me about *House*, but the one thing that frustrated me about the appearance of it was that the walls were still embedded in the actual sculpture.

It was a solid chunk and therefore it went against your idea of expressing the void rather than the structure?

Exactly, yeah. I didn't really know that at the time. I knew I was a bit irritated that I had to keep these walls in, and it's just since then, through the kind of plodding nature of my practice, that I've realised that's what it was that annoyed me.

I want to go back to the personal background that you mentioned. The sort of things that are written about you, the memories of crawling into a dark cupboard as a child and that then led to your first significant cast piece; you were heavily influenced by your father's death and another piece was driven by that. Did these experiences really influence your work, or have the critics kind of retro-fitted a lot of experiences and cast you as this rather gloomy, traumatised artist?

I'm not in the least bit gloomy and traumatised! When I made *Closet*, which was the piece that is always referred to as the childhood experience, I said when I made it that I had this memory of sitting inside wardrobes. It wasn't a traumatic thing; it's the way in which kids crawl under beds – my son does exactly the same thing, finds little spaces – and you'd go in them because they're kind of cosy and interesting, and you can close a door and it's dark and you can see a chink of light, and it's private and secret. That's what that was about. It was cast in plaster and then it was covered in black felt, and people immediately thought it was incredibly morbid, which I don't think it was. I think it was quite celebratory!

A perfectly innocent memory, not a memory of trauma.

An innocent memory but to do with reverie as a child rather than trauma, so that was that. I made *Shallow Breath*.

Which was of a mattress . . .

Which was soon after my father died, and that was very much to do with my father's death, which, as someone in their mid twenties, it was a very traumatic thing. I make no apologies for these things and I don't think that it's necessarily painted me as being kind of morbid. But, you know, I'm a very honest, straightforward person and I think that's somehow where the waters maybe get a little bit muddied, because people can't quite believe that I can be that straightforward about my father's death, and not illustrate it, but somehow bring the pain out and physically make something with it.

I was struck by the fact that when some of these pieces were displayed, you said 'Really, some of these pieces still break my heart' and doing it as an exorcism of emotion. This is an unfashionably candid and honest thing for an artist to say.

Yeah, I think that's still true, actually. The first show that I did when I left college was in a gallery called the Carlisle Gallery, that doesn't exist any more. And in the show there was a cast of the inside of a hot-water bottle, that was called *Torso*; there was *Closet*, there was *Shallow Breath* and there was another piece called *Manty*, which was the cast of the dressing table, and it was a really quiet show in a very small gallery that had a wooden floor, it was a very domestic space. And for me it was the first time that I felt that I'd made sculpture. Throughout all my time at college, I was struggling with trying to make things that stood in the middle of a room and never really managed it – not that I think that's what sculpture is – but for me that was a starting point. From that, I'd made these four things that you might find in a sort of little domestic space, and then I thought, 'Well, I'd like to cast the space inside a room,' and I described that as mummifying the air in a room. And again people thought that was really morbid, you know mummifying . . . ! But for me it was just a way of poetically describing it and being able to make grant applications, to be able to fund doing it!

As you describe it, that is a perfectly innocent and logical progression of a young artist and what's she doing, dealing with a material which first comes to hand.

Yeah, throughout my time at college, especially in post-grad when I kind of knew what I was doing a bit more, in the last year of college I would say I knew what I was doing, and I was using a lot of materials, blankets from my childhood and chairs and tables. And so all of the things that I use now, but I didn't quite know what I was doing with them, so I made all this very strange work with furniture and hung them upside down and stuffed things into them and it's work that I still stand by but it was very naïve in a way. And I think the actual struggle of leaving college and getting a studio and someone putting their faith in you and saying that they'd like to give you a show . . . !

Can I just try to get a basic definition for my own benefit? Sometimes the impression is given that you cast a particular kind of space, i.e. the inside of a building, as in House. *But you also cast spaces below – as with your chairs and tables – and, in the case of* Sarcophagus, *you cast the space, the imprint that the bath makes on a block of material. So you're playing with the idea of the volumes that you cast in a fairly complicated set of ways.*

It's something that I've developed over the years. As an artist, you develop a language. It's like learning to talk and over the years you gradually move this language a little further and you start thinking about what happened to that, how that refers to the floor, how that refers to something else. Once you've got all of that language together, you can then play with it and I think that's what I'm doing now. When I first made the bathtub pieces, which were called *Ether* and various other things, they were never called 'Sarcophagus', actually!

Yes, people say it looks like a sarcophagus; there you are!

I stopped titling things a long time ago, but I was always very careful about my titles, that they were never that direct. But these were using a cast-iron bathtub, I always used cast-iron because that was what I could get to rust into the material properly, and to get this very rich surface on the final piece, and I had the bathtub, I turned it upside down in the studio and I just worked on proportions and how something could look when it was finally a lump in my studio. So I was trying to decide what height it would be and they were also always based on weight and how I could physically move them around the studio, maybe myself and someone else next door that I could knock on the door to help me just shift something for ten minutes. So all of those things were considerations; and they all become part of your working practice.

If you had just been – I use the word 'just' deliberately – casting the space inside, you would have put the resin inside the bathtub, rather than putting the bathtub into a block of resin?

Yeah, but I've never found that space very interesting!

Right, that disposed of that! But you find the space beneath chairs and tables and stools is interesting?

I think it's for a number of reasons. One, that they're quite architectural lumps once they're made, and they also stand for the absence of a body. Chairs are made to be sat on, whereas the inside of a bathtub is water!

And the body?

Yeah, but then you have to put the body in it, don't you, and that would then become a very complicated cast and would look very figurative. You know, I've never used the body other than when I was a student, in my work, and I'm always looking for ways of representing the body but not actually physically putting it there.

It's the presence of the body and the spaces that the body inhabits that you're interested in?

Yes, the presence and the absence, whether it's casting the space underneath a table and really enjoying the fact that there are pieces of chewing gum and all sorts of other things that actually become part of the sculpture. But I think that the physical way in which people are absent, that's one way to read the work. But I think it's something that I very much played with especially in a lot of the chair pieces; making a hundred chairs together and it's almost like an audience, an absent audience. I think in the room pieces, especially I think with *Ghost*, when I first looked at it in the studio and saw it for the first time after I'd been spending three months making it, I was completely alarmed when I realised that I was the wall, as the viewer. And I thought 'What have I done?' You know, I've actually made everybody absent from everything, and it was quite an odd moment, an epiphany.

But you don't dehumanise?

No, I don't think I dehumanise; no, not at all. But it is about becoming the wall a lot of the time and maybe that's just the place that I think more people should be, behind the wall.

Now going back to your great piece, the House *of 1993, what strikes me is that it must have involved a huge amount of preparation and planning. It was an engineering and a building operation. Were you prepared for that; are you particularly good at doing that sort of thing?*

No, I certainly wasn't prepared for it. I've got better at doing it. I work with Artangel, so an awful lot of the stuff was organised by them. They found the construction firm and they found the engineers, so, you know, that was all taken care of. I had to work very closely with everybody and the most important part was getting the internal structure of the building right before we actually cast it. So I went in with a group of people, we had to strip a lot of things out and make good and make decisions about what should be kept, what should go.

What sort of things did you take out? I hadn't realised that you had interfered in the inside of House *so much.*

Well, there were some very interesting 1950s–1970s DIY bits. There was a bar, built-in bar, in there and things like that which didn't really resonate as a structure that you wanted to cast or have as part of the building, so things like that you just needed to think about. There was actually a valley roof on the building and I made a decision to just block that off and not actually cast into the roof space, because it would have looked too complicated, it would have looked like there was a crown on the roof rather than just being this very kind of severe flat top to it.

So there were some 'unadmitted interventions', as architects would say?

Yeah; they were very slight, actually, but there were. We had to cut the staircase in half, because we had to cast around the staircase, things like that.

Would it make a huge difference to the validity of the piece in your terms, if the amount of intervention you had introduced was very significant, if you had tinkered with the space too much before casting it?

Well, I think it would have been a very different thing and I would never have done that. I think we'd been working on it for about a week and we came in one night and two of the fireplaces had been ripped out by someone who'd just gone in and nicked them, so we had to rebuild the fireplaces. Things like that happened that we didn't really expect to happen and then you had to deal with once they had happened.

Was it physically hard work?

It was completely exhausting. I actually got very sick making that piece, because I just overdid it.

But do you like getting involved with the physical side of sculpture?

Completely, yeah. More recently I've had to stand back a little bit from that. I organise an awful lot of the making these days on the larger works rather than physically doing it, but I make all of the decisions, all of the decisions of how it's going to finally look. But I have a great kind of team of people that I work with, not all the time by any means, but they come in and work on specific projects with me.

But you no longer need to get some of your satisfaction from getting physically tired?

I get physically tired in other ways now. Of course I love it, it's like you move into a new place and you spend all night unpacking books, that's very part of it. And one needs to move into a new piece of sculpture in the way you need to do with anything else, so I do very much enjoy doing that, but it's a kind of necessity to not have to do it sometimes these days.

Your nature, your character as an artist, are you a realist or a symbolist, and I suppose you don't have to make the choice between the two?

I would say I could easily make a choice. I would say I was definitely a realist.

Unqualified?

I don't think I'm romantic enough to be a symbolist.

But people read huge symbolic values into your work.

Yeah, they do.

So do they think of you as an unadmitted symbolist?

I don't know, I've never asked them! It's an interesting question. I'm not responsible for how people respond to works, you can't dictate how people respond to works. A long time ago when I was first making sculpture, maybe for about three years maximum, I titled works and I was very careful about titling them, I spent hours pontificating about what the words should be. And then I decided that it made the reading of it very specific, which is why I stopped titling things. And now everything, which makes life very complicated, is untitled and then maybe 'Grey Bed' in brackets or something. It's much more specific rather than having a kind of poetry to the reading of it.

People rather like me then go round and label a piece 'Sarcophagus', which it isn't!

Well, that's fine, that's fine. But I just remember as a student, I'd be puzzling over something and then you'd go and read the label and then you'd think 'Oh,' and it could be incredibly disappointing because you got it, you know. And I think the interesting thing about looking at work is that you don't necessarily get it, you don't necessarily understand what the artist is trying to say, or you can completely put your own interpretation on to it.

Let me try another -ism while we're here. Do you see yourself at all as a minimalist?

Yes, I work in a very specific kind of way and I have a debt certainly to the minimalists.

And one final one, a concern for pure form, formalism, how much does that drive what you do?

I don't think it does really, I think that proportion maybe is more of . . . proportion with making the works and that comes very much from drawing and a sort of physical thing. For me it's to do with being able to move things around and in and out of buildings, and I enjoy playing with that. And I think the works often are very formal looking, but I think that was never an intention. It's not that I'm trying to make the straightest line or the most beautiful curve; it really comes from the thing that I'm physically casting and have chosen to cast. So maybe the formalism comes from the actual spaces and the interpretation for me, but not finally the sculpture, if that makes sense.

Do you set out to do something which is beautiful? But you have sometimes specifically said that art should not be beautiful.

I've never set out to make things beautiful, no. I kind of enjoy it when they are sometimes but I also like making ugly things!

Which of your pieces would you regard as being successfully ugly?

Strangely enough, I could be very specific about a piece, which was called *Untitled: Black Bed* I think, which was made a long time ago now. And it was the cast of the space underneath a bed and it was cast in two sections, it was a large double bed which could be folded in half to get it up and down stairs, kind of utility furniture. And then I made this bit in the area in the middle which I didn't do anything with at all; I just bunged this black rubber down it and it came out as this horrible hairy lip, which was in the centre of the piece. A friend of mine, an artist called Alison Wilding, came to see me in the studio and she said 'That reminds me of the stuff you find underneath your fingernail'! And I thought that was a really great way of sort of describing something. And yeah, I think it was successfully ugly, and it was very sort of female. There were all sorts of things about it that made it deliciously ugly I'd say, yes!

Some people have described the spaces you work with and express as meaningless spaces. Now as we're talking about the chairs or the tables, they are not meaningless to you; they may seem arbitrary but they're not meaningless.

No, everything that I cast I make a very clear-cut decision about casting it. It may be to do with physically what it looks like, it may have come from a place that I'm familiar with. There's all sorts of things that can inform each piece that I choose, but they're certainly not meaningless. I always see furniture, especially furniture that's chucked out in the street, almost like people, just sort of derelict and chucked out in the street; they've been loved and used, and then they have no purpose any more in someone's life and they just chuck them there. It's something that you see in Hackney and in Tower Hamlets everywhere, it's just part of street life, street furniture, it's just part of the city.

From that point of view there's the random element in what you do that you could see something that's been rejected and say . . . ?

No, I would very rarely actually pick something up from the street; that might have been something that I've done as a student but somehow it's a little bit too arbitrary. I need to go and choose something. I'll photograph stuff in the street but I wouldn't necessarily bring it back and work on it.

What's your working day like?

Get up around seven and that's because I've a little boy, and do all that kind of stuff, get into the studio by about nine-fifteen and finish by six. And then after my evening's activity, maybe come back into the studio and have a think, do some drawing, you know, or maybe not.

But then what about the nine hours between the nine-fifteen and the six? What is your life? I know every day is different.

During my working day, over the past year it's been involved with builders and architects a lot. But usually my working day consists of getting up, maybe going through some sort of correspondence, doing some admin stuff and then going into the studio and start thinking and drawing and making things in the drawing space of my studio; getting it to a stage, and then going downstairs and actually start physically kind of making things.

Do you work in a very steady way throughout the day?

Life's been quite different over the past few years, but I used to have a very steady way of working. When I had a studio in Hackney Wick and I'd cycle to the studio and I'd cycle to second-hand shops and it was a very fluid way of working. And now the older I've got, the busier I am, trying to work everything into one day can be quite hard.

Do you try to avoid work at times?

I go for a walk, I go and try and find things in shops, I go for a swim, I maybe go for a run. You know, I've got lots of avoiding tactics.

Have you ever been seriously blocked, where you thought you just didn't know what you were going to do with any of your pieces?

It hasn't happened for a while, actually; but I think it's a very healthy moment when that happens, where you think, 'I just don't know what I'm going to do next,' and you sort of back yourself right into a corner. And then you just have to work your way out of it, and I think it only happens through work, actually. I don't know what writers feel about this when they have writer's block, but I think with artists you have to just somehow do it; even if it's just an hour a day, you need to do something, because you need to keep thinking in order to get yourself out of a blockage. I do a lot of drawings when I'm stuck.

And then finally you realise that you're not stuck, that actually just the process of putting ideas on to paper works, works you through?

Exactly, exactly.

And did you get very depressed, or were you frustrated?

I have, yes, I think you do, especially if you've got deadlines coming up for things and you just think, 'I don't know what I'm doing,' you know. But I think generally you work through it, and it's difficult. But depression comes in all sorts of forms and misery comes in all sorts of forms, and people have different ways of dealing with it.

You've said of your work that it's quiet, spiritual, poetic. Is that a description of you as well?

Of me personally? I don't know really, I'm certainly quite sort of contemplative. I wouldn't really necessarily say that I was, what was it, quiet, spiritual and poetic?

Quiet, spiritual and poetic.

No I'll just stick to contemplative!

Obviously, you're also a very determined person or you would have given up on the Holocaust Memorial in Vienna. Rather than me trying to describe it, why don't you describe it for me?

The Holocaust Memorial is a concrete sculpture made from cases of books. So it's like a library but it's inside out, it has a kind of double reading to it. It has two doors on the front. It has a ceiling rose in the roof which acts as drainage, and it has this concrete plinth around it with an inscription and names of all of the concentration camps in which people died in Austria. I'd lived in Berlin for a long time. When I lived there I thought a lot about what had happened during the war, and I think that if I hadn't had that experience I wouldn't have even approached or begun to approach such a subject. And when I was asked to put in a proposal, which I did, I hadn't a clue that I would get it. I really didn't think that I would get it because it was against all sorts of other people that were much more experienced than I was. It was a piece that was to be in a square called Judenplatz, which is a quite domestic-scale square, and it was as if one of the rooms from the surrounding buildings had been taken and put in the centre of the square, and all of the books were completely blank. You had no idea what was supposedly in them, and the pages were facing outwards so you couldn't read the spines of the books, so that was essentially the idea, a sort of blank library. There's all sorts of interpretations of it.

The Jews as the people of the book?

Exactly, and various other things which I obviously thought about when I was making the piece or thinking about making the piece, but it's also quite like a bunker and it was something that I thought about and something that I was accused of. I remember at the jury when I went and stood in this very terrifying room and I said, 'What do you mean it's like a bunker? I've no idea what you're talking about!' And acted completely innocently, but it was something that I really felt quite strongly about. I'd been to see a lot of the bunkers around the Atlantic Wall and I didn't want to give the city of Vienna a beautiful object. I wanted to give them something that they had to think about and that wasn't ugly but that had a presence and quite a severe presence in the city, which I've done very successfully I'd say, in terms of how people have to look at it, and it's not an easy thing to look at and I would hope it makes people quite uncomfortable. But it's also quite poetic, you know; it has all sorts of different ways and layerings to reading it. I'm finally very proud of it, but it took an awful lot of doing and it wasn't a pleasant thing to go through.

Were you ever tempted to give up?

I certainly was tempted to give up, but what drove me through that was I think the nature of the attack on it. I felt even more clear that it should happen, because there was a lot of racism involved and it was pretty nasty. But I also had a wonderful woman called Andrea Schlieker who worked with me through it and helped me through the whole thing, and she's German-speaking but lives here. And she had a good handle on it all and she was able to nanny me through it a little bit. I think if she hadn't been a part of it I would have chucked it in, because I just couldn't handle the attack all the time. It was just driving me slightly kind of insane.

How much was it the attacks on you and the piece rather than a huge piece of internal Austrian faction-fighting?

It was both. The internal fighting was extraordinary and

everybody was so excited that it should happen under their political umbrella, that they could be seen to be making a Holocaust memorial. But the government changed three or four times and everybody was trying to make it their political baby. But there was a lot of local opposition in the square in which the piece was made, in Judenplatz; and there were ideas that it should be moved to a place called Heldenplatz, a Hero's Place, which I refused to let happen and said, 'If you want a piece for there, then you have to have another competition. This was specifically designed for this intimate place.' So there were all sorts of fights that went on. I got to a stage where I would go over there for day trips, and going to Vienna for a day trip is quite hard work, and then eventually I refused to go until they sorted themselves out. And they would all come over here and turn up with their chocolates, trying to make me feel very much a part of it. But it's extraordinary. The piece was finally opened maybe two years ago. I haven't been back since. I will go back but I haven't gone back.

You're associated with these big pieces, the House, *the plinth in Trafalgar Square, Holocaust, but are you in danger of being branded as the sculptor of the monumental?*

I don't know. I don't intend to do that, and as I said to you earlier, I'm resisting making more large works just simply because I want to become a bit quieter about the way I make work, and I want to be in the studio more, physically doing it myself and just changing things a little bit. I think constantly working in other people's studios or in other countries, all of these things really take their toll mentally and physically. And I think that it's very important to try and keep a kind of handle on the things that maybe you want to do, and you can lose sight of that a little bit if you're flying around the globe. But I've actually made very few very large works. People think that I've made a lot but I'm not a sculptor that makes enormous pieces for bank buildings or lobbies, I haven't really done that.

So you need to rediscover for your own purposes, or to reconnect yourself with, the smaller more intimate works?

I think it's something that I'm about to sort of start.

Does this actually amount to a change of direction, because somebody said, I think it was Francis Bacon, 'An artist must deepen their game.' Do you feel at the age of forty that you're at the stage when you want to deepen your game?

I'm not sure what that means, 'deepen your game'; what does that mean?

Extend the range, perhaps?

Extend the range; I'm not sure if extending the range is something that I want to do. Some of the most interesting artists have done more or less the same thing their entire lives. I think that by reinvestigating things, you can just draw that little bit more from something. I don't want to start making vast metal sculptures, you know; I'm not going to start doing that.

And you see no need to abandon the idea of casting or something connected with it?

No. I see no need at all to do that; no. It's what I do.

You're not running out of themes, ideas, subjects?

We'll see. I hope not.

Because you've just done a room, Room 101, *which is George Orwell's supposed room at the BBC, a room in Broadcasting House, I think that's now been destroyed. What attracted you to that commission? That's a fairly monumental piece, isn't it?*

Yeah, it wasn't really a commission, it was more a question of 'would I think about it?'. And then I decided that it was an opportunity not to be missed, and actually when I was starting to think about making it was during the time that the war was about to happen here, rather in Iraq! And I wasn't a great supporter of the war by any stretch of the imagination, and somehow it felt a kind of good thing to do because it felt connected to that. By casting this room and the way in which rooms get bombed out, because all of this plant machinery had been taken out of the room and there were these big gaping holes in the walls, so it's almost like a cartoon of a room. There's all this kind of brickwork that you can see and it felt somehow connected. It felt a little kind of Orwellian in some way.

And as a piece of evocation and nostalgia for anybody who's been inside Broadcasting House, it's very powerful on that level alone!

I don't know what's really going to happen with it. We put it in the cast courts, the cast courts are an extraordinary place in the V & A, and it's going to be standing alongside gargantuan Michelangelo and various other things, and I'm moving some of the works around, not a great deal of them but what we can, and somehow making a relationship with the works that are in the cast courts with *Room 101*. So that's an interesting thing to play with as well.

And you're also doing something which really is rather different. You will be working with snow and ice in Finland and that will have nothing whatever to do with casting but it will use some of your corridor and staircase themes, won't it?

That's going to be something which happens in February, and it was really for me a way of being able to make something very large without actually physically having to do it myself. And also working alongside an architect who can make all the drawings and understand how this structure can go together and tell the builders what to do. But it will be working with snow and ice, and making a kind of cavity of where a staircase was rather than a sort of hole, so it will be an architectural space but it will be unusable. You'll be able to go inside it and from the outside it will be very straightforward, very formal.

Can you see other ways in which what you've done over the last twenty years and what you've learned can be turned into new kinds of work?

I don't know, actually; I mean, I'm sort of about to start. I'm very much a kind of open book with it all. This was partly one of the reasons why I'm doing this interview with you. It's often very good to think things through and just try and work on the whole of something or the whole of what I'd done, and try and work out what it is that I'm going to be doing. I've got some ideas; I'm thinking things through and we'll see. I'm about to start playing with lots of new materials, different types of rubbers and different types of clear plastics, felt. All sorts of things. So there's all sorts of things that are going on that are kind of related. I've used them a bit, but, you know, colours have changed, materials have changed, so we'll see.

So if you're in this taking-stock mood, you look back over twenty years, what's your sense of the journey that you've come?

A long and arduous one, but very good, you know a very good journey. I've achieved an awful lot and I'm looking forward to my mid career. That might sound like a strange thing to say but I think no one can continue at that pace. Some artists have three good years in them, some have ten, some have fifty. We'll just see what happens. I can't really say what it is that will happen but I'm still looking forward to continuing the journey.

But you're not facing block at the moment?

No. I'll let you know in a few months' time, but at the moment no.

And you don't feel that casting has run its route for you?

No, I definitely don't feel that. People say, 'What else can you do with casting?' but, you know, the staircase pieces that I made very recently, they completely surprised me, and I felt absolutely ecstatic that I'd made them and it felt like the first sculpture I'd made once again. So if that can happen every five, ten years then that's a great feeling, that's what keeps you going.

You mentioned the YBAs, Young British Artists, many of whom have led and continue to lead legendarily rackety lives. You've never done that and you described yourself, or have been described, as being very grounded. What keeps you grounded?

I don't know. It may be something to do with the background that I came from. You know my mother's an artist and my father was involved in it. Maybe the artists that my parents knew weren't necessarily all mad and crazy, drinking, drug-taking people, so maybe it comes from there. But I've done my fair share of partying as well, I just hide from the cameras. I just haven't done it for a while, I'm just not interested, really, any more. I like doing it sometimes but I have a different kind of life now.

Do you mind fame? Would you quite like it?

The fame thing I find quite difficult. I'm getting used to it now but there were times when I've really not enjoyed it, being followed. You know some people love it, they court it, they actively enjoy it. I just don't, really. I don't like being available to people all the time, which comes with fame. I don't like people saying, 'Oh, I've got a great idea, cast the inside of a telephone box!' One, because that's not a very good idea!

I've got a great idea, cast the inside of a motorcar!

That's not a good idea either!